Public Budgeting in Search for an Identity

Public Budgeting in Search for an Identity: State of the Art and Future Challenges provides a state-of-the-art reflection on current trends in international public budgeting, representing an important pillar in the accumulation of knowledge on public sector budgeting processes, contents, evolutions and critical issues.

Budgeting is central in public sector organizations. It performs a complex variety of functions, being the arena where multiple actors, cultures and professional identities interact, making it an extremely fascinating field and topic of investigation. There is a significant need and scope for exploring budgeting processes in the public sector today, as a consequence of the managerial waves of reforms that have taken place over the last few decades and the implementation of austerity programmes – as well as in light of current trends, including emerging challenges related to community care and well-being, rising inequality, people flows, climate change, pandemics, and the persistence of democratic deficits. The chapters in this volume address critical issues on this broad topic, offering new perspectives on current evolutions in public budgeting, including, among others, participatory budgeting, performance budgeting, the budgetary slack resources and the need to ensure balance between budget control and flexibility. These contributions show that public budgeting can, and must remain, the subject of enduring interest in our studies.

The chapters in this book were originally published as a special issue of *Public Management Review*.

Mariafrancesca Sicilia is Associate Professor of Public Sector Accounting and Management at the University of Bergamo, Italy. She has published extensively on public sector accounting, accountability, performance measurement and management and co-production of public services.

Ileana Steccolini is Full Professor of Accounting at the University of Essex, UK. She is the Co-editor of *Financial Accountability and Management* and the Chair and Founder of the International Research Society for Public Management (IRSPM) Public Service Accounting and Accountability Group. She has published extensively on public sector accounting, accountability, performance measurement and governmental financial resilience.

Public Budgeting in Search for an Identity

State of the Art and Future Challenges

Edited by
**Mariafrancesca Sicilia and
Ileana Steccolini**

Routledge
Taylor & Francis Group

LONDON AND NEW YORK

First published 2021
by Routledge
2 Park Square, Milton Park, Abingdon, Oxon OX14 4RN

and by Routledge
52 Vanderbilt Avenue, New York, NY 10017

Routledge is an imprint of the Taylor & Francis Group, an informa business

British Library Cataloguing in Publication Data
A catalogue record for this book is available from the British Library

ISBN 13: 978-0-367-67965-1

Typeset in MinionPro
by Newgen Publishing UK

Publisher's Note
The publisher accepts responsibility for any inconsistencies that may have arisen during the conversion of this book from journal articles to book chapters, namely the inclusion of journal terminology.

Disclaimer
Every effort has been made to contact copyright holders for their permission to reprint material in this book. The publishers would be grateful to hear from any copyright holder who is not here acknowledged and will undertake to rectify any errors or omissions in future editions of this book.

Contents

Citation Information

The chapters in this book were originally published in *Public Management Review*, volume 19, issue 7 (2017). When citing this material, please use the original page numbering for each article, as follows:

Introduction

Public budgeting in search for an identity: state of the art and future challenges
Mariafrancesca Sicilia and Ileana Steccolini
Public Management Review, volume 19, issue 7 (2017), pp. 905–910

Chapter 1

Insights into performance-based budgeting in the public sector: a literature review and a research agenda
Sara Giovanna Mauro, Lino Cinquini and Giuseppe Grossi
Public Management Review, volume 19, issue 7 (2017), pp. 911–931

Chapter 2

Linking budgeting to results? Evidence about performance budgets in European municipalities based on a comparative analytical model
Pieter Bleyen, Daniel Klimovský, Geert Bouckaert and Christoph Reichard
Public Management Review, volume 19, issue 7 (2017), pp. 932–953

Chapter 3

The design of performance budgeting processes and managerial accountability relationships
Suresh Cuganesan
Public Management Review, volume 19, issue 7 (2017), pp. 954–971

For any permission-related enquiries please visit:
www.tandfonline.com/page/help/permissions

Notes on Contributors

John Alford, Honorary Professorial Fellow at the Melbourne School of Government, University of Melbourne, Australia.

Roland Almqvist, Stockholm Business School, Stockholm University, Sweden.

Pieter Bleyen, Public Governance Institute, KU Leuven, Belgium.

Geert Bouckaert, Public Governance Institute, KU Leuven, Belgium.

Maria Isabel Brun-Martos, Department of Economics and Business, University CEU Cardenal Herrera, Valencia, Spain.

Lino Cinquini, Institute of Management, Scuola Superiore Sant'Anna, Pisa, Italy.

Suresh Cuganesan, The University of Sydney Business School, University of Sydney, Australia.

Michael Di Francesco, The Australia and New Zealand School of Government, Carlton, Australia; School of Social Sciences, University of New South Wales (UNSW), Sydney, Australia.

Abhisekh Ghosh Moulick, Department of Political Science, University of Oklahoma, Norman, OK, USA.

Giuseppe Grossi, Top Scholar and Research Professor of Accounting, Nord University, Norway, and Professor of Public Management and Accounting, Kristianstad University, Sweden.

Daniel Klimovský, Faculty of Social and Economic Sciences, Comenius University, Bratislava, Slovakia.

Irvine Lapsley, Institute for Public Sector Accounting Research (IPSAR), Business School, University of Edinburgh, UK.

Sara Giovanna Mauro, Institute of Management, Scuola Superiore Sant'Anna, Pisa, Italy.

Christoph Reichard, LS Public and Nonprofit Management, University of Potsdam, Germany.

Mariafrancesca Sicilia, Department of Management, University of Bergamo, Italy.

Ileana Steccolini, Essex Business School, University of Essex, Colchester, UK.

Lori L. Taylor, The Bush School of Government and Public Service, Texas A&M University, College Station, TX, USA.

Niklas Wällstedt, Stockholm Business School, Stockholm University, Sweden.

INTRODUCTION

Public budgeting in search for an identity: state of the art and future challenges

Budgeting has traditionally been the process through which governments decide how much to spend on what, limiting expenditures to the revenues available and preventing overspending. Over time, public budgets have taken on different roles, becoming tools for bargaining and allocating power, for planning and controlling, for providing impulses to the economic and social environment and for ensuring transparency and stakeholder involvement (Saliterer, Sicilia, and Steccolini Forthcoming). As such, budgets play, among others, political, economic, managerial and accountability functions. They perform a *political function* as they reflect stakeholders' preferences and power positions, representing the same time the result of past decisions and bargains, and the basis for future discussions. They define the boundaries of public intervention in the economy, and the degree of redistribution of wealth in the economic system, fulfilling an *economic* function. They are also increasingly used to hold managers accountable for the attainment of results and use of public resources, thus filling a *managerial* function, and to hold public organizations accountable to the general public, satisfying an *external accountability* function.

The multifaceted nature of budgeting has generally translated into its being the subject of enduring interest by different disciplines, including political science, public administration, accounting, psychology, management and organization studies. At the same time, budgeting is an arena where different rationalities, logics, competencies and professional identities interact. The complexity and variety of functions of budgeting, and its being an arena of interaction of different actors, cultures, professional identities and disciplines probably account for the variety of approaches and forms taken on by budget documents and budgeting processes (Saliterer, Sicilia, and Steccolini Forthcoming) and by its variable nature over time. These same features also contribute to make public budgeting an extremely fascinating field and topic of investigation, which can provide a number of insights on political, social, economic and psychological processes. It may thus represent the ideal setting for bringing in views from different scholarly communities and disciplines to show what can be learnt by accepting that social, political and economic processes are complex and rich arenas, where deterministic and simplistic explanations limit our views and possibilities, and accepting that the challenge of complexity can be risky in the current 'publish and perish' culture, but also extremely rewarding and stimulating.

This is the challenge that the authors of this special issue accepted to take up, contributing to offer a rich and in-depth view of current trends in the studies and practices of public budgeting at a time when New Public Management (NPM) influence still appears to remain important (Lapsley 2009), but claims have increasingly emerged that either other paradigms may be emerging (e.g., Osborne 2006, 2009), or that we may be witnessing a paradigmatic gap (Coen and Roberts 2012).

A recent review of public budgeting studies in Europe (Anessi et al. 2016) confirms that NPM and modernization movements have significantly influenced the study and practice of public budgeting over the last two decades, showing that most European studies of public budgeting published in the main public administration and accounting journals refer to NPM not only as the context of their analyses, but very often as the main conceptual framework informing them. While this appears to have offered a good opportunity for feeding a debate on managerialism in the public sector, and for accumulating contextual knowledge on public sector reforms, it may have also crowded out scholarly attention from the development of alternative conceptual frameworks. Moreover, far from providing evidence that NPM-type reforms have solved public administration problems, most studies have highlighted that changes in public budgeting, including shifts to performance-based and accruals-based budgeting, are still under way, or their expected benefits are yet to be fully reaped and understood, while a number of unexpected and even undesired effects have arisen.

This suggests that there is an enormous need and scope for exploring budgeting processes in the public sector today, both as a consequence of the managerial waves of reforms that have taken place over the last few decades, and in the light of current emerging trends. The post-crisis and austerity context, the growing inequalities emerging in many countries, the rising emphasis on new forms of service delivery such as co-production and inter-organizational collaborations, the widespread shift from *representative* to *participative* democracy, are among the current trends that may present new challenges for public organizations and the related budgeting processes. In the light of its multifaceted nature, budgeting may be an ideal place to look at the impacts and implications of such trends in the public realm.

First, managerial reforms have suggested the move to an increased reliance on accruals- and performance-based budgets. However, the integration of financial and non-financial aspects of performance, and of budgeting and performance management are still underway and not fully understood by scholars. Indeed, an increasing body of literature shows that accruals data are not necessarily preferred by either managers or politicians (for a review of relevant literature, see Liguori, Sicilia, and Steccolini 2012, 2014), as non-financial performance measures and cash-based data may appeal more to their users' needs. In this respect, some authors suggest that the accruals basis of accounting may be useful for reporting and as an analytical tool, but still may not be needed as a basis for budgeting (Caiden 2010). Thus, while the literature on the adoption of accruals accounting has become increasingly wide, much less attention has been devoted so far, both in the literature and in practice, to how accruals-based budgeting should work and actually works, or to its impacts for political as well as managerial decision-making (for a few notable exceptions, see Ezzamel et al. 2007; Hyndman and Connolly 2011). Similarly, the role of non-financial performance information in the formulation and execution stages of budgeting goals still remains unclear.

Second, austerity and the consequences of the global financial crisis have often caused a re-centralization of budgeting processes (Bracci et al. 2015), while the emergence of increasing complex and non-routine problems to deal with may have generated fragmented decision-making and the need of continuous changes and adjustments to budgets, both in their formulation and in their execution. Practitioners and scholars should devote more attention to requirements of stability and how fiscal rules and constraints, and a search for stability in public finances (macro-budgeting), can go hand in hand, or even require, increased flexibility in budget execution (micro-budgeting).

Third, public management reforms have emphasized the importance of accountability and have promoted transparency and communication of numbers about public organizations. This logic initially has been promoted in a situation in which citizens were mainly viewed as passive actors that receive services and elect their representatives. With the emergence of ideas of 'active citizenship' and new forms of participatory democracy (Hendriks 2010), as well as of wider views of co-production as co-planning and co-design (Bovaird 2007; Sicilia et al. 2016; Barbera, Sicilia, and Steccolini 2016) citizens are increasingly seen as active players in public governance, directly involved in deliberations and provisions of services. In the light of such developments, the potential contribution of budgeting to external accountability, both in terms of transparency and communication and in terms of stakeholder involvement and participation requires further investigation.

Fourth, public service delivery is increasingly requiring the involvement of multiple actors, including other governments or public sector entities, as well as private and nonprofit organizations. Budgeting may play an important role in the distribution and representation of resources and responsibilities, as well as in the discharge of accountability in such emerging inter-organizational arrangements. However, its role in inter-organizational relationships has largely been neglected (e.g., Marvel and Marvel 2007; Miller, Kurunmäki, and O'Leary 2008; Cristofoli et al. 2010; Ditillo et al. 2015). This gap needs to be filled through an in-depth analysis of uses and impacts of new tools such as pooled or consolidated budgets, as well as a better understanding of the factors affecting the choice and design of the related practices and processes.

The seven papers of this special issue contribute to fill some of the gaps in the literature on public sector budgeting highlighted earlier.

Among them, three papers unearth the under-researched relationship among budgeting and performance measurement and management. Mauro, Cinquini and Grossi (this issue) provide a systematic literature review of studies on performance-based budgeting (PBB) published in international academic journals from 1990 to 2014. The analysis highlights that the majority of such studies are US-based and tend to focus on the description and explanation of implementation issues and obstacles of PBB and the extent and breadth of the use of performance information in budgeting processes. The paper identifies interesting future avenues of research, also advocating the adoption of mixed methods and comparative approaches.

The article by Bleyen et al. (this issue) empirically contributes to a better understanding of the phenomenon of incorporation of performance information in budgets by examining and comparing the cases of 10 European cities. Performance structures and the dimensions of performance taken into consideration differ significantly across the cases analysed. This variety can be explained considering varying degrees of reform implementation, experience with performance budget and prevailing institutional arrangements. However, the paper highlights that a few similarities exists: those municipalities that left the phase of embryonic performance budgeting linked performance information hundred per cent to their expenditures; performance objectives are almost always more focused on outcomes and outputs than the underlying performance indicators. This finding suggests similar learning trajectories when performance objectives and indicators are incorporated in the budget.

Drawing on a constructionist approach and applying discourse analysis, the paper of Cuganesan (this issue) seeks to investigate how the design of performance budgeting might shape managerial accountability relationships. Presenting a case study of performance budgeting reforms in the Commonwealth Government of Australia, it reveals that the proposed alternative designs for performance budgeting have shaped the managerial accountability relationships in terms of the obligation of actors to inform; forum identity; a forum's ability to discuss and interrogate; and, albeit to a limited extent, potential forum judgements and consequences.

The next four articles offer interesting insights on how budgets respond to contextual features, requests and changes, as they enhance or constrain flexibility in the face of non-routine problems, uncertainty and shocks, provide tools for strengthening participatory accountability, and can be central in strengthening or hampering a relational or transactional culture in the public realm.

Alford and Di Francesco (this issue) investigate how budget systems can be designed to enable greater situational flexibility while ensuring that public money is managed consistently with the purposes of the government. The authors offer a range of regulatory options for balancing these imperatives of control and flexibility. These options include the leadership/cultural role of central finance agencies in facilitating voluntary rule compliance, performance control, and earned autonomy as a variant of responsive regulation. Whilst each of these options depends crucially on trust building, responsive regulation is seen as a potentially significant change in the practice of budgeting and financial management within government. It assumes that regulators should apply different instruments to regulatees according to their postures towards compliance.

The paper by Ghosh Moulick and Taylor (this issue) investigates if and how the roles of absorbed and unabsorbed slack resources are different in buffering against budgetary shocks. The findings suggest that higher transparency and visibility of slack resources will play a beneficial buffering role against fiscal shock. At the same time, absorbed slack does not seem to provide a meaningful buffer for negative budget shocks.

The paper by Brun-Martos and Lapsley (this issue) tackles with the external accountability role of budgeting. In contributing to fill this gap, the authors examine the experience of participatory budgeting in the city of Edinburgh. They show how participatory budgeting enhances participative democracy and transparency, giving to citizens not only accessibility to information, but also the possibility of participating in a process of construction and sharing of meanings. They also highlight that participatory budgeting acts as a mediating instrument between the two worlds of city management and citizens, forging a bridge across the worlds of management and democratic accountability.

The paper by Wällstedt and Almqvist (this issue) investigates how budgeting can contribute or hamper the diffusion of a relational culture of cooperation, sharing and outcome-based management advocated in the New Public Governance paradigm. Using a constructivist approach to analyse budgeting and control systems in three Swedish municipalities, the authors show that budgeting and its reinforcement of traditional and transactional systems makes it difficult to employ relational approaches in practice.

The papers included in this special issue represent yet another pillar in the accumulation of knowledge on public sector budgeting. They address a number of critical issues on this broad topic, offering new perspectives on current evolutions in public budgeting, but also showing that public budgeting can and must remain the subject of enduring interest in our studies and thus opening new possibilities of research. We hope that this special issue, far from being a closure, will represent an opening of further future debates, reflections and studies on this topic.

Disclosure statement

No potential conflict of interest was reported by the authors.

References

Anessi Pessina, E., C. Barbera, M. Sicilia, and I. Steccolini. 2016. "Public Sector Budgeting: A European Review of Accounting and Public-Management Journals." *Accounting, Auditing & Accountability Journal* 29 (3): 491–519. doi:10.1108/AAAJ-11-2013-1532.

Barbera, C., M. Sicilia, and I. Steccolini. 2016. "What Mr. Rossi Wants in Participatory Budgeting: Two R's (Responsiveness and Representation) and Two I's (Inclusiveness and Interaction)." *International Journal of Public Administration*. doi:10.1080/01900692.2016.1177839.

Bovaird, T. 2007. "Beyond Engagement and Participation: User and Community Coproduction of Public Services." *Public Administration Review* 67 (5): 846–860. doi:10.1111/puar.2007.67.issue-5.

Bracci, E., C. Humphrey, J. Moll, and I. Steccolini. 2015. "Public Sector Accounting, Accountability and Austerity: More than Balancing the Books?" *Accounting, Auditing & Accountability Journal* 28 (6): 878–908. doi:10.1108/AAAJ-06-2015-2090.

Caiden, N. 2010. "Challenges Confronting Contemporary Public Budgeting: Retrospectives/Prospectives from Allen Schick." *Public Administration Review* 70 (2): 203–210. doi:10.1111/puar.2010.70.issue-2.

Coen, D., and A. Roberts. 2012. "A New Age of Uncertainty." *Governance* 25 (1): 5–9. doi:10.1111/gove.2012.25.issue-1.

Cristofoli, D., A. Ditillo, M. Liguori, M. Sicilia, and I. Steccolini. 2010. "Do Environmental and Task Characteristics Matter in the Control of Externalized Public Services? Unveiling the Relevance of Party Characteristics and Citizens' Offstage Voice?" *Accounting, Auditing & Accountability Journal* 23 (3): 350–372. doi:10.1108/09513571011034334.

Ditillo, A., M. Liguori, M. Sicilia, and I. Steccolini. 2015. "Control Patterns in Contracting-Out Relationships: It Matters What You Do, Not Who You Are." *Public Administration* 93 (1): 212–229. doi:10.1111/padm.2015.93.issue-1.

Ezzamel, M., N. Hyndman, Å. Johnsen, I. Lapsley, and J. Pallot. 2007. "Experiencing Institutionalization: The Development of New Budgets in the UK Devolved Bodies." *Accounting, Auditing & Accountability Journal* 20 (1): 11–40. doi:10.1108/09513570710731191.

Hendriks, F. 2010. *Vital Democracy: A Theory of Democracy in Action*. Oxford: Oxford University Press.

Hyndman, N., and C. Connolly. 2011. "Accruals Accounting in the Public Sector: A Road Not Always Taken." *Management Accounting Research* 22 (1): 36–45. doi:10.1016/j.mar.2010.10.008.

Lapsley, I. 2009. "New Public Management: The Cruellest Invention of the Human Spirit?" *Abacus* 45 (1): 1–21. doi:10.1111/abac.2009.45.issue-1.

Liguori, M., M. Sicilia, and I. Steccolini. 2012. "Some like It Non-Financial Politicians' and Managers' Views on the Importance of Performance Information." *Public Management Review* 14 (7): 903–922. doi:10.1080/14719037.2011.650054.

Liguori, M., M. Sicilia, and I. Steccolini. 2014. "Public Value as "Performance": Politicians' and Managers' Perspectives on the Importance of Budgetary, Accruals and Non-Financial Measures." In *Public Value and Performance Management, Measurement and Reporting Studies in Public and*

Non-Profit Governance, Volume 3, edited by J. Guthrie, G. Marcon, S. Russo, and F. Farneti, 85–104. Bingley: Emerald.

Marvel, M., and H. Marvel. 2007. "Outsourcing Oversight: A Comparison of Monitoring for In-House and Contracted Services." *Public Administration Review* 67 (3): 521–530. doi:10.1111/puar.2007.67.issue-3.

Miller, P., L. Kurunmäki, and T. O'Leary. 2008. "Accounting, Hybrids and the Management of Risk." *Accounting, Organizations and Society* 33 (7–8): 942–967. doi:10.1016/j.aos.2007.02.005.

Osborne, S. P. 2006. "The New Public Governance?" *Public Management Review* 8 (3): 377–387. doi:10.1080/14719030600853022.

Osborne, S. P. 2009. "Debate: Delivering Public Services: Are We Asking the Right Questions?" *Public Money & Management* 29 (1): 5–7. doi:10.1080/09540960802617269.

Saliterer, I., M. Sicilia, and I. Steccolini. Forthcoming. "Public Budgets and Budgeting: State of the Art and Future Challenges." In *Handbook of Public Administration and Management in Europe*, edited by E. Ongaro and S. Van Thiel. Palgrave.

Sicilia, M., E. Guarini, A. Sancino, M. Andreani, and R. Ruffini. 2016. "Public Services Management and Co-Production in Multi-Level Governance Settings." *International Review of Administrative Sciences* 82 (1): 8–27. doi:10.1177/0020852314566008.

Mariafrancesca Sicilia

Ileana Steccolini

Insights into performance-based budgeting in the public sector: a literature review and a research agenda

Sara Giovanna Mauro, Lino Cinquini and Giuseppe Grossi

ABSTRACT

In the spirit of New Public Management (NPM), performance-based budgeting (PBB) has (re-)attracted the interest of both academics and practitioners. A wide variety of approaches and results have enlivened the debate on this topic, but the growing amount of theoretical and empirical works calls for systematization. Therefore, a systematic review is carried out on public management and accounting studies published in international academic journals from 1990 to 2014. Through descriptive and thematic investigations, this article explores the results achieved to date and identifies gaps and avenues for future research, answering two questions: What has been done? What else should be done?

Introduction

During the New Public Management (NPM) era, the shift from a focus on input to a focus on results has led to an 'increase in the amount of information and change in the type of information generated and used for budgeting and management purposes' (Kristensen, Groszyk, and Buhler 2002, 10). It has renewed the attention by both practitioners and academics to the budgetary use of performance information (OECD 2007), which this work refers to as performance-based budgeting (PBB). PBB is designed to develop information about results and use it in both the budgeting process and the allocation of resources.

Despite the relevant body of literature on PBB and the wide variety of research findings, surprisingly there has not been any systematization of the knowledge regarding PBB. Previous academic reviews have broadly investigated the research patterns in accounting (Broadbent and Guthrie 2008; Goddard 2010), focused on the more general stream of literature on performance measurement and management (Modell 2009; Van Helden, Johnsen, and Vakkuri 2008; Van Helden and Reichard 2013), or alternatively, on the evolution of the public budget (Anessi-Pessina et al. 2016). In these works, PBB has played only a marginal role. Robinson and Brumby (2005) conducted a review of the topic, but focusing on the empirical literature on output-based hospital funding systems. Therefore, the claim of the paper is that not enough attention has been given to reviewing and systematizing empirical and theoretical knowledge regarding PBB, and this work is thus an attempt to fill this gap through a systematic review of the literature (Tranfield, Denyer, and Smart 2003).

Systematic review may be defined as 'a review of the literature according to an explicit, rigorous, and transparent methodology' (Greenhalgh et al. 2004, 582). Widely used in the medical sciences, it has been applied more recently to management research to counteract the bias of traditional literature reviews and enhance the 'legitimacy and authority of the resultant evidence' (Tranfield, Denyer, and Smart 2003, 208). Therefore, a contribution of this work is methodological since a systematic review of the literature in the field of public management/administration and accounting is conducted to guarantee the reliability of the evidence produced (De Vries, Bekkers, and Tummers 2015).

Similar to Broadbent and Guthrie, who reviewed 20 years of accounting research, the current work is designed to answer two questions: 'What has been done?' and 'What could be done?' (Broadbent and Guthrie 2008). Indeed, the review has a twofold purpose: (a) to understand PBB by systematizing the results achieved until now; and (b) to map relevant previous contributions to highlight overstated and overlooked areas and thus address a possible future agenda. Accordingly, the review is designed to contribute to the current body of knowledge by describing how previous works have addressed the topic under investigation (*Descriptive analysis*), synthesizing the main themes investigated until now and determining new research questions (*Thematic analysis*).

To fulfil these purposes, the research process underwent different phases. First, the research protocol was defined and the search process carried out (*Review design*). This process resulted in a set of papers that were analysed and codified (*Descriptive analysis*). Then, the content of these papers was subjected to further investigation in an attempt to provide an answer to the first research question, '*What has been done?*', as discussed in the section with the same name. According to the analysis, relevant issues were suggested for further analysis, thus addressing the second research question, '*What could be done?*' (*Discussion: What could be done?*). In the last working phase, the main findings were summarized and conclusions were drawn (*Conclusion*).

Review design

A systematic review designed to be both methodologically rigorous and theoretically sound was carried out through a well-documented process (Tranfield, Denyer, and Smart 2003). Each of the following subsections illustrates a stage of this process.

Search strategy

The systematic search began with an identification of the keywords. This was a dynamic process aimed at finding search terms suitable for reflecting the variety of labels coined and used by practitioners and scholars. As demonstrated by the scoping study (Tranfield, Denyer, and Smart 2003), *performance, output, outcome* and *results* are all concepts at the heart of the current debate on the topic and partly explain the different expressions used (e.g., Diamond 2005). Our search process used these terms and some acronyms (Appendix 1).

We were interested in discovering the different contributions from the fields of public management/administration and accounting, which are the most relevant disciplines in studies of public sector performance measurement and management (Modell 2009; Van Helden, Johnsen, and Vakkuri 2008). Thus, a variety of databases, powered by Google (Google Scholar), EBSCOHost (Business Source Complete), Jstor (Jstor: Arts and Science I and II collection – Business collection) and Thomson Reuters (Web of Science), were selected to frame the search. They were used in combination, or alternatively, by previous literature reviews on adjacent topics (e.g., Boyne 2003; Kroll 2015).

In addition, four search strings guided the selection of papers:

- *First parameter (language)*: To avoid translation problems, only papers written in English were selected.
- *Second parameter (time frame)*: The review included papers published from 1990 to 2014 to take into account studies conducted throughout the NPM era (Hood and Peters 2004).
- *Third parameter (topic)*: The papers should address PBB in the public sector to ensure an in-depth analysis of comparable studies (Kroll 2015).
- *Fourth parameter (source)*: The review included only papers published in international academic journals in the fields of public management/administration and accounting to guarantee that all the selected papers meet the basic requirements of theoretical and methodological rigor (Anessi- Pessina et al. 2016). A systematic review is usually characterized by the quality assessment of the papers, but researchers often rely on the assessment of the journals rather than formally applying any quality assessment criteria to the articles, particularly in the field of management (Tranfield, Denyer, and Smart 2003). Thus, the journal rankings powered by ABS (2015) and SCJmago (http://www.scimagojr.com/) were used as a reference point in order to include in the review data set only papers published in academic journals.

Search rounds

A representative data set of the literature was constructed by conducting six search queries in each web-search engine selected, using Boolean logic to frame the search and specific keywords for each search round and limiting the search according to language, time frame, and, if possible, type of paper.

Screening and assessment

During this third phase, three main activities were carried out, each of which is described below and depicted in Figure 1.

Check all the eligibility criteria
The records identified were manually scanned, and their general information, title and, when required, abstract/introduction were screened to include in the data set

Stage 3a: Check of all the eligibility criteria (records selected)							
Databases	Search Rounds						
	S1	S2	S3	S4	S5	S6	S7
Google Scholar	8	42	14	5	4	2	19
Business Source Complete	5	50	43	17	24	8	-
JStor	1	19	13	3	4	2	-
Web of Science	13	17	8	6	9	0	-
Tot.	27	128	78	31	41	12	19

Stage 3b: Elimination of duplicated papers

Net number of papers selected: N= 90

Stage 3c: Elimination of loosely focused papers

Final number of papers selected: **N= 60**

Figure 1. Stage 3: screening and assessment.

(*Records selected*) those that met all four inclusion parameters, with specific attention paid to topic and source.

A preliminary analysis of the selected records highlighted a significant predominance of public management/administration journals compared to accounting journals in the data set. To achieve a more balanced portrayal of the two fields of research, additional searches were launched through Google Scholar in accounting journals most often used in previous accounting literature reviews (e.g., Broadbent and Guthrie 2008; Goddard 2010). The results of these rounds are summarized in Figure 1(*S7*).

Elimination of duplicated papers
The records selected from the different search queries and databases were compared, and duplicate papers were eliminated.

Elimination of loosely focused papers
The final listing included ninety papers. These works were further screened and categorized through deeper analysis to attain a more focused selection of papers. In the final data set, papers whose main purpose was the study of PBB were included, and papers where PBB appeared to be a contextual or marginal factor were excluded. While the number of selected papers, sixty, might appear limited, it is in line with the size of previous reviews (Kroll 2015; Van Helden, Johnsen, and Vakkuri 2008). Furthermore, it is the result of multiple searches conducted with multiple web engines and is consistent with the purpose of the work.

Data analysis
The last stage of the process involved descriptive and conceptual analyses conducted on the sixty papers of the final data set, as explained in the following sections.

Descriptive analysis

The review selected the main parameters used by previous classification frameworks (Anessi- Pessina et al. 2016; Broadbent and Guthrie 2008; Goddard 2010; Van Helden 2005; Van Helden, Johnsen, and Vakkuri 2008) and adapted them to the features of the current data set. The resulting following dimensions were included in the analysis scheme:

- DATA SOURCE, which is the journal and year of publication.
- RESEARCH SETTING, which is the context of the analysis. This dimension considered the continent and distinguished: (a) *federal level*, referring to the federal level of government in a federation; (b) *state level*, referring to the state level in a federation; (c) *central level*, referring to the central level of government in a unitary state; (d) *local level*, referring, for instance, to a county or munici- pality; (e) *cross level*, referring to different levels of government (e.g., federal and central levels; cantonal and municipal); (f) *agency level*, referring to studies built primarily on an agency's role and perspective; and (g) *other*, that is, for instance, research referring generally to the public sector.
- RESEARCH METHOD, which is the data-collection and methodological approaches used. The research identified the following main categories: (a) *survey-based analysis*, referring to papers focused primarily on developing a statistical/mathematical analysis of data gathered from a survey; (b) *official data-based analysis*, referring to papers focused primarily on developing a statistical/mathematical analysis of data gathered from an official data set; (c) *experiment*; (d) *case study*, referring to research conducted through the use of qualitative – and often multiple – methods of data collection, such as interviews and document analysis (this category also included a few works based on interviews); (e) *document analysis*; (f) *reviews/reflections*, referring to studies that described, elaborated on, reflected on or critically analysed previous studies and/or official, legislative, and historical data; and (g) *mixed methods*, referring to papers that combined different methods of data collection, such as surveys and interviews. When one method was predominant, the study was classified accordingly.
- THEORETICAL FRAMEWORK, which is the use of (a) a *single theory*, (b) *multiple theories*, or (c) *no explicit theory*, when explicit or clearly identifiable theoretical frameworks lack. Stating what a theory is or is not is a challenging issue (Jacobs 2012; Weick 1995), and the categorization of different theoretical approaches is even more difficult (Goddard 2010). Our review distinguishes between the papers that adopted a distinctive discipline (Van Helden, Johnsen, and Vakkuri 2008), formally and explicitly, from papers that adopted account- ing concepts, theorized about concepts such as accountability or provided descriptions of practices (Jacobs 2012). The latter type of work was classified as 'no explicit theory', although 'in studying performance anyone explicitly or implicitly adopts a stance on important ontological, epistemological and meth- odological issues' (Talbot 2010, 53).

The sixty works were published in the 1990–2014 (Figure 2) volumes of sixteen journals classified according to their fields on the basis of scientific journal rankings

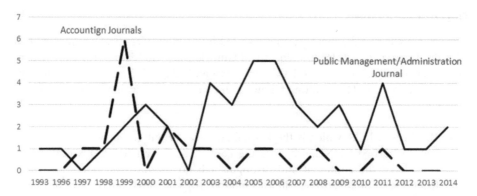

Figure 2. Analysis of papers by year of publication and journal.

(ABS 2010, 2015; SJR 2013; AIDEA 2011) and by comparing the classification with those elaborated by previous literature reviews (Anessi- Pessina et al. 2016; Van Helden, Johnsen, and Vakkuri 2008) (Figure 3).

Table 1 presents the findings of the descriptive analysis, which will be recalled in the subsequent paragraphs in order to discuss research gaps and avenues.

What has been done?

The full text of the papers was read and codified. According to prior reviews on performance measurement (Van Helden, Johnsen, and Vakkuri 2008), the research followed two main dimensions to analyse the papers: 'stage' and 'topic'. 'Stage' refers to the step in the life cycle of PBB on which the papers focused. Among the different frameworks developed by researchers (Van Dooren 2005; De Lancer Julnes and Holzer 2001), our model is similar to the one designed by Johnsen and Vakkuri (2006), who identified four steps: adoption, implementation, use, and impact. 'Topic' refers to the main issues noted by the researchers in relation to each stage.

As shown in Table 2, this analysis provides an overview of a set of issues. The scheme cross-tabulates the publications according to the stage analysed and to their source. It takes into account both the field of research and the research setting. Since the descriptive analysis indicated that the majority of works referred to the US experiences, a distinction is made between studies based exclusively in the United States (US-based) and studies conducted elsewhere (non US-based). Although this coding system involves subjectivity, the resulting classification could be useful as an analytical tool for guiding the appraisal of findings (De Vries, Bekkers, and Tummers 2015).

This section underlines the results of this analysis according to the four stages under investigation, each of which corresponds to a subsection.

Adoption

Few papers addressed this step. Despite the theoretical and, sometimes, rhetorical claims regarding why PBB should be introduced (e.g., Carlin 2003, 2006), the papers

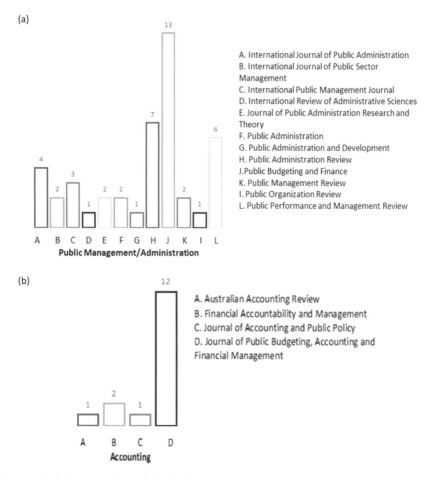

Figure 3. (a), (b): Analysis of journals by discipline.

investigating the goals of the reform pointed out how different motivations may be, even within the same state (Berry and Flowers 1999).

Nevertheless, according to the US studies, the main reasons perceived by the actors were related to programme accountability, effectiveness, and efficiency (Jordan and Hackbart 2005; Melkers and Willoughby 2001).

Implementation

Both disciplines have shown significant interest in the description and explanation of implementation issues and obstacles. PBB is not a universal concept, and it is affected by several variables (Helmuth 2010). Therefore, its design can and should change across countries and even within the same country since there is no 'one size fits all' approach (Flowers, Kundin, and Brower 1999). Variations exist about the role played by several variables in the design of the system, as demonstrated by the contrasting opinion on the costing system (e.g., Hendon 1999; Kong 2005; Martí 2013;

Table 1. Classification of papers.

	Public management and administration	Accounting	Tot.
Continent			
Europe			5
- *Estonia*	1	–	*1*
- *Germany*	2	1	*3*
- *Switzerland*	1	–	*1*
North America			42
- *USA*	30	12	*42*
Central and South America			2
- *Latin American countries*	1	–	*1*
- *Chile*	1	–	*1*
Asia			1
- *Singapore*	–	1	*1*
Oceania			4
- *Australia*	1	2	*3*
- *New Zealand*	1	–	*1*
Across continents			6
- *North America & Asia*	1	–	*1*
- *North America, South America, Asia & Africa*	1	–	*1*
- *North America, Europe & Oceania*	2	–	*2*
- *Europe & Oceania*	1	–	*1*
- *Other*	1	–	*1*
Tot.	*44*	*16*	*60*
Research setting			
Federal level	10	1	11
State level	11	9	20
Central level	3	1	4
Local level	6	2	8
Across level	8	–	8
Agency level	4	2	6
Other	2	1	3
Tot.	*44*	*16*	*60*
Research method			
Survey-based analysis	9	2	11
Official data-based analysis	4	2	6
Experiment	1	1	2
Case study	9	4	13
Document analysis	3	0	3
Reviews/reflections	14	7	21
Mixed methods	4	–	4
Tot.	*44*	*16*	*60*
Theoretical framework			
Single theory	9	2	11
Multiple theories	4	–	4
No explicit theory	31	14	45
Tot.	*44*	*16*	*60*

Wang 2008), while, at the same time, different approaches share similar problems and challenges.

Use

The extent and breadth of the use of performance information have been mainly investigated in the field of public management and administration. In this regard, the US studies have often investigated the effect of data on budget allocations through statistical analysis (e.g., Gilmour and Lewis 2006a, 2006b). The findings reveal a limited impact of information on budget recommendations and appropriations.

Table 2. Analysis of papers by content and origin.

	Accounting		Public management/administration	
	US-based	Non US-based	US-based	Non US-based
Adoption	*Reasons* • Berry and Flowers 1999; Jordan and Hackbart 2005 *Actors involved, influencing conditions and tactics to adopt* • Berry and Flowers 1999		*Reasons* • Melkers and Willoughby 2001 *Requirements* • Melkers and Willoughby 1998 *Drivers* • Andrews 2004; Andrews and Hill 2003 *Overview* • Joyce 2011	*Reasons* • Sterck and Scheers 2006 *Drivers* • Andrews 2006
Implementation	*Actors involved, influencing conditions and tactics to adopt* • Berry and Flowers 1999 *Design* • Flowers, Kundin, and Brower 1999 • Martin 1997 *Implementation issues* • Berry and Flowers 1999; Easterling 1999; Hendon 1999; Lu 1998; Pitsvada and LoStracco 2002; Sheffield 1999; Wang 1999	*Gap between adoption and implementation* • Carlin 2003, 2006 *Design* • Jones 2001	*Design* • Kong 2005; Joyce 1993; Melkers and Willoughby 1998 *Extent of implementation* • Melkers and Willoughby 2001 *Implementation issues* • Courty and Marschke 2003; Kong 2005; Joyce 1993; Lu 2007, 2011; McNab and Melese 2003; Melkers and Willoughby 2001; Posner and Fantone 2007; Smith 1999; VanLandingham, Wellman, and Andrews 2005; Wang 2008	*Gap between adoption and implementation* • Carlin and Guthrie 2003 *Design* • Martí 2013; Mascarenhas 1996; Sterck and Scheers 2006 *Implementation issues* • Arellano – Gault and Gil – Garcia 2004; Mascarenhas 1996; McGill 2001; Ridder, Bruns, and Spier 2005, 2006; Sterck and Scheers 2006

(Continued)

Table 2. (Continued).

	Accounting		Public management/administration	
	US-based	Non US-based	US-based	Non US-based
Use	*Extent of use* • Reck 2001 *Purposes of use* • Wang 1999		*Extent of use* • Gilmour and Lewis 2006a, 2006b; Jordan and Hackbart 1999; Joyce 1993; Frisco and Stalebrink 2008; Moynihan 2006; Rhee 2014 *Use over time* • Lee and Burns 2000. *Purposes of use* • Ho 2011; Lu 2007; Wang 2000 *Drivers/conditions* Hou et al. 2011; Kong 2005; Lu, Willoughby, and Arnett 2009; Rivenbark and Kelly 2006; Williamson and Snow 2014	*Extent of use* • Raudla 2012; Sterck 2007; Sterck and Scheers 2006; Zaltsman 2009
Impact	*Subjective impact* • Jordan and Hackbart 2005. *Objective impact* • Klase and Dougherty 2008	*Subjective impact* • Jagalla, Becker, and Weber 2011	*Subjective impact* • Melkers and Willoughby 2001; Willoughby 2004; Willoughby and Melkers 2000; Wang 2000	*Subjective impact* • Sterck 2007 *Factors influencing the perceived PBB success* • Helmuth 2010 *Objective impact* • Lee and Wang 2009

More positive results can be identified at the local level, where the decisions could be less political (Ho 2011; Kong 2005). Non-US studies have adopted a different perspective but shown similar results. Indeed, a partial and limited use of information has also emerged by qualitative studies on the use of performance information by different actors (Raudla 2012; Sterck 2007; Sterck and Scheers 2006).

Finally, although only two accounting studies address this stage, their results confirm a limited impact of information on resource allocations.

Impact

In both disciplines, few studies have explored the effects of the reform and have used perceptual measures more than factual measures. The latter are used by in both the fields demonstrating differentiated PBB's effect (Klase and Dougherty 2008; Lee and Wang 2009). According to the perceptions of users, particularly budgeters, PBB seems to have a greater effect on organizational and programme-related factors, such as programme accountability and effectiveness, as well as general decision-making (Jordan and Hackbart 2005; Melkers and Willoughby 2001; Willoughby and Melkers 2000), and the impact appears to be more positive at the local level (Wang 2000). Non US studies (e.g., Jagalla, Becker, and Weber 2011; Helmuth 2010) have investigated more varied topics.

Discussion: what could be done?

The thematic analysis of the issues summarized in Table 2 contributed to identifying overlooked and overstated areas and to creating a research agenda. In the following pages, we highlight the main issues regarded as a cause for reflection and a starting point for future investigation.

Context and level of analysis

The descriptive analysis shows the predominance of the US experiences, consistently with the role the country has played in the process of public sector reform over a long period of time. Only more recently, different continents and the local level did attract more attention. Thus, future research could adopt a wider approach and take into greater account different countries and organizational levels. The rationale is to enrich the understanding of PBB through more extensive use of comparative analysis between countries and national and sub-national levels.

Since our descriptive analysis shows that most studies were based on examination of PBB at the organizational level, future research could focus on specific policy areas, or programmes (e.g., Ho 2011). The rationale is to find out whether and how PBB strengths and weaknesses might vary across sectors. Consequently, the combination of macro and micro perspectives (e.g., Grossi, Reichard, and Ruggiero 2016) may provide new interesting insights.

Literature contribution and theoretical and methodological approaches

The low attention paid to the topic by accounting literature underlines the need to reinforce the contribution by mainstream accounting journals to PBB. This gap should be filled through a dialogue between accounting and public management/ administration literature in order to exploit the role of accounting in finding appropriate mechanisms to allocate resources (Goddard 2010) and thus improving PBB.

In terms of research method, the findings of the descriptive analysis show that few works used mixed methods to investigate the phenomenon. Our research suggests using different approaches to increase the likelihood of contributing in an original way to the current debate on PBB. Our findings also show that most papers seemed not to rely explicitly on a formal theoretical framework, partly consistently with previous investigations on the use of theory in public sector accounting research (Van Helden and Reichard 2013; Jacobs 2012). The papers that refer explicitly to formal theories use several theoretical approaches: economics theory (e.g., agency theory), organization theory (e.g., organizational theory and organizational learning theory), resource-based theory, institutional theory, psychological theory (e.g., self-determination theory), budget theory (e.g., dialogue theory), political theory (e.g., the political theory of Klitgaard), and accounting theory (Miller's interpretive theory of financial management), among others. Accounting studies prefer the first two theoretical approaches, while public management studies are the only ones that combine different approaches. As Van Helden (2005) stated, performance management attracts the attention of scholars with a more pragmatic view. The use of theory is extremely relevant in order to clarify conceptual issues and explain empirical experiences. Future research could contribute greatly to the topic by linking theory and practice more explicitly.

Conceptual issues

A first suggestion for future research is to pay attention to clearly defining the conceptual issues that distinguish current practice from broader reforms undertaken by the public sector under NPM. Indeed, it is crucial to differentiate performance measurement, management, and budgeting, which are not always clearly distinguished (Easterling 1999). Although 'performance budgeting cannot stand without performance management' (Rivenbark and Kelly 2006, 37), the concepts should be understood as distinct notions, such that the latter could be interpreted as a prerequisite for PB, as the analysis of the implementation drivers confirms (Lu 2007; Wang 1999).

As many authors recognize, performance budgeting lacks a standard definition and a unique interpretation. In parts of the literature, labels such as 'performance-based budgeting', 'performance budgeting', 'outcome-based budgeting', and 'results-oriented budgeting' are used interchangeably, showing basically only semantic differences (Klase and Dougherty 2008; Melkers and Willoughby 2001; Willoughby and Melkers 2000). Some researchers consider activity-based budgeting, programme budgeting (Kong 2005), entrepreneurial budgeting, and one-line budgeting to be 'all common names for concepts that share similar features' (Helmuth 2010, 409).

Conversely, researchers note the need to differentiate concepts based on the type of information used or the type of usage. For instance, it is opportune to differentiate outcome budgeting from previous reforms because of its distinctive focus on outcomes (Martin 1997; Wang 1999). With regard to type of use, consistent with the OECD (2007) classification, 'semantic splitting' has been justified as a useful tool to distinguish between practices according to their level of sophistication in the use of information (Joyce 2011, 357), thus differentiating PBB and performance-informed budgeting, or performance budgeting and performance funding (Jordan and Hackbart 1999). In addition, some labels, such as accrual output based budgeting (AOBB) and performance-based programme budgeting, appear to be context related, and their definitions imply distinctive features. AOBB has been defined as a way to change the basis for funding agencies according to the output they produce for governments (Carlin and Guthrie 2003).

Thus, at first sight, these findings give cause to ask whether it is important to develop a more standardized approach to the topic and whether there is a need for a higher level of differentiation. As McGill (2001) noted, the ambiguity of terms and definitions has paved the way for the development of different procedures to link results and resources. In our opinion, a balanced level of differentiation in the terms used could be justified if it reflects significant differences in the interpretation and operationalization of the concept of PBB. Future studies should try to build consensus on this issue.

Nature, purposes, and impacts

The exploration of PBB should consider the nature of the tool, that is, whether PBB is a management or budgeting tool (e.g., Ho 2011; Hou et al. 2011). Some results have demonstrated that PBB can be viewed as an integral part of management *and* budgeting reform (Ho 2011), although the initiative is more popular as a management and accountability tool than as an allocative tool (e.g., Jordan and Hackbart 2005; Lu 1998; Melkers and Willoughby 1998, 2001; Wang 2000).

The issue of how best to use performance information seems still unresolved. A few researchers have underlined the difficulties in determining the causal linkage between funds and results (e.g., Joyce 1993; Wang 2008) and have attempted to provide alternatives, such as the purchase or linking approaches (Martin 1997). As Posner and Fantone said, 'the relationship between performance levels and budget dimension is not one-dimensional' (2007, 357), and the uses of performance information can vary (Ho 2011; Zaltsman 2009). Thus, given that performance information might play different roles during the budgeting process, the purposes and impacts of its use may vary. A unique focus on changes in the allocation of resources to prove the use of information could be misleading. A few studies on the stage of use have focused on the dichotomy between PBB as a managerial or budgeting tool and on its impact on changes in resource allocation. In this regard, our review suggests moving forward and investigating PBB through a new lens that takes into account the following issues, explicitly and systematically. First, Key's question on how to allocate funding (1940) should not necessarily be addressed in a direct and strict way through PBB (Moynihan 2006). As Joyce (1993) explained, performance information could be used as a motivational tool, assisting in the management of resources without directly affecting the allocation of resources. '[T]he fact that performance-based budgeting has not gained widespread acceptance is not reason enough to discount its potential' (Joyce 1993, 14). In this regard, more attention in future research should be paid to the wide range of uses of performance information and their potential impact (Nielsen and

Baekgaard 2015), taking into account the different steps of the budget cycle and its different functions.

Indeed, the public budget can play different roles and fulfil different functions, such as planning, management, and control functions (Schick 1966) and each function can correspond to a phase of the budget cycle (McNab and Melese 2003). As demonstrated in a recent review of public budgets (Anessi- Pessina et al. 2016) and confirmed by our data set, the different functions of a public budget are rarely covered in the same research. Specifically, in the case of PBB, further attention should be devoted to examining how and whether performance budgeting can contribute to the fulfilment of those different functions and during the different steps of the budget cycle (Joyce 2011; Sterck 2007). Particularly, the use dimension should prevail over the measurement dimension. To address this gap, future studies should investigate further the budgetary use of performance information. We suggest looking at practice in a systematic and critical way to link the analysis of PBB throughout the budget cycle with the different functions and goals it can fulfil.

It is worth recognizing that the reform can have multiple goals. As Jordan and Hackbart (2005) noted, the lack of a standard definition implies that different perceptions are developed regarding the definition of PBB and the reasons motivating its adoption. According to some authors (Sterck and Scheers 2006; Reck 2001), the need to improve efficiency and effectiveness goes hand in hand with the need to improve accountability; other scholars see these goals as contrasting (Arellano – Gault and Gil – Garcia 2004; Smith 1999). According to Carlin and Guthrie (2003), AOBB has been presented as a tool suitable for managing this challenge. However, the evidence demonstrates how challenging and difficult this task can be. Future studies should contribute by deepening the investigation of the potential different goals of the reform and assessing its results.

From design to use

If there are problems regarding definition, different information can generate confusion, the translation of the concept into practice becomes challenging, and the chances of success decrease. Indeed, the evidence indicates the existence of a gap between what is formally declared and what is practically achieved (Andrews and Hill 2003; Carlin 2003, 2006; Carlin and Guthrie 2003; Pitsvada and LoStracco 2002; Sterck 2007). Is the gap unintentional or is it the consequence of voluntary decisions? Carlin (2003) stated that the description of deviations from initial plans as 'unintended effects' has become difficult to sustain. Is the partial implementation of the reform a consequence of intrinsic challenges? Can actors' decisions help create a gap between discourses and actions?

We suggest the development of a comprehensive and systematic approach to the topic, from the analysis of the reform's meaning and reasons to the assessment of its results. In this framework, the role played by the different actors is crucial. Opinions and perceptions can change across units and departments (Easterling 1999; Moynihan 2006), but differences exist also because of the different 'public entrepreneurs' involved in the various stages of reform (Berry and Flowers 1999). A further step could be the study of participation patterns (e.g., Lu 2011) during all stages of the process and interactions among the different users. Therefore, it is important to investigate how each category of actor perceives, interprets, and enacts the reform, looking also at external stakeholders.

Conclusion

The use of performance information for budgeting has appeared as a challenging research theme. Indeed, the integration of budgeting and performance management has been recognized as a 'promising research avenue' by previous analysis (Anessi-Pessina et al. 2016, 14) and has attracted growing attention in recent years because of its potentially multi-faceted impacts. Nevertheless, it has not been the object of systematic or ad hoc analysis of the related literature. Our paper contributes to the body of knowledge on this relevant issue by providing both an attempt to systematize previous research and stimulate future studies.

The review has searched for both empirical and theoretical works, that have studied PBB in the public sector without focusing only on a specific type of public organization, policy field, or country (e.g., Robinson and Brumby 2005). Furthermore, it has enriched the understanding and development of PBB by investigating the contributions made to the topic by accounting and public management/administration studies. Indeed, previous reviews of public sector performance management research have underlined the shift from the examination of performance information design to that of performance information use (Van Helden and Reichard 2013), and thus the crucial role of the 'use' dimension (Van Helden, Johnsen, and Vakkuri 2008), but with few references to budgeting. Equally, a review of studies on public budget in the two fields of research has pointed out their limited references to performance budgeting (Anessi- Pessina et al. 2016). Previous examinations of public sector accounting literature have recognized performance measurement and management as key 'accounting topics' (Broadbent and Guthrie 2008; Goddard 2010; Van Helden 2005) and have identified accounting as a vital ingredient in the agenda of public sector organizations to address key questions, such as the search for the most effective mechanisms to allocate resources (Goddard 2010). The references to budgeting in these studies have been modest. Our work has shed new light on this topic by conducting a highly focused review that deeply analyses studies on the integration of performance information and budgeting and illustrates how the two streams of literature have contributed and can still contribute to the development of the topic.

In order to guarantee the reliability and validity of findings and implications, we adopted an explicit, transparent, and rigorous methodology (De Vries, Bekkers, and Tummers 2015; Greenhalgh et al. 2004). Our work has provided an additional systematic review of management research in order to reinforce its use in a field where it is relatively more recent and less frequently used than in other fields (Tranfield, Denyer, and Smart 2003).

By conducting this systematic review, our work has achieved a twofold objective of contributing to the current body of knowledge from two perspectives, represented by the following questions: 'What has been done?' and 'What could be done?' (Broadbent and Guthrie 2008, 130).

First, through the implementation of a descriptive analysis, our work has provided a picture of the main features of the studies included in the data set. The predominance of US papers and public management/administration literature on the topic have meant the call for a more differentiated approach and greater attention to the topic in the field of accounting. Then, the review has suggested the adoption of mixed methods, comparative approaches, and more theoretical investigations to move forward the dialogue on PBB.

Furthermore, to overcome the lack of systematization, our work has proposed a framework of analysis based on a previous study (Johnsen and Vakkuri 2006) and has enriched this model with a distinction between the different streams of research in order to clarify the previous contributions. This classification has provided a tool to look at previous research and identify overlooked and overstated issues. Through its thematic analysis the review has contributed to identifying research gaps and future research avenues by providing several stimuli for researchers. These latter include the call for higher conceptual clarity; exploration of diverse purposes and uses of performance information throughout the budget cycle; focus on the assessment of the impact of the reforms; and systematic analysis of the link between PBB's interpretations, goals, and results.

We acknowledge that the present literature review has some limitations. It was based on a selection of papers published only in international academic journals. We found a number of relevant studies published in non-academic journals or elaborated by practitioners, but these practical works fell outside the scope of our review. Consequently, could be the object of future research to compare between different approaches and complement the current findings. The gaps and problems identified and the research directions outlined are the personal views of the authors, as do the decisions about the review's parameters. Notwithstanding these issues, this work could be considered an attempt to review previous studies on PBB and suggest a research agenda. Indeed, the use of performance information in budgeting processes has been a critical topic and still represents an issue that requires further clarification, as the debate on the phenomenon and the present review demonstrate.

Acknowledgements

The authors wish to acknowledge helpful feedbacks from the participants at EAA Annual Congress (Glasgow, 2015), XIX IRSPM Conference (Birmingham, 2015), and AIDEA Annual Congress (Piacenza, 2015), and thank Prof. Jan van Helden (University of Groningen) for his precious comments on a previous version of the paper, the anonymous reviewers and the guest editors of the special issue for their priceless advices.

Disclosure statement

No potential conflict of interest was reported by the authors.

References

ABS. 2010. *Academic Journal Quality Guide 2010*. Version 4. London: The Association of Business School.

ABS. 2015. *Academic Journal Guide 2015*. London: The Association of Business School.

AIDEA. 2011. *Journal Rating*. Accademia Italiana di Economia Aziendale. http://www.accademiaai dea.it/

Andrews, M. 2004. "Authority, Acceptance, Ability and Performance- Based Budgeting Reforms." *The International Journal of Public Sector Management* 17 (4): 332–344. doi:10.1108/09513550410539811.

Andrews, M. 2006. "Beyond 'Best Practice' and 'Basics First' in Adopting Performance Budgeting Reform." *Public Administration and Development* 26 (2): 147–161. doi:10.1002/(ISSN)1099-162X.

Andrews, M., and H. Hill. 2003. "The Impact of Traditional Budgeting Systems on the Effectiveness of Performance- Based Budgeting: A Different Viewpoint on Recent Findings." *International Journal of Public Administration* 26 (2): 135–155. doi:10.1081/PAD-120018299.

Anessi- Pessina, E., C. Barbera, S. Rota, M. Sicilia, and I. Steccolini. 2016. "Public Sector Budgeting: A European Review of Accounting and Public-Management Journals." *Accounting, Auditing, & Accountability Journal* 29 (3). doi:10.1108/AAAJ-11-2013-1532.

Arellano – Gault, D., and J. R. Gil – Garcia. 2004. "Public Management Policy and Accountability in Latin America: Performance- Oriented Budgeting in Colombia, Mexico, and Venezuela (1994-2000)." *International Public Management Journal* 7 (1): 49–71.

Berry, S. F., and G. Flowers. 1999. "Public Entrepreneurs in the Policy Process: Performance – Based Budgeting Reform in Florida." *Journal of Public Budgeting, Accounting and Financial Management* 11 (4): 578–617.

Boyne, G. A. 2003. "Sources of Public Service Improvement: A Critical Review and Research Agenda." *Journal of Public Administration Research and Theory* 13 (3): 367–394. doi:10.1093/jopart/mug027.

Broadbent, J., and J. Guthrie. 2008. "Public Sector to Public Services: 20 Years of Contextual Accounting Research." *Accounting, Auditing & Accountability Journal* 21 (2): 129–169. doi:10.1108/09513570810854383.

Carlin, T. M. 2003. "Accrual Output- Based Budgeting Systems in Australia – A Great Leap Backwards?" *Australian Accounting Review* 13 (30): 41–47. doi:10.1111/j.1835-2561.2003.tb00399.x.

Carlin, T. M. 2006. "Victoria's Accrual Output Based Budgeting System- Delivering as Promised? Some Empirical Evidence." *Financial Accountability & Management* 22 (1): 1–19. doi:10.1111/fam.2006.22.issue-1.

Carlin, T., and J. Guthrie. 2003. "Accrual Output Based Budgeting Systems in Australia. The Rhetoric- Reality Gap." *Public Management Review* 5 (2): 145–162. doi:10.1080/1461667032000066372.

Courty, P., and G. Marschke. 2003. "Performance Funding in Federal Agencies: A Case Study of a Federal Job Training Program." *Public Budgeting & Finance* 23 (3): 22–48. doi:10.1111/1540-5850.2303002.

De Lancer Julnes, P., and M. Holzer. 2001. "Promoting the Utilization of Performance Measures in Public Organizations: An Empirical Study of Factors Affecting Adoption and Implementation." *Public Administration Review* 61 (6): 693–708. doi:10.1111/puar.2001.61.issue-6.

De Vries, H., V. Bekkers, and L. Tummers. 2015. "Innovation in the Public Sector: A Systematic Review and Future Research Agenda." *Public Administration*. Advance online publication. doi:10.1111/padm.12209.

Diamond, J. 2005. *Establishing a Performance Management Framework for Government*. Working Paper No. 5-50. Washington, DC: International Monetary Fund.

Easterling, N. C. 1999. "Performance Budgeting in Florida: To Muddle or Not to Muddle, that is the Question." *Journal of Public Budgeting, Accounting and Financial Management* 11 (4): 559–577.

Flowers, G., E. Kundin, and R. S. Brower. 1999. "How Agency Conditions Facilitate and Constrain Performance- Based Program Systems: A Qualitative Inquiry." *Journal of Public Budgeting, Accounting and Financial Management* 11 (4): 618–648.

Frisco, V., and O. Stalebrink. 2008. "Congressional Use of the Program Assessment Rating Tool." *Public Budgeting & Finance* 28 (2): 1–19. doi:10.1111/j.1540-5850.2008.00902.x.

Gilmour, J., and D. Lewis. 2006a. "Assessing Performance Budgeting at OMB: The Influence of Politics, Performance and Program Size." *Journal of Public Administration Research and Theory* 16 (2): 169–186. doi:10.1093/jopart/muj002.

Gilmour, J., and D. Lewis. 2006b. "Does Performance Budgeting Work? An Examination of the Office of Management and Budget's PART Scores." *Public Administration Review* 66 (5): 742–752. doi:10.1111/puar.2006.66.issue-5.

Goddard, A. 2010. "Contemporary Public Sector Accounting Research – an International Comparison of Journal Papers." *The British Accounting Review* 42 (2): 75–87. doi:10.1016/j.bar.2010.02.006.

Greenhalgh, T., G. Robert, F. Macfarlane, P. Bate, and O. Kyriakidou. 2004. "Diffusion of Innovations in Service Organizations: Systematic Review and Recommendations." *Milbank Quarterly* 82 (4): 581–629. doi:10.1111/milq.2004.82.issue-4.

Grossi, G., C. Reichard, and P. Ruggiero. 2016. "Appropriateness and Use of Performance Information in the Budgeting Process: Some experiences from German and Italian municipalities." *Public Performance & Management Review* 39 (3): 581–606. doi:10.1080/15309576.2015.1137770.

Helmuth, U. 2010. "Better Performance with Performance Budgeting? Analyzing Cases of Success and Failure in Public Administrations." *International Public Management Journal* 13 (4): 408–428. doi:10.1080/10967494.2010.524833.

Hendon, C. 1999. "Performance Budgeting in Florida- Half Way There." *Journal of Public Budgeting, Accounting and Financial Management* 11 (4): 670–679.

Ho, A. T. K. 2011. "PBB in American Local Governments: It's More than a Management Tool." *Public Administration Review* 71 (3): 391–401. doi:10.1111/j.1540-6210.2011.02359.x.

Hood, C., and G. Peters. 2004. "The Middle Aging of New Public Management: Into the Age of Paradox?" *Journal of Public Administration Research and Theory* 14 (3): 267–282. doi:10.1093/jopart/muh019.

Hou, Y., R. S. Lunsford, K. C. Sides, and K. A. Jones. 2011. "State Performance-Based Budgeting in Boom and Bust Years: An Analytical Framework and Survey of the States." *Public Administration Review* 71 (3): 370–388. doi:10.1111/j.1540-6210.2011.02357.x.

Jacobs, K. 2012. "Making Sense of Social Practice: Theoretical Pluralism in Public Sector Accounting Research." *Financial Accountability & Management* 28 (1): 1–25. doi:10.1111/faam.2012.28.issue-1.

Jagalla, T., S. D. Becker, and J. Weber. 2011. "A Taxonomy of the Perceived Benefits of Accrual Accounting and Budgeting: Evidence from German States." *Financial Accountability & Management* 27 (2): 134–165. doi:10.1111/faam.2011.27.issue-2.

Johnsen, A., and J. Vakkuri. 2006. "Is There a Nordic Perspective on Public Sector Performance Measurement?" *Financial Accountability and Management* 22 (3): 291–308. doi:10.1111/fam.2006.22.issue-3.

Jones, D. S. 2001. "Performance Measurement and Budgetary Reform in the Singapore Civil Service." *Journal of Public Budgeting, Accounting & Financial Management* 13 (4): 485–511.

Jordan, M. M., and M. H. Hackbart. 1999. "Performance Budgeting and Performance Funding in the States: A Status Assessment." *Public Budgeting and Finance* 19 (1): 68–88. doi:10.1046/j.0275-1100.1999.01157.x.

Jordan, M. M., and M. Hackbart. 2005. "The Goals and Implementation Success of State Performance-Based Budgeting." *Journal of Public Budgeting, Accounting and Financial Management* 17 (4): 471–487.

Joyce, P. G. 1993. "Using Performance Measures for Federal Budgeting: Proposal and Prospects." *Public Budgeting & Finance* 13 (4): 3–17. doi:10.1111/1540-5850.00987.

Joyce, P. G. 2011. "The Obama Administration and PBB: Building on the Legacy of Federal Performance- Informed Budgeting?" *Public Administration Review* 71 (3): 356–367. doi:10.1111/j.1540-6210.2011.02355.x.

Key, V. O. 1940. "The Lack of a Budgetary Theory." *American Political Science Review* 34 (6): 1137–1144. doi:10.2307/1948194.

Klase, K. A., and M. J. Dougherty. 2008. "The Impact of Performance Budgeting on State Budget Outcomes." *Journal of Public Budgeting, Accounting and Financial Management* 20 (3): 277–298.

Kong, D. 2005. "Performance-Based Budgeting: The U.S. Experience." *Public Organization Review* 5 (2): 91–107. doi:10.1007/s11115-005-1782-6.

Kristensen, J. K., W. Groszyk, and B. Buhler. 2002. "Outcome- Focused Management and Budgeting." *OECD Journal on Budgeting* 1 (4): 7–34. doi:10.1787/budget-v1-art20-en.

Kroll, A. 2015. "Drivers of Performance Information Use: Systematic Literature Review and Directions for Future Research." *Public Performance & Management Review* 38 (3): 459–486. doi:10.1080/15309576.2015.1006469.

Lee Jr, R. D., and R. C. Burns. 2000. "Performance measurement in State Budgeting: Advancement and Backsliding from 1990 to 1995." *Public Budgeting and Finance* 20 (1): 38–54. doi:10.1111/0275-1100.00003.

Lee, J. Y. J., and X. Wang. 2009. "Assessing the Impact of Performance- Based Budgeting: A Comparative Analysis across the United States, Taiwan, and China." *Public Administration Review* 69 (s1): 60–66. doi:10.1111/j.1540-6210.2009.02090.x.

Lu, H. 1998. "Performance Budgeting Resuscitated: Why is it Still Inviable?" *Journal of Public Budgeting, Accounting and Financial Management* 10 (2): 151–172.

Lu, Y. 2007. "Performance- Budgeting: The Perspective of State Agencies." *Public Budgeting & Finance* 27 (4): 1–17. doi:10.1111/pbaf.2007.27.issue-4.

Lu, Y. 2011. "Individual Engagement to Collective Participation: The Dynamics of Participation Pattern in Performance Budgeting." *Public Budgeting & Finance* 31 (2): 79–98. doi:10.1111/pbaf.2011.31.issue-2.

Lu, Y., K. Willoughby, and S. Arnett. 2009. "Legislating results: Examining the Legal Foundations of PBB Systems in the States." *Public Performance & Management Review* 33 (2): 266–287. doi:10.2753/PMR1530-9576330206.

Martí, C. 2013. "Performance Budgeting and Accrual Budgeting." *Public Performance & Management Review* 37 (1): 33–58. doi:10.2753/PMR1530-9576370102.

Martin, L. L. 1997. "Outcome Budgeting: A New Entrepreneurial Approach to Budgeting." *Journal of Public Budgeting, Accounting and Financial Management* 9 (1): 108–126.

Mascarenhas, R. C. 1996. "Searching for Efficiency in Public Sector: Interim Evaluation of Performance Budgeting in New Zealand." *Public Budgeting & Finance* 16 (3): 13–27. doi:10.1111/1540-5850.01074.

McGill, R. 2001. "Performance Budgeting." *The International Journal of Public Sector Management* 14 (5): 376–390. doi:10.1108/09513550110404633.

McNab, R. M., and F. Melese. 2003. "Implementing the GPRA: Examining the Prospects for Performance Budgeting in the Federal Government." *Public Budgeting and Finance* 23 (2): 73–95. doi:10.1111/1540-5850.2302006.

Melkers, J., and K. Willoughby. 1998. "The State of the States: Performance-Based Budgeting Requirements in 47 out of 50." *Public Administration Review* 58 (1): 66–73. doi:10.2307/976891.

Melkers, J. E., and K. Willoughby. 2001. "Budgeters' Views of State Performance- Budgeting Systems: Distinctions across Branches." *Public Administration Review* 61 (1): 54–64. doi:10.1111/puar.2001.61.issue-1.

Modell, S. 2009. "Institutional Research on Performance Measurement and Management in the Public Sector Accounting Literature: A Review and Assessment." *Financial Accountability & Management* 25 (3): 277–303. doi:10.1111/fam.2009.25.issue-3.

Moynihan, D. P. 2006. "What Do We Talk About When We Talk About Performance? Dialogue Theory and Performance Budgeting." *Journal of Public Administration Research and Theory* 16 (2): 151–168. doi:10.1093/jopart/muj003.

Nielsen, P. A., and M. Baekgaard. 2015. "Performance Information, Blame Avoidance, and Politicians' Attitudes to Spending and Reform: Evidence from an Experiment." *Journal of Public Administration Research and Theory* 25 (2): 545–569. doi:10.1093/jopart/mut051.

OECD. 2007. *Performance Budgeting in OECD Countries*. Paris: OECD Publishing.

Pitsvada, B., and F. LoStracco. 2002. "Performance Budgeting- the Next Budgetary Answer. But What is the Question?" *Journal of Public Budgeting, Accounting and Financial Management* 14 (1): 53–73.

Posner, P. L., and D. M. Fantone. 2007. "Assessing Federal Program Performance: Observations on the U.S. Office of Management and Budget's Program Assessment Rating Tool and its Use in the Budget Process." *Public Performance & Management Review* 30 (3): 351–368. doi:10.2753/PMR1530-9576300303.

Raudla, R. 2012. "The Use of Performance Information in Budgetary Decision-Making by Legislators: Is Estonia Any Different?" *Public Administration* 90 (4): 1000–1015. doi:10.1111/padm.2012.90.issue-4.

Reck, J. L. 2001. "The Usefulness of Financial and Nonfinancial Performance Information in Resource Allocation Decisions." *Journal of Accounting and Public Policy* 20 (1): 45–71. doi:10.1016/S0278-4254(01)00018-7.

Rhee, D.-Y.. 2014. "The Impact of Performance Information on Congressional Appropriations." *Public Performance & Management Review* 38 (1): 100–124. doi:10.2753/PMR1530-9576380105.

Ridder, H.-G., H.-J. Bruns, and F. Spier. 2005. "Analysis of Public Management Change Processes: The Case of Local Government Accounting Reforms in Germany." *Public Administration* 83 (2): 443–471. doi:10.1111/padm.2005.83.issue-2.

Ridder, H.-G., H.-J. Bruns, and F. Spier. 2006. "Managing Implementation Processes: The Role of Public Managers in the Implementation of Accrual Accounting–Evidence from Six Case Studies in Germany." *Public Management Review* 8 (1): 87–118. doi:10.1080/14719030500518857.

Rivenbark, W. C., and J. M. Kelly. 2006. "Performance Budgeting in Municipal Government." *Public Performance & Management Review* 30 (1): 35–46. doi:10.2753/PMR1530-9576300102.

Robinson, M., and J. Brumby. 2005. *Does Performance Budgeting Work? An Analytical Review of the Empirical Literature*. Working Paper No. 5-210. Washington, DC: International Monetary Fund.

Schick, A. 1966. "The Road to PPB: The Stages of Budget Reform." *Public Administration Review* 26 (4): 243–258. doi:10.2307/973296.

Sheffield, S. R. 1999. "Implementing Florida's Performance and Accountability Act: A Focus on Program Measurement and Evaluation." *Journal of Public Budgeting, Accounting and Financial Management* 11 (4): 649–669.

Smith, J. F. 1999. "The Benefits and Threats of PBB: An Assessment of Modern Reform." *Public Budgeting & Finance* 19 (3): 3–15. doi:10.1046/j.0275-1100.1999.01168.x.

Sterck, M. 2007. "The Impact of Performance Budgeting on the Role of the Legislature: A Four-Country Study." *International Review of Administrative Sciences* 73 (2): 189–203. doi:10.1177/0020852307077960.

Sterck, M., and B. Scheers. 2006. "Trends in Performance Budgeting in Seven OECD Countries." *Public Performance & Management Review* 30 (1): 47–72. doi:10.2753/PMR1530-9576300103.

Talbot, C. 2010. *Theories of Performance: Organizational and Service Improvement in the Public Domain*. Oxford: Oxford University Press.

Tranfield, D. R., D. Denyer, and P. Smart. 2003. "Towards a Methodology for Developing Evidence-Informed Management Knowledge by Means of Systematic Review." *British Journal of Management* 14 (3): 207–222. doi:10.1111/bjom.2003.14.issue-3.

Van Dooren, W. 2005. "What Makes Organisations Measure? Hypotheses on the Causes and Conditions for Performance Measurement." *Financial and Accountability Management* 21 (3): 363–383. doi:10.1111/fam.2005.21.issue-3.

Van Helden, G. J. 2005. "Researching Public Sector Transformation: The Role of Management Accounting." *Financial Accountability and Management* 21 (1): 99–133. doi:10.1111/fam.2005.21.issue-1.

Van Helden, G. J., A. Johnsen, and J. Vakkuri. 2008. "Distinctive Research Patterns on Public Sector Performance Measurement of Public Administration and Accounting Disciplines." *Public Management Review* 10 (5): 641–651. doi:10.1080/14719030802264366.

Van Helden, G. J., and C. Reichard. 2013. "A Meta-Review of Public Sector Performance Management Research." *Tékhne* 11 (1): 10–20. doi:10.1016/j.tekhne.2013.03.001.

VanLandingham, G., M. Wellman, and M. Andrews. 2005. "Useful but Not a Panacea: Performance-Based Program Budgeting in Florida." *International Journal of Public Administration* 28 (3–4): 233–253. doi:10.1081/PAD-200047313.

Wang, X. 1999. "Conditions to Implement Outcome- Oriented Performance Budgeting: Some Empirical Evidence." *Journal of Public Budgeting, Accounting & Financial Management* 11 (4): 533–552.

Wang, X. 2000. "Performance Measurement in Budgeting: A Study of County Governments." *Public Budgeting and Finance* 20 (3): 102–118. doi:10.1111/0275-1100.00022.

Wang, X. 2008. "Convincing Legislators with Performance Measures." *International Journal of Public Administration* 31 (6): 654–667. doi:10.1080/01900690701641232.

Weick, K. E. 1995. "What Theory is Not, Theorizing is." *Administrative Science Quarterly* 40 (3): 385–390. doi:10.2307/2393789.

Williamson, A., and D. Snow. 2014. "From Accountability to Decision-Making? Budgeting with Mandated Performance Measures." *International Journal of Public Administration* 37 (4): 202–214. doi:10.1080/01900692.2013.809593.

Willoughby, K. G. 2004. "Performance Measurement and Budget Balancing: State Government Perspective." *Public Budgeting & Finance* 24 (2): 21–39. doi:10.1111/j.0275-1100.2004.02402002.x.

Willoughby, K. G., and J. E. Melkers. 2000. "Implementing PBB: Conflicting Views of Success." *Public Budgeting and Finance* 20 (1): 105–120. doi:10.1111/0275-1100.00006.

Zaltsman, A. 2009. "The Effects of Performance Information on Public Resource Allocations: A Study of Chile's Performance-Based Budgeting System." *International Public Management Journal* 12 (4): 450–483. doi:10.1080/10967490903328931.

Appendix 1

Search 1 (S1): 'performance-budgeting' AND 'public sector organizations'

Search 2 (S2): 'performance budgeting'

Search 3 (S3): 'performance-based budgeting' OR 'performance-informed budgeting' OR 'programme performance budgeting' OR 'performance-oriented budgeting'

Search 4 (S4): 'output budgeting' OR 'outcome budgeting' OR 'outcome-based budgeting' OR 'output-based budgeting' OR 'output-focused budget' OR 'outcome focused budget'

Search 5 (S5): 'PBB' OR 'PPBB' OR 'AOBB'

Search 6 (S6): 'results-oriented budgeting' OR 'results- focused budgeting'

Search 7 (S7): 'performance-based budgeting' OR 'output-based budgeting' OR 'use of performance information' (throughout the paper)

Linking budgeting to results? Evidence about performance budgets in European municipalities based on a comparative analytical model

Pieter Bleyen, Daniel Klimovský, Geert Bouckaert and Christoph Reichard

ABSTRACT

This article contributes to the debate on the incorporation of performance information in European local government budgets. At the core is the development of an analytical model for comparing efforts of performance budgeting (PB). Evidence in ten cases indicates that performance structures and the span of performance differ, that performance indicators are far from always measuring outcomes or outputs, and that future and past performance figures are often absent. Nevertheless similar learning trajectories do exist. Possible explanations for the variation involve the varying degrees of reform implementation, experience with PB and prevailing institutional arrangements.

Introduction

Since the 1980s, several European countries have established result-oriented administrative reforms. In these reforms new public management (NPM) and post-NPM management ideas play an important role (Humphrey et al. 2005; Kuhlmann and Bouckaert 2016). Within these developments, performance budgeting is specifically relevant. It is an indicator of the integration of performance measurement into management, and of non-financial and measurable information into budgeting (Robinson 2007; Curristine and Flynn 2013).

The concepts, implementation and use of performance budgeting have been studied, though only to a limited extent from a local government and/or comparative point of view (e.g. Sterck 2007; Mussari et al. 2016; Grossi, Reichard, and Ruggiero 2016). Although there is some empirical evidence about the general features and the dissemination of performance budgets (PBs), there is still a lack of information about details on the design of these budgets and about their incorporation and use into municipal practice (e.g. ter Bogt, van Helden, and van der Kolk 2015). As Grossi, Reichard and Ruggiero (2016) conclude, there is still plenty of room for more research to cover additional issues of performance budgeting practices, for applying different methods and for expanding the regional and comparative scope by including additional countries.

Taking these facts into account, this article intends to shed more light on the design and the incorporation of performance budgeting at local level in Europe. The budgets will be studied with a special focus at the incorporation of performance information by analysing ten 'good' practice municipalities in a selection of European countries. Moreover, a general model will be developed to compare performance budgets. The research is based on the following research questions: RQ1: How can we design a general model to map and compare performance budgets of local governments? RQ2: What are the major characteristics of the implemented performance budgets in the selected municipalities? RQ3: How can we explain observed differences in the structure and performance orientation of the analysed budgets?

Evolution of performance budgeting

PBs are linking financial resources allocated in the budget period with some kind of information about the expected results of policies. This type of budgeting requires information about strategic planning regarding the mission and objectives of an organisation and requests quantifiable data together with the allocation of resources providing meaningful information about program outcomes (Jordan and Hackbart 1999). The degree of linkage between financial resources and performance may differ in PBs between very loose coupling and a strict 'mechanical' connection between both sides (OECD 2008; Pollitt and Bouckaert 2011).

PB is not a new issue, it is known in public financial management since several decades (e.g. under the label of the 'Planning-Programming-Budgeting-System' of the 1960s and 1970s) and it has undergone several metamorphoses (Schick 2013). In the era of NPM, the PB-concept has been revitalised and became increasingly attractive for various governments (Anessi-Pessina et al. 2016). The manifold initiatives associated with NPM to strengthen performance measurement and management in public sector were an important driver for the design and implementation of PBs (see e.g. Bouckaert and Halligan 2008; Moynihan 2008; Van Dooren, Bouckaert, and Halligan 2015).

Various governments around the world have introduced PBs at national as well as at subnational and local level during the last decades. The scientific debate about PB dealt primarily with the design of PBs, with experiences implementing such concepts and – more recently – with the use of PBs during the budget cycle for budget planning and for monitoring budget execution (see e.g. Bourdeaux 2008; Carlins and Guthrie 2003; Jordan and Hackbart 1999; Raudla 2012; Robinson 2007; Schick 2013; Sterck 2007; ter Bogt, van Helden, and van der Kolk 2015; Yi Lu, Mohr, and Tat-Kei Ho 2015; for studies about PBs at local level, see particularly e.g. Anessi-Pessina and Steccolini 2007; Grossi, Reichard, and Ruggiero 2016; Kelly and Rivenbark 2011; Mussari et al. 2016; Saliterer and Korac 2013). Most of these publications focus at the managerial function of budgeting whereas the allocative and particularly the external accountability functions of the budget seem to be less developed in research (Schick 2009; Anessi-Pessina et al. 2016).

A large proportion of PB articles is dealing with the design, implementation and use of PBs in a rather general manner. Not much evidence was found on details of the performance side of PBs. The composition of a performance budget, particularly its ability to inform about past results and future ambitions with regard to the policies and services of a public sector organisation, has not often been studied in a detailed way (e.g. Curristine 2005; Conings, Sterck, and Bouckaert 2007; Weets 2012; Bleyen, Lombaert, and Bouckaert 2015). Which forms of qualitative policy objectives and corresponding quantitative performance data (performance indicators) can be discerned? To which extent are performance indicators applied to clarify achieved outcomes and performed outputs and processes? Are the interrelations between ambitions and performance indicators balanced or blurred? To which extent do PBs inform with a view at past and future developments about resource consumption (inputs), transformation pro-cesses within the organisation, direct outputs and also about policy outcomes of a public sector organisation? These are some of the issues we want to study in our research.

The existing body of research suggests that the implementation of performance budgets has not always been equally successful (for general reform results see e.g. OECD 2013; Schick 2013). Despite some exceptions, most governments face difficulties in providing decision makers with credible and relevant information in a timely manner, especially in the first years after the reform (e.g. Johnsen 2005; Jackson 2011). Also the functional use of performance information proves to be contestable (e.g. Grossi, Reichard, and Ruggiero 2016; Raudla 2012; Sterck 2007; Taylor 2009). Moreover, the information is used more for accountability purposes than for steering and control, and sometimes users just lack the exper-tise to use performance information properly (Taylor 2009; Hyndman 2008; Van Helden and Reichard 2016). A varying degree of reform implementation, external pressure by third parties or pressures to look modern, institutional arrangements, path dependencies, experience and internal political-administrative culture are all possible explanations for implementation and usage gaps (e.g. DiMaggio and Powell 1991; Olsen and Peters 1996; Christensen and Lægreid 2001).

Method and case selection

To achieve our research objectives, a qualitative research design was chosen. In the framework of COST Action "Local Public Sector Reforms (LocRef),"[1] the authors have conducted an in-depth document analysis of the budgets of ten European municipalities from Northern, Eastern, Western and Southern Europe. The munici-palities were chosen by the team members because they are considered as being 'good' practice cases in the respective country. Although the mix of countries represented in the sample is depending on the regional origin of the team members and thus is somewhat random, we consider the composition of countries as repre-sentative for the various regional patterns and models of European local government (Kuhlmann and Wollmann 2014).

Obviously, the concentration on the selected countries and municipalities has some limitations. First, selection bias may occur because of the non-random and deliberative choice of only a handful of municipalities out of several thousand across Europe (Landman 2008).

Second, the selection criterion of a 'good' practice municipality is somewhat ambiguous. The team members have selected municipalities which are well known among practitioners in the respective country for their reputation and 'good' practice in public (financial) management. Consequently, the selection process was based on the experience and the practice network of the authors.

The research was conducted between the end of 2014 and the beginning of 2016 and was based on the most recent available budget documents for each case. The fact that all budgets were available online was a coincidence and not part of the initial selection process. The following table provides a general overview of the selected countries and municipalities and why the municipalities are considered as being 'good' practice (Table 1).

Operationalisation

Measuring performance in the public sector is mostly a highly complex exercise as the major factors influencing performance are difficult to quantify and to assess (e.g. Bouckaert and Halligan 2008; Jackson 2011; Johnsen 2005; Van Dooren, Bouckaert, and Halligan 2015). In this article, a picture is provided of how municipalities cope with this complexity in the context of budgeting. Consequently, evidence is presented in two main parts: (1) context of performance budgeting reform and (2) level of incorporation of performance information in the budget. In order to analyse *the context* of performance budgeting reform in the selected European municipalities, the authors have discerned seven variables (see Table 2). These seven variables were derived from the analytical framework on the design and implementation of performance budgeting system reforms as developed by Mussari et al. (2016). Unlike the focus of that framework on the more general elements and trajectories of reform, including main causes, antecedents and drivers, this article only focuses on the current state of affairs regarding budgeting in the ten municipalities.

The extent to which performance information is *incorporated* in the budget is operationalized by seven variables that enable the assessment of what may be called the span of performance in the budget (Table 3) (Bouckaert and Halligan 2008).

The nature and embeddedness of the link between financial and non-financial performance information needs to be assessed (B.LINK). As such, the distinction is made between four types of linking practices: no link at all (traditional line-item budget without any kind of performance information); an unclear link between the financial items and (usually separated) non-financial performance information; a clear link between the financial items and separated non-financial performance information; and a clear link by means of fully integrated non-financial performance information.

In order to assess the different types of performance information in the budget, three main concepts and corresponding variables are applied throughout the analysis. First, performance objectives describe a desirable future performance situation. These pieces of performance information are usually defined in a qualitative and general way (T.OBJE). The following example is a typical performance objective: 'Increasing the well-being of citizens by providing a sufficient supply in municipal daycare units'. The measurement of performance objectives is complex and difficult because of intermediate factors and involvement of many actors within and outside the organisation. As such it is often impossible to measure the net policy outcome (e.g. Padovani and Young 2012).

On top of this, performance objectives are often multi-layered since most objectives are further detailed into several sub items or grouping items and are often grouped to some logic (i.e. policy domains, products). The budget structures of the ten selected cases confirm this complexity. Zero to seven categorical layers are discerned of which the structures of Bari[2] and Bonn are the most complex. In

Table 1. Ten 'good' practice local governments.

Country	Slovakia 5.5 million	Italy 60.8 million	Germany 81.0 million	The Netherlands 17.0 million	Ireland 4.8 million	Belgium 11.2 million	Norway 5.1 million	The Czech Rep. 10.5 million	Lithuania 3.7 million	Poland 38.7 million
Number of municipalities	2,891	8,117	11,534	390	31	589	428	6,249	60	2,478
Municipality	B. Bystrica 79,000 ±	Bari 320,000 ±+/-	Bonn 311,000 ±+/-	Eindhoven 223,000 ±+/-	Galway City 75,000 ±+/-	Genk 65,000 ±+/-	Leenskog 35,000 ± +/-	Olomouc 101,000 ±+/-	Vilnius 531,000 ±+/-	Warsaw 1.,737,000 ±+/-
Within country	6th largest city	9th largest city	19th largest city	5th largest city	3rdth largest city	24th largest city	24th largest city	6th largest city	Largest city	Largest city
'Good' practice	One of the most transparent municipalities in Slovakia according to Transparency International Slovakia (2014); Pilot project budget reform (2008)	Oscar for Budget (2014); Finalist Oscar for Budget (2012, 2013); Pilot project accounting and budgeting reform (2012–2014)	Frontrunner according to German think tank KGSt; Pilot in introducing outcome-oriented performance data	Frontrunner and best practice according to Dutch budget specialist from the Nijmegen School of Management (2015)	A represen-tative council in terms of size which prepared and published an Annual Service Plan for first time in 2015 in accordance with new legislation	Frontrunner according to Flemish performance management research (Bleyen, Lombaert and Bouckaert, 2015) Government of the Year (2014); Manager of the year (2008)	Winner of European Council price for innovation and good local governance 2014	One of the most transparent municipalities in the Czech Republic and winner of the 'Nice-City-Web 2014 Award'	First pilot project introducing strategic management plan in which financial and non-financial performance information is linked (2002)	One of the most developed performance budgets in Poland, officially published contrary to the majority of other local governments
The budget time frame	2014–2016	2014–2016	2015–2016	2015–2018	2015	2014–2019	2016–2019	2015	2014–2017	2015

Table 2. Assessment of the context of performance budgeting reform.

Variable	Question(s)
(1) Latest budget reform	When was the latest performance-oriented budgeting reform put into place?
(2) Existence of legal PB frameworks	Is a top-down framework decided by the central government or do multiple local frameworks exist?
(3) Implementation trajectory	How is the implementation trajectory organized?
(4) Obligation of performance budgeting	Is this reform obligatory for all municipalities?
(5) Budget time horizon	What is the time horizon of (non-)financial information in the budget?
(6) Budget format(s)	Are there alternative budget formats to inform the different stakeholders?
(7) Monitoring and evaluation of performance	Is performance information also included in interim reports and in the annual report?

Table 3. Assessment of incorporation of performance information in the budget.

Variable	Abbr.	Operationalization
(1) Budget link with PI	B.LINK	(1) No link, (2) Unclear link to (separate) PI, (3) Clear link to separate PI, (4) Fully Integrated PI
(2) Type of performance objectives	T.OBJE	(1) Outcome, (2) output, (3) process, (4) input (performance ambitions, strategic)
(3) Type of performance indicators	T.INDI	(1) Outcome, (2) output, (3) process, (4) input (performance ambitions, measurable)
(4) Availability of future performance figures	A.FFIG	% of performance indicators with future performance figures
(5) Availability of past performance figures	A.PFIG	% of performance indicators with past performance figures
(6) Budget coverage	B.COVE	% of expenditures covered with qualitative or quantitative performance information
(7) Performance coverage	P.COVE	% of performance objectives covered with performance indicators

order to structure the analysis only those layers that fit most closely to the definition of performance objectives as presented in this article have been selected (marked in grey in Table 4). The remaining layers are left out of the scope of the analysis, since they represent more general categories (e.g. general programmes or policy domains) or underlying and more detailed activities and actions. No evidence of any layered structure was found in Olomouc. As illustrated further in the results of this article, Olomouc is a special case. Although it is considered as being a 'good' practice municipality, Olomouc does not have a PB. Nevertheless, it is a useful case that will serve as a baseline where all findings about PB are valued as zero.

Second, performance indicators describe the way to measure a certain performance objective, usually by indicating the variables of a ratio (T.INDI). A typical example is 'increasing the number of children that make use of municipal daycare units'. The assessment of the types of performance objectives and corresponding performance indicators is based on the logical framework of input, process, output and outcome (e.g. Kirkpatrick 1998; Bennett 1975; Robinson 2013). Based on this framework, it is possible to get a comparable insight into the linkages between performance information (objectives and indicators) and funding in the (multi-)annual budgets. Inputs define the amount of resources (money, staff, research, equipment) that are used for executing a process or a programme. Processes define

Table 4. Variation of performance structures in the budget.

	Layer 1	Layer 2	Layer 3	Layer 4	Layer 5	Layer 6	Layer 7
Lørenskog[a]	8 Policy spheres	51 Policy objectives	180 Activities				
Eindhoven	6 Programs *(19 indicators)*	30 Subprograms *(78 indicators)*					
B. Bystrica	16 Programs	89 Subprograms	96 Elements *(313 indicators)*				
Genk	11 Policy domains	38 Policy objectives	162 Action plans	1,101 Actions *(150 indicators)*			
Warsaw	11 Spheres	35 Programs	190 Tasks *(173 indicators)*	140 Sub-tasks *(388 indicators)*			
Galway	8 Policy domains	57 Strategy obj.	108 Service obj.	114 Strategies	114 Perf. Standards		
Vilnius	10 Policy domains	17 Programs	62 Strategic aims *(63 indicators)*	85 Program obj. *(185 indicators)*	62 Activities		
Bonn[b]	17 Product areas	144 Product groups	X Strategic obj. *(indicators)*	X Activities	1,400 Products	X Operational obj. *(indicators)*	
Bari	4 Policy domains	99 Policy objectives	23 Missions	99 Programmes	54 Operational obj. *(57 indicators)*	95 Organization obj. *(100 indicators)*	525 Activities
Olomouc	No layered performance structure available						

[a] Fifty-four performance indicators were counted, but these were only partly linked to the layers in the budget.
[b] The number of strategic objectives, activities, operational objectives and indicators in the Bonn budget are too manifold to count.

the actions that need to be undertaken. Outputs define the products and services that are delivered through the processes that are carried out. Note that the distinction between processes and outputs is sometimes blurred. Both concepts are often confused or labelled as outputs. In this article, the authors distinguish between processes – activities undertaken to deliver an output – and the output itself, e.g. the number of participants to an organized activity. Finally, outcomes define the desired consequences of and societal reactions to public goods and services. Theoretically, the distinction is made between short-, medium- and long-term outcomes, and between direct and indirect outcomes. Important to note is that output–input (efficiency) and outcome–output ratios (effectiveness) were not included in the analysis (Van Dooren, Bouckaert, and Halligan 2015).

Third, performance figures quantify performance indicators since those figures contain a specification of the measurement of the respective indicator, either in the past or in the future (A.FFIG and A.PFIG). A typical example of a performance figure is that 'We expect the number of children that make use of municipal daycare units to increase by 5 percent in 2015 (2014: 20%)'.

Apart from how resources are linked to performance information and what kind of performance information is linked, the linking practice as such may be more or less intense. Following this idea, the concept of budget coverage is applied to estimate both the amount of expenditures that are backed with non-financial performance information (B.COVE), while the concept of performance coverage indicates the amount of performance information for which at least one clear and unambiguous performance indicator is defined (P.COVE) (e.g. Curristine 2005).

Results part 1 – budgeting reform

The countries under consideration have followed different paths of reform (see also Brusca et al. 2015) from no performance budgeting initiatives at all (e.g. the Czech Republic) to years of experience (Table 5). The Netherlands (1988), Poland (1994), Lithuania (2000), Norway (2001) and Germany (2003) are early adopters. In The Netherlands, performance budgeting and performance indicators were introduced between 1988 and 1995. Since 2003, all municipalities are obliged to start using outcome budgets in addition to output budgets, although they are free to determine the form of the budgets themselves (ter Bogt, van Helden, and van der Kolk 2015). The first Polish local performance budget was implemented voluntarily in Krakow in 1994. Although other cities like Warsaw (2007) also started to implement performance budgeting, the pace of reforms is slow due to the absence of compulsory legal provisions (Krajewska and Andrzan 2013).

In Lithuania, programme-based budgeting was introduced at the local level in 2000. By 2008 almost all municipalities were on track because they were driven by Lithuania's preparation to absorb EU financial assistance in the pre-accession and post-accession period (Nakrošis 2008). In Norway the municipal financial and performance reporting to central government (the KOSTRA system) was installed in 2001 and required local authorities to report performance indicators in a benchmarking system. Prior to KOSTRA pilot cases experimented with performance reporting. Today, the legislation requires municipalities and counties to report financial accounts, activities and results, but the framework leaves freedom as to how to establish the link with expenditures and objectives (Bernt 2012). From 2003

Table 5. Performance budgeting frameworks and reform implementation.

Municipality	B. Bystrica	Bari	Bonn	Eindhoven	Galway City	Genk	Lorenskog	Olomouc	Vilnius	Warsaw
Latest PB reform	2008–2009	2014	2003–today	2002–2003	2014	2011–2014	2002	NA	2014	2008–2009
Introduction in case	2008 (pilot)	2012	2003	2003	2014	2014	2002	NA	2014	2007
Legislation	Yes (central)	Yes (central)	Yes (regional)	Yes (central)	Yes (central)	Yes (regional)	Yes (central)	NA	Yes (central)	No
Obligation	Municipalities (>2,000)	Municipalities, provinces, regions (>5,000)	Municipalities, counties	Municipalities, provinces	Municipalities	Municipalities, provinces	Municipalities	NA	Municipalities	No
Time horizon	3–5 years (1-year binding)	3–5 years (1-year binding)	3–5 years (1-year binding)	3 years (1-year binding)	1-year binding	6 years (1-year binding)	4 years (1-year binding)	1-year binding	3 years (1-year binding)	1-year binding
Format	Same for council and management + aldermen	Different for council and management + aldermen	Same for council and management + aldermen	Different for council and management + aldermen	Same for council and management + aldermen	Different for council and management + aldermen	Same for council and management + aldermen	Same for council and management + aldermen	Same for council and management + aldermen	Same for council and management + aldermen
PI in financial documents	Budget includes PI, interim reports and annual account without PI	Budget, interim reports and annual account include PI	Budget includes PI, interim reports and annual account without PI	Budget, interim reports and annual account include PI	Formal budget, interim reports and annual account do not include PI, Annual Service Plans will include PI	Budget, interim reports and annual account include PI	Budget includes PI, interim reports without PI, annual account include PI	NA	Budget, interim reporting and annual account include PI	Budget, interim reporting and annual account include PI

onwards, all German municipalities were incrementally forced to introduce a performance budget. While some Länder established legal frameworks just after 2003, others only started recently; these developments led to the present state when only 25 per cent of municipalities so far have introduced performance information in their budgets (Burth and Hilgers 2014).

In Belgium (2007), Slovakia (2008), Italy (2009) and Ireland (2014), performance budgeting reforms were more recently initiated. In Belgium, the Flemish government has jurisdiction with regard to local matters. With an NPM-inspired decree (2007), the municipalities were given the opportunity to formally link financial and non-financial strategic and performance plans. Since 2014, all local governments are obliged to present performance-oriented budgets. However, regarding non-financial performance information legislation remains free of obligations (Bleyen, Lombaert, and Bouckaert 2016). The aim of the Italian financial management reforms was to integrate strategic planning and budgeting at all levels of the public sector. Since 2015, after a pilot phase of 2 years (2012–2014) all municipalities, provinces and regions are for the first time obliged to develop a programme budget (Mussari et al. 2016). In Slovakia, thirty local governments were chosen as pilot projects in 2008 for the implementation of performance budgeting. Since 2009, all municipalities with a population of over 2,000 inhabitants have had to implement this reform (MFSR 2010). Irish local governments include limited performance information in their new annual service delivery plans which are required since 2015, and which must be presented to and adopted consecutively by local governments at the start of the budgetary year. However, this information is only informally linked at domain level.

All examined legislations require municipalities to propose medium-term financial plans whereas only funding of the first year is binding, except for the case of Ireland. Unlike in the other countries, Flemish local governments in Belgium have to make 6-year budgetary forecasts including both financial and non-financial performance information. Also, the way budget documents are presented to different stakeholders differs between the cases under scrutiny. The Flemish, Dutch and Italian local governments present different budget documents to the council than they present to the aldermen (and management). The idea of such differentiation is to present summarized data to the council, whereas the policy implementers receive detailed documents. This differentiation does not exist in the other cases.

In Germany, local monitoring reports and the annual accounts do not include performance information and thus they are solely driven by information on expenditures and revenues. The same goes for the Irish local level although reporting against the Annual Service Plans will be guided by performance information from 2015 on. The Slovak local governments do not inform in any way about achieved performance in their annual reports, although they do in their subsequent budget. In most cases, however, monitoring reports and/or the annual accounts include performance information. In Genk (Belgium), for instance, monitoring of expenditures and revenues takes place formally each month, while performance monitoring is conducted half-yearly when performance dashboards are presented to the council. In the Netherlands and in Lithuania, monitoring reports including performance results are presented to the council during the budget year and performance information is presented in the annual account. In Norway, local governments only include this information in the annual account.

Results part 2 – performance incorporation

With regard to the link between financial budget information and non-financial performance information (B.LINK), the municipal systems show divergence. Whereas Eindhoven, Bonn, Banská Bystrica, Vilnius, Genk and Warsaw present performance budgets in which performance information is fully integrated in one budget document together with financial information, the budgets of Lørenskog, Bari, Galway and Olomouc are built in different ways. Olomouc does not include any performance information at all. In Lørenskog, financial and performance information are found in a single budget document, but the link is unclear since performance objectives are not linked to expenditures and only serve a general informative purpose. The budgeting framework of Bari consists of two separate budget documents. The 'official' budget includes missions in its strategic section and detailed programmes in its operative section. More detailed objectives, indicators and processes are found in the Management Executive Plan (MEP) which is a separate document addressed to the municipal management. A similar approach is found in the Galway budgeting framework where some performance information (objectives) is included in a separate annual service plan. Contrary to the case of Bari the link between both documents is much more ambiguous and general since only a high-level link exists between financials and policy domains in the service plan. The annual service plan serves more like a separate strategic plan that is only indirectly linked to the budget.

According to our case studies, seven out of ten municipalities have added non-financial performance objectives to all expenditures in the budget. In all seven cases, budget coverage equals 100 per cent (B.COVE). In Lørenskog and Galway, performance objectives assist the budget but are by no means linked to expenditures. No coverage is found in Olomouc since no elements of performance budgeting were found.

The analysed performance budgets show a lot of variation in both performance objectives (T.OBJE) and performance indicators (T.INDI). The values shown in Table 6 and Figure 1 range from 0 (no objectives or indicators at all) to 1 (exclusively outcome objectives and indicators). They serve an analytical purpose and should not be interpreted in an absolute way since outcomes are not 'better' than, but different from outputs, processes and inputs. The Bonn budget is by far the most detailed; it covers a countless number of performance objectives and related performance indicators. For this reason, the authors have chosen to include only one representative product area (child-care). The highest percentages of outcome and output performance objectives were found in the budgets of Eindhoven, Vilnius and Banská Bystrica. In these budgets, input and process objectives are less common or even absent. In contrast, performance objectives in the other cities are more balanced between outcomes, outputs, processes and inputs. When it comes to the quantification of performance objectives in performance indicators, the most outcome and output performance information were found in the budgets of Eindhoven and Vilnius. Bonn and Warsaw do not present a single outcome indicator. In all municipalities except for Galway where no performance indicators are available, performance indicators are at least partially measured by the municipal administration.

The municipalities with the longest performance budgeting tradition (i.e. Eindhoven and Vilnius) present the most outcome performance information, both in terms of performance objectives and performance indicators (see Figure 1). This is in line with

Table 6. Type of performance objectives and performance indicators.

	B. Bystrica	Bari	Bonn[a]	Eindhoven	Galway	Genk	Lørenskog	Olomouc	Vilnius	Warsaw
Performance objectives	105 objectives (%)	173 objectives (%)	85 objectives (%)	36 objectives (%)	279 objectives (%)	200 objectives (%)	51 objectives (%)	NA	147 objectives (%)	197 objectives (%)
% Outcome (1)	49	18	18	50	0	30	25	NA	42	23
% Output (0.75)	28	47	42	47	46	38	27	NA	58	25
% Process (0.5)	13	32	12	3	54	32	31	NA	0	51
% Input (0.25)	10	2	26	0	0	0	16	NA	0	1
Value	**0.78**	**0.70**	**0.62**	**0.86**	**0.61**	**0.75**	**0.66**	**0**	**0.86**	**0.67**
Performance indicators	313 Indicators (%)	157 Indicators (%)	50 Indicators (1,000+ in total) (%)	91 Indicators (%)	0 Indicators	160 Indicators (%)	54 Indicators (%)	NA	248 Indicators (%)	561 Indicators (%)
% Outcome (1)	16	22	0	67	NA	9	13	NA	25	0
% Output (0.75)	36	62	66	13	NA	41	26	NA	55	12
% Process (0.5)	27	13	14	15	NA	44	28	NA	17	47
% Input (0.25)	20	3	20	4	NA	6	33	NA	3	41
Value	**0.62**	**0.76**	**0.59**	**0.85**	**0**	**0.63**	**0.55**	**0**	**0.76**	**0.45**

[a]Only the product area of 'Children, Youth and Family' of the budget of Bonn was covered.

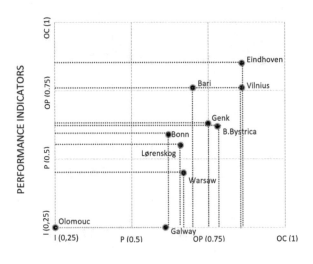

Figure 1. Symmetry between performance objectives and indicators.

findings from earlier comparative research at the national level of the OECD countries (Curristine 2005). Moreover, the analysis of the symmetry between performance objectives and indicators reveals that in all but one municipality (Bari), performance objectives tend to be more outcome and output-related than are the indicators. As such, performance indicators do not always mirror the objectives. This observation is most striking in the budgets of Genk, Banská Bystrica and Bonn. In Genk for instance 30 per cent of the performance objectives are outcome-related, whereas only 9 per cent of the performance indicators are outcome-related. It seems that local governments have less difficulties to identify outcome and output objectives than they have to define outcome and output indicators to measure goal achievement. A possible explanation may be that municipalities focus at first on process and output indicators because of their measurability and that local governments – although not avoiding outcomes – tend to limit the efforts to measure them (e.g. Moynihan 2006).

Except from Genk, all municipalities present clear future quantitative performance figures (A.FFIG). In Bari, Banská Bystrica and Warsaw, such quantitative figures are defined for every performance indicator. In Bonn, Eindhoven and Vilnius, the future-related figures are mostly but not always available. The main reason for their absence is the fact that sometimes new performance indicators are defined, for which no indication or baseline yet exist. However, one must be aware of the fact that for instance in the Bonn case the analysed budget does not report all actual or planned values for future years, since the outcome focus was introduced in the 2014 budget for the very first time. In Lørenskog, only 7 per cent of the presented performance indicators contain future performance figures. In the case of Genk, some future performance figures are available within most of the municipal departments, but they are not formally incorporated in the budget because of time and software constraints during the first budget cycle with the new system. In those cases that have presented future quantitative performance figures, the time frame to which these figures apply differs between $N + 1$ and $N + 3$ years, mainly depending on the time horizon of the budgets.

As for past performance figures in the budget, four out of ten municipalities have formally incorporated result-based performance figures to a great extent (with time frames between $N - 1$ and $N - 6$) (A.PFIG). If past performance figures are not available, this may have been due to the lack of capacity to measure and collect them, due to the impossibility to collect them in time or due to the introduction of new indicators for which no results are available. In the other cases, past performance figures are absent.

With the last variable, the authors aim to assess the performance coverage of the budgets, by which is meant (1) the number of performance objectives for which at least one clear and unambiguous performance indicator is defined and (2) the average number of indicators that are defined per performance objective (P. COVE). Performance indicators are not provided at the level of performance objectives in the budget of Genk and Banská Bystrica. In both cases, indicators are related to 'actions' or 'elements' which are sub items of performance objectives and thus out of scope of the analysis. Performance coverage is highest in Vilnius, Eindhoven, Warsaw and Bari. With regard to the average number of indicators per performance objective Warsaw and Eindhoven and to a lesser extent Vilnius have the highest score in our sample (Table 7).

To conclude this section, recapitulative performance budgeting positioning maps have been designed for each of the municipalities including Olomouc although its position is negligible and becomes a baseline (see Figure 2). The rationale for these positioning maps is that the more a municipality is moving to the outside perimeter, the more its budget is to be judged as being performance based. Based on these positioning maps, three performance budgeting incorporation patterns or phases are observed.

First, the cases of Lørenskog and Galway show symptoms of what is labelled 'embryonic performance budgeting'. A preliminary and unclear link between financial and non-financial information exists without any budget coverage. Whereas performance information in Galway is not directly included in the budget, the Lørenskog budget is somewhat more developed because the budget includes performance objectives, figures and even benchmarks. However, this information lacks a clear link to expenditures. Second, four cases seem to be more mature, since the link between financial and non-financial performance information is much more developed and all parts of the budget are covered with future performance objectives. Although all these cases have in common that they fail to present past performance information, there are clear differences between, on the one hand, the budgets of Bari, Warsaw and Bonn in which performance coverage is high, and future performance figures are common, and, on the other hand, the transitioning budget of Genk in which performance coverage is very low and future performance figures are practically absent. Since only information about future performances is provided, the budgeting practices of these cases are labelled as 'target performance budgeting'. Third, Vilnius, Eindhoven and to a lesser extent Banská Bystrica have the most inclusive, and outcome and output focused performance budgeting systems. Not only they incorporated both qualitative and quantitative data, but they also include both future and past performance information. As such, these budgeting practices are labelled 'performance budgeting for results'.

Table 7. Availability of performance figures in the budget and performance coverage.

	B. Bystrica	Bari	Bonn	Eindhoven	Galway	Genk	Lørenskog	Olomouc	Vilnius	Warsaw
% Future figures	100%	100%	60%	74%	NA	0%	7%	NA	96%	100%
Future time frame	N + 2	N + 1	N + 1	N + 3	NA	NA	N + 4	NA	N + 2	N + 1
% Past figures	71%	NA	NA	80%	NA	NA	93%	NA	98%	NA
Past time frame	N − 6	NA	NA	N − 2	NA	NA	N − 1 or N − 5	NA	N − 1	NA
Amount of objectives with at least one indicator	0% (0 out of 105) (indirect: 100%)	86% (149 out of 173)	59% (50 out of 85)	97% (35 out of 36)	NA	0% (0 out of 200) (indirect: 14%)	33% (17 out of 51)	NA	100% (147 out of 147)	100% (197 out of 197)
Average of indicators per objective	0 (0/105) (indirect: 3.2)	0.9 (157/173)	0.6 (50/85)	2.7 (97/36)	NA	0 (0/200) (indirect: 0.14)	1.1 (54/51)	NA	1.7 (248/147)	2.8 (561/197)

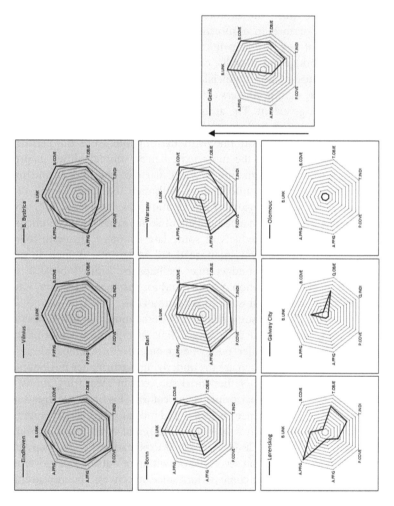

Figure 2. Comparison of performance budgeting in ten European municipalities.

Discussion and conclusions

This article contributes to the conceptualisation and measurement of performance budgeting based on a general model (RQ1) as well as to the debate on the implementation of performance budgeting reforms and (differences in) incorporation of performance information in the budget of European local governments (RQ2 and RQ3). The analysis is based on (1) a concise literature review of the evolution of performance budgeting, (2) the framework for analysing the structure of performance budgeting systems and its reform trajectories (Mussari et al. 2016), and (3) the general analytical model which the authors developed for the comparative analysis of the incorporation of performance information in the budgets at local level.

Overall, eight out of ten municipalities have introduced consistent elements towards performance budgeting. Results of the analysis linked to the RQ2 show however that the structure of non-financial performance information in the budget as well as type (outcome, output, process or input) and measurability of performance information vary to a large extent. The authors therefore differentiate between three types: 'embryonic performance budgeting', 'target performance budgeting' and 'performance budgeting for results'. In line with existing literature on performance budgeting one would expect that the more experienced municipalities incorporate more outcome performance information in more parts of the budget and provide both future and past performance information. Although the small sample of cases excludes solid conclusions with regard to this relation, results do not fully confirm the expectations, since the performance budgets of some experienced municipalities are less developed than are the budgets of some late adopters. In-depth follow-up research could explore this relation in more detail. Attempts to include detailed performance information in the budget may perhaps be limited because of the possible trade-off between information quantity and for instance, relevance, information overload and measurement efforts and reporting costs.

Apart from the differences, also some similarities were found. Municipalities that left the phase of embryonic performance budgeting all linked performance information 100 per cent to their expenditures. Further, performance objectives are almost always more focused on outcomes and outputs than are the underlying performance indicators. Only one municipality (Eindhoven, The Netherlands) succeeds in measuring almost every performance objective by outcome performance indicators. This finding suggests similar learning trajectories when performance objectives and indicators are incorporated in the budget and it confirms earlier research of Weets (2012) and of Bleyen, Lombaert, and Bouckaert (2016) at Flemish local level. A possible explanation for this gap between objectives and indicators (RQ3) is that several actors within or outside local governments contribute to the achievement of outcome performance objectives. The measurement of results as well as defining who is accountable for achieved results is complex in such circumstances. In addition, measurement of outcome indicators is very often time- and money-consuming. Therefore, local governments may tend to avoid the collection and evaluation of those data.

It should be kept in mind that the applied research setting has some noteworthy limitations. First, only ten municipalities out of a population of several thousand municipalities were taken under consideration. As a consequence, results of this exploratory study are by no means to be generalized. However, the general model has been developed in a way which allows its further utilization for similar analytical purposes.

Second, the selection of the sample is prone to criticism since the concept of a 'good' practice case is potentially subjective and blurred. A different selection rationale in the same set of countries would potentially lead to different results, since municipalities do not exactly practise the same budgetary concept within the given legislative framework. The developed general analytical model with its set of criteria is nevertheless able to help describing the major features of a performance budgeting system and helps to draw a meaningful picture of such systems showing both strengths and deficits. Therefore, as mentioned earlier, the model is a potential basis for qualitative or quantitative research activities in the future.

Third, data gathering must not be restricted to incorporation processes and quality of performance information, since this information is only valuable when effectively used. Thus, an extension of the research focus on the analysis of the use of performance information within the various stages of the budget cycle and for the different purposes of budgeting would be an important future research challenge.

Fourth, our analysis of the budgets of the selected municipalities has primarily resulted in descriptive research findings. The collected data only allow to draw limited conclusions to explain the examined differences of performance budgeting and thus restricts our response to RQ3. Different time frames, internal and external pressures, path dependencies, institutional arrangements and political-administrative cultures all are plausible explanations for the observed differences. The applied method of document analysis of published budgets does, however, not allow to identify more detailed explanatory factors for deeper understanding of these differences and to undoubtedly explain all identified differences. This article only gives some insights about the role of external pressures on the reform of municipal budgets. Central or state governments of the Netherlands, Belgium, Norway and Germany have introduced elements of performance budgeting at the local level as part of broader NPM-reforms, whereas in Slovakia, Lithuania and Italy external (EU) authorities put pressure on the respective governments. However, similar pressures did not move the Czech and Irish local governments towards performance budgeting, whilst in Poland some local governments like Warsaw did not await those pressures to act.

Despite these limitations, the results in this article prove to be a new step towards a better understanding of performance budgeting in local government. This kind of comparative performance budgeting research is still scarce and a general analytical model to assess the incorporation of performance information in the budget did not previously exist. Our model helps to collect more specific data about the incorporation of performance information in municipal budgets, e.g. about the amount of performance objectives and its related indicators, about the availability of past and future performance measures and about the predominant focus of such measures on outcomes, outputs, processes and inputs. The article supports earlier research conclusions at country level that although performance budgeting systems differ in their approach, they can be characterized by similar basic features. In this article, those common features have been operationalized and pooled by introducing positioning maps based on the seven variables of a general model. This research setting seems to be solid and enables comparative and longitudinal research since it offers a simplified but comparative first insight into the state of affairs of the incorporation of performance information in local government budgets.

Notes

1. This network studies Local Public Sector Reforms and stimulates International Comparison.
2. Moreover, the seven layers of Bari are allocated to two different budget documents, the 'official' budget and the MEP (see below).

Declaration of interest

No potential conflict of interest was reported by the authors.

Funding

This work is supported by the COST Action "Local Public Sector Reforms (LocRef)": [Grant Number IS 1207]. This network studies Local Public Sector Reforms and stimulates International Comparison (for more information, see http://www.uni-potsdam.de/cost-locref/). This research would not have been possible without the contribution of the following team members: *Riccardo Mussari* and *Alfredo Ettore Tranfaglia* (University of Siena), *Christian Schwab* (University of Potsdam), *Nicole Küchler-Stahn* (Frankfurt University of Applied Sciences), *Åge Johnsen* and *Lillian Oterholt* (Oslo and Akershus), *Urszula Zawadzka-Pąk* (University of Bialystok), *Vitalis Nakrošis* (Vilnius University), *Geraldine Robbins* (National University of Ireland Galway) and *Johan de Kruijf* (Radboud University of Nijmegen).

References

Anessi-Pessina, E., C. Barbera, M. Sicilia, and I. Steccolini. 2016. "Public Sector Budgeting: A European Review of Accounting and Public Management Journals." *Accounting, Auditing & Accountability Journal* 29 (3): 491–519. doi:10.1108/AAAJ-11-2013-1532.

Anessi-Pessina, E., and I. Steccolini. 2007. "Effects of Budgetary and Accruals Accounting Coexistence: Evidence from Italian Local Governments." *Financial Accountability & Management* 23 (2): 113–131. doi:10.1111/j.1468-0408.2007.00422.x.

Bennett, C. F. 1975. "Up the Hierarchy. – A Staircase to Measuring Extension's Impact." *Journal of Extension* 13 (2): 6–12.

Bernt, J. F. 2012. *Kommunelovens fødsel, oppvekst og fremtid. Kommuneloven 20 år. Artikkelsamling.* Oslo: Kommunal- og Regionaldepartementet.

Bleyen, P., S. Lombaert, and G. Bouckaert. 2015. "De Beleids- en Beheerscyclus: zes stellingen over strategische en prestatie-informatie in de meerjarenplannen van gemeenten, OCMW's en provincies." *Vlaams Tijdschrift voor Overheidsmanagement* 15 (3): 21–40.

Bleyen, P., S. Lombaert, and G. Bouckaert. 2016. "Measurement, Incorporation and Use of Performance Information in the Budget. A Methodological Survey Approach to Map Performance Budgeting Practices in Local Government." *Society and Economy* 37 (3): 337–355. doi:10.1556/204.2015.37.3.2.

Bouckaert, G., and J. Halligan. 2008. *Managing Performance. International Comparisons.* Oxon: Routledge.

Bourdeaux, C. 2008. "Integrating Performance Information into Legislative Budget Processes." *Public Performance & Management Review* 31 (4): 547–569. doi:10.2753/PMR1530-9576310403.

Brusca, I., E. Caperchione, E. S. Cohen, and F. Manes Rossi, eds. 2015. *Public Sector Accounting and Auditing in Europe: The Challenge of Harmonization. Governance and Public Management Series.* New York: Palgrave Macmillan.

Burth, A., and D. Hilgers. 2014. "Cui Bono? Depicting the Benefits of the New Municipal Budgeting and Accounting Regime in Germany." *Journal of Business Economics* 84 (4): 531–570. doi:10.1007/s11573-013-0698-9.

Carlins, T. M., and J. Guthrie. 2003. "Accrual Output Based Budgeting Systems in Australia. The Rhetoric-Reality Gap." *Public Management Review* 5 (2): 145–162. doi:10.1080/1461667032000066372.

Christensen, T., and P. Lægreid. 2001. *New Public Management. The Transformation of Ideas and Practice.* Aldershot: Ashgate.

Conings, V., M. Sterck, and G. Bouckaert. 2007. *Budgeting, Accounting and Auditing for Results. Towards Integrated Financial Management.* Leuven: Steunpunt Beleidsrelevant Onderzoek - Bestuurlijke Organisatie Vlaanderen.

Curristine, T. 2005. "Performance Information in the Budget Process: Results of the OECD 2005 Questionnaire." *OECD Journal on Budgeting* 5 (2): 87–131. doi:10.1787/16812336.

Curristine, T., and S. Flynn. 2013. "In Search of Results: Strengthening Public Sector Performance." In *Public Financial Management and its Emerging Architecture*, edited by M. Cangiano, T. Curristine, and M. Lazare. Washington, DC: International Monetary Fund.

DiMaggio, P. J., and W. W. Powell. 1991. *The New Institutionalism in Organization Analysis.* Chicago: University of Chicago Press.

Grossi, G., C. Reichard, and P. Ruggiero. 2016. "Appropriateness and Use of Performance Information in the Budgeting Process: Some Experiences from German and Italian Municipalities." *Public Performance & Management Review* 39 (3): 581–606. doi:10.1080/15309576.2015.1137770.

Humphrey, C., J. Guthrie, L. R. Jones, and O. Olsen. 2005. "The Dynamics of Public Financial Management Change in an International Context." In *International Public Financial Management Reform: Progress, Contradictions, and Challenges*, edited by J. Guthrie, C. Humphrey, L. R. Jones, and O. Olsen. Greenwich: Information Age Publishing.

Hyndman, N. 2008. "Accounting and Democratic Accountability in Northern Ireland." In *Accounting in Politics: Devolution and Democratic Accountability*, edited by M. Ezzamel, N. Hyndman, A. Johnsen, and I. Lapsley. New York: Routledge.

Jackson, P. M. 2011. "Governance by Numbers: What Have We Learned Over the Past 30 Years?" *Public Money & Management* 31 (1): 13–26. doi:10.1080/09540962.2011.545542.

Johnsen, Å. 2005. "What Does 25 Years of Experience Tell Us About the State of Performance Measurement in Public Policy and Management?" *Public Money & Management* 25 (1): 9–17. doi:10.1111/j.1467-9302.2005.00445.x.

Jordan, M., and M. Hackbart. 1999. "Performance Budgeting and Performance Funding in the States: A States Assessment." *Public Budgeting Finance* 19 (1): 68–88. doi:10.1046/j.0275-1100.1999.01157.x.

Kelly, J. M., and W. C. Rivenbark. 2011. *Performance Budgeting for State and local Government.* London: M. E. Sharpe.

Kirkpatrick, D. L. 1998. *Evaluating Training Programs.* 2nd ed. San Francisco: Berrett-Koehler.

Krajewska, M., and K. Andrzan. 2013. "Budżet Zadaniowy - Instrument Zarządzania Finansami miasta Stołecznego Warszawy." *Studia Biura Analiz Sejmowych* 33 (1): 189–208.

Kuhlmann, S., and G. Bouckaert, eds. 2016. *Local Public Sector Reforms in Times of Crisis: National Trajectories and International Comparisons*. New York: Palgrave Macmillan.

Kuhlmann, S., and H. Wollmann. 2014. *Introduction to Comparative Public Administration*. Cheltenham: Edward Elgar.

Landman, T. 2008. *Issues and Methods in Comparative Politics. An Introduction*. 3rd ed. New York: Routledge.

MFSR. 2010. "Projekt Pilotnej Implementácie Programového Rozpočtovania na úrovni územnej Samosprávy: Informácie o Projekte." Accessed 30 July 2015. http://rozpocet.finance.gov.sk

Moynihan, D. P. 2006. "What Do We Talk about When We Talk about Performance? Dialogue Theory and Performance Budgeting." *Journal of Public Administration Research and Theory* 16 (2): 151–168. doi:10.1093/jopart/muj003.

Moynihan, D. P. 2008. *The Dynamics of Performance Management: Constructing Information and Reform*. Washington, DC: Georgetown University Press.

Mussari, R., A. E. Tranfaglia, C. Reichard, H. Bjørnå, V. Nakrošis, and S. Bankauskaitė-Grigaliūnienė. 2016. "Design, Trajectories of Reform and Implementation of Performance Budgeting in Local Governments: A Comparative Study of Germany, Italy, Lithuania and Norway." In *Local Public Sector Reforms in Times of Crisis. National Trajectories and International Comparisons*, edited by S. Kuhlmann and G. Bouckaert. New York: Palgrave Macmillan.

Nakrošis, V. 2008. "Reforming Performance Management in Lithuania: Towards Result-based Government." In *Mixes, Matches and Mistakes: New Public Management in Russia and the Former Soviet Republics*, edited by B. G. Peters. Budapest: Open Society Institute.

OECD. 2008. *Performance Budgeting: A Users' Guide*. Paris: OECD.

OECD. 2013. *Government at a Glance 2013*. Paris: OECD.

Olsen, J. P., and B. G. Peters. 1996. *Lessons from Experience: Experimental Learning in Administrative Reforms in Eight Democracies*. Oslo: Scandinavian University Press.

Padovani, E., and D. W. Young. 2012. *Managing Local Governments. Designing Management Control Systems that Deliver Value*. London: Routledge.

Pollitt, C., and G. Bouckaert. 2011. *Public Sector Reform, NPM, Governance and the Neo-Weberian State*. Oxford: Oxford University Press.

Raudla, R. 2012. "The Use of Performance Information in Budgetary Decision-Making by Legislators: Is Estonia any Different?" Public Administration 90 (4): 1000–1015.

Robinson, M. 2007. *Performance Budgeting. Linking Funding and Results*. New York: Palgrave Macmillan.

Robinson, M. 2013. *Program Classification for Performance-Based Budgeting: How to Structure Budgets to Enable the Use of Evidence*. Washington, DC: World Bank.

Saliterer, I., and S. Korac. 2013. "Performance Information Use by Politicians and Public Managers for Internal Control and External Accountability Purposes." *Critical Perspectives on Accounting* 24 (7–8): 502–517. doi:10.1016/j.cpa.2013.08.001.

Schick, A. 2009. "Performance Budgeting and Accrual Budgeting: Decision Rules or Analytical Tools?" *OECD Journal on Budgeting* 7 (2): 109–138. doi:10.1787/budget-v7-art11-en.

Schick, A. 2013. "The Metamorphoses of Performance Budgeting." *OECD Journal on Budgeting* 12 (3): 1–29. doi:10.1787/16812336.

Sterck, M. 2007. "The Impact of Performance Budgeting on the Role of the Legislature: A Four-Country Study." *International Review of Administrative Sciences* 73 (2): 189–203. doi:10.1177/0020852307077960.

Taylor, J. 2009. "Strengthening the Link Between Performance Measurement and Decision Making." *Public Administration* 87 (4): 853–871. doi:10.1111/padm.2009.87.issue-4.

ter Bogt, H. J., J. van Helden, and B. van der Kolk. 2015. "Challenging the NPM Ideas About Performance Management: Selectivity and Differentiation in Outcome-Oriented Performance Budgeting." *Financial Accountability & Management* 31 (3): 287–315. doi:10.1111/faam.12058.

Van Dooren, W., G. Bouckaert, and J. Halligan. 2015. *Performance Management in the Public Sector*. 2nd ed. London: Routledge.

Van Helden, G. J., and C. Reichard. 2016. "Commonalities and Differences in Public and Private Sector Performance Management Practices: A Literature Review." In *Performance Management and Management Control: Contemporary Issues (Studies in Managerial and Financial Accounting Vol 31)*, edited by M. Epstein, F. Verbeeten, and S. Widener. Bingley: Emerald Publishers.

Weets, K. 2012. *Van Decreet tot Praktijk? – Een Onderzoek naar de Invoering van Elementen van Prestatiebegroting in Vlaamse gemeenten.* Leuven: Faculty of Social Sciences.

Yi Lu, E., Z. Mohr, and A. Tat-Kei Ho. 2015. "Taking Stock: Assessing and Improving Performance Budgeting Theory and Practice." *Public Performance & Management Review* 38 (3): 426–458. doi:10.1080/15309576.2015.1006470.

The design of performance budgeting processes and managerial accountability relationships

Suresh Cuganesan

ABSTRACT
Performance budgeting (PB) can play an important role in managerial accountability. Prior research focuses on the operation of PB as an information production device and concludes that its effects are shaped by context. Through a case study of reforms to government PB processes, the study extends understandings of how PB processes affect managerial accountability by showing how the design of PB shapes important elements of managerial accountability relationships that extend beyond information provision. A second contribution is in revealing how accountability arrangements come about through 'micro-level' interactions, comprising contests between participants in redesign processes.

1. Introduction

Performance budgeting (PB) engenders managerial accountability, where those with delegated authority are held to account for the effective and efficient use of public resources (Day and Klein 1987; Christensen and Lægreid 2015). Prior research on PB and accountability focuses on whether PB arrangements produce information that allows conclusions about efficient and effective public expenditure and the factors that influence the use of PB information (Lu, Mohr, and Ho 2015). It conceptualises PB largely as an information production device that meets (or not) the demands of managerial accountability.

However, important elements of accountability relationships extend beyond information concerns to also include the underlying obligation to provide an account, as well as the identity of the account receiver and its ability to interrogate information, pass judgement and impose consequences (Bovens 2007, 2010; Willems and Van Dooren 2012). Understanding PB in terms of managerial accountability requires attention to all of these elements. Importantly, these elements are not features of a context that exists independently of PB, but can also be affected by the way PB processes are designed, as broader research on accounting processes suggests (Hopwood 1987; Ezzamel, Robson, and Stapleton 2012). The implication is that PB not only operates within an existing accountability context, but also helps to shape it.

Hence, the research question this study pursues is how does the design of PB processes affect managerial accountability relationships? It presents a case study of PB process reforms in the Commonwealth (national) Government of Australia.[1] From this, the paper makes two main contributions. It extends understandings of how PB affects managerial accountability by showing how PB processes constitute the accountability context when one considers their design rather than operation. The study also complements prior research adopting a macro-focus when explaining variation in accountability arrangements over time and across jurisidictions by illustrating how accountability arrangements come about through interactions at the 'micro-level', comprising contests between participants in redesign processes as they interpret accountability in different ways and seek to persuade others to their points of view.

The next section of the paper reviews relevant PB and public accountability research. This is followed by a discussion of the study's specific perspective on accountability relationships and its constituent elements. The research method and empirical results are presented next before the paper ends with a discussion of its main findings and contributions.

2. Performance budgeting and managerial accountability

Governments in many countries have implemented PB in some form or another (Posner and Fantone 2007), largely on the basis that better public spending and budgetary allocations decisions occur from being informed about performance achievements. Accordingly, the majority of public management research on PB has focused on it as a budgetary decision-making tool with recent reviews recognizing that more work needs to be done on PB and accountability (Lu, Mohr, and Ho 2015):

Accountability as a concept has long been recognized as chameleon-like in terms of the multiple forms it comprises (Sinclair 1995). However, as Mulgan (2000, 555) notes, 'One sense of "accountability", on which all are agreed, is that associated with the process of being called "to account" to some authority for one's actions'. One important form of accountability is that of 'managerial accountability', where those with delegated authority are answerable according to agreed performance criteria (Day and Klein 1987).

In many countries new public management (NPM) reforms, including PB, have aimed to improve managerial accountability. NPM envisioned government entities being held accountable by the political executive as well as the broader legislature for the results generated from public expenditure. *Inter alia*, managerial accountability is concerned with questions of whether public money is being used efficiently and effectively (Christensen and Lægreid 2015), although it must also be acknowledged that this form of accountability can be subjectively constructed contingent on an individual's personal experiences and perspectives (Sinclair 1995).

Prior literature focuses on the operation of PB as an information production device, and see an independent context – in particular, the dynamics between the executive and legislature (for example, Johnson and Talbot 2007; Lu and Xue 2011; Ward 2015) – as determining its information effects for managerial accountability purposes. However, important aspects of managerial accountability relationships include information but also other elements (see next section), all of which require examination if PB's effects for managerial accountability are to be fully understood.

Furthermore, attention must also be devoted to how the design of PB processes may shape context comprising these elements of accountability relationships.

Indeed, broader studies on accounting indicate that processes such as PB are much more constitutive than the public management research discussed earlier acknowledges, shaping the types of accounts that might be undertaken and the identity of actors involved in the process of accountability. A long tradition of research establishes how accounting processes create particular visibilities and mediate the recognition of problems and alters relationships between actors (Hopwood 1987; Miller 1992; Ezzamel, Robson, and Stapleton 2012). The view of this research can be summarized as follows: 'Accounting and budgeting technologies perform, and contribute to the construction of the "reality" of which they speak'. (Ezzamel, Robson, and Stapleton 2012, 285). Accordingly, the study pays attention to the constitutive effects of PB processes for managerial accountability relationships. Its perspective on accountability relationships and the specific elements that it examines are discussed next.

3. Elements of accountability relationships

Accountability as a concept has undergone such significant expansion and diverse application that it requires conceptual coherence (Willems and Van Dooren 2012). Although a review of the various frameworks and typologies is beyond the scope of this paper, it is relevant to note that one important way in which accountability is understood in the literature is as a relation through which an actor is held accountable (Mulgan 2000; Bovens 2007; Willems and Van Dooren 2012). Here, the focus is 'not whether the agents have acted in an accountable way, but whether they are or can be held accountable *ex post facto*' (Bovens 2010, 948).

This study draws on the work of Bovens (2007, 2010) who sees accountability as:

> A relationship between an actor and a forum, in which the actor has an obligation to explain and to justify his or her conduct, the forum can pose questions and pass judgement, and the actor may face consequences. (Bovens 2007, 450)

The study of accountability relationships thus needs to concern itself with the identity of the actor (account giver) and the accountability forum (account receiver), both of which can be individuals (or aggregations of individuals) and organizations. In public accountability relationships, actors potentially comprise individual officials or government departments while forums include individual ministers, parliaments and related committees, and the citizenry or 'public'.

Bovens (2010; see also Bovens, Schillemans, and Goodin 2014) proposes attention to three elements of the relationship between actor and forum. The first involves the obligation to inform forums about and explain conduct, performance and/or outcomes. These obligations can be based in legislation, administrative policy and procedure or grounded in informal understandings or expectations, such as when accounts are provided on a voluntary basis on the presumption that it is good to do so. How this obligation is interpreted influences account giving and the aspects of the actor's conduct to be accounted for. Second, forums must be able to question actors (Bovens 2010; Bovens, Schillemans, and Goodin 2014). This involves interrogating the adequacy and accuracy of the provided accounts and could extend to discussions about the underlying behaviour of the actor.

Finally, the forum may pass judgement from which actors face consequences. While some accountability scholars see actual rewards and sanctions as central to accountability relationships (Gray and Jenkins 1993; Smyth 2012, 2016), Bovens (2010) is careful to specify that it is the possibility of consequences that is important. Here, the study adopts this perspective on the basis that many accountability arrangements are not targeted exclusively towards providing reward or imposing sanctions (although this might happen) while consequences can also be emergent, comprising positive/negative publicity and the voicing of approval/disapproval.

In summary, this study applies Boven's (2007, 2010; also Bovens, Schillemans, and Goodin 2014) framework to understand managerial accountability relationships in terms of the identity of actors and forums as well as the constituent elements of obligation to inform, ability to question and interrogate, and possible judgements and consequences as discussed above. In so doing, it is consistent with a number of other studies on public accountability that likewise utilize the work of Bovens to character-ize accountability relationships (for example, Brenton 2014; Overman, Van Genugten, and Van Thiel 2015; Christensen and Lægreid 2015). The following section explains the framework's application in discussing the research method used in the study.

4. Research method

4.1 *Case details: the public management reform agenda*

The case study comprises multi-faceted reforms of the national public sector in Australia (the Commonwealth government) that were eventually labelled the 'Public Management Reform Agenda' (PMRA). The PMRA envisioned a different approach to the management of public resources in an effort to improve the opera-tion of the Commonwealth Government. PB process reforms were a central aspect of this. Examining a reform is particularly appropriate given the study's focus on the design of PB processes.

4.2 *Data collection and analysis*

In examining how the design of PB processes shapes managerial accountability relationships the study is constructionist in nature. It employs discourse analysis on the basis that oral (talk) and written text 'do not neutrally reflect our world, identities and social relations but, rather, play an active role in creating and changing them' (Phillips and Jorgensen 2002, 1). Analysis of discourse allows access to versions of social reality that are progressively brought into being through the production, dissemination, and consumption of written and oral material (Hardy 2004).

The study applies discourse analysis to understand different proposals for the design of PB processes and how these shape managerial accountability relationships. The first step comprised the selection of texts for closer analysis. This was achieved by focusing on texts that appeared to be most central and connected to reforming the design of PB processes. Examining the reform process revealed that the key partici-pants were the Department of Finance (referred to as 'Finance') responsible for the PB process and leading the reforms, the Australian National Audit Office (ANAO), and the Joint Committee of Public Accounts and Audit (JCPAA), which was made up of members of Parliament 'to hold Commonwealth agencies to account for the lawfulness, efficiency and effectiveness with which they use public monies' (Parliament of Australia 2015). Consequently, texts produced by Finance about the reforms were selected. The JCPAA also announced inquiries into the PMRA reforms as part of its mandate, with these inquiries providing focal points for the circulation of texts (including those from the ANAO) through submissions, hearings and reports. These texts were also selected for analysis.

Although the case for reforms was being made as early as 2010, specific propositions about the form that PB might take did not manifest in significant ways until 2012 and later. The date of production of selected texts ranged from 2012 to 2015 when data collection concluded. Oral texts comprised transcripts of hearings conducted by the JCPAA as it inquired into the PMRA reforms, including how the PB process was to be redesigned. Written texts related to documentation announcing the reform, discussion papers, guidance documents, submissions to JCPAA, and JCPAA inquiry reports. Table 1 summarizes the data sources that were collected.

Inter alia, discourse analysis requires attention to how texts relate entities and events to one another and the interests, values, and positions of their authors (Fairclough 2003). Accordingly, the various data sources were analysed with a particular focus on differentiating between the texts of Finance, ANAO, and JCPAA once their significance to the reform process became clearer. Texts were reviewed first to identify segments concerned with PB process design and managerial accountability. These various segments were subsequently reviewed and analysed in how they referred to the identity of actors and forums and the elements of accountability relationships discussed in Section Three. Attention was also paid to intertextuality or how 'texts draw upon, incorporate, recontextualize and dialogue with other texts' (Fairclough 2003, 17). This was done through consideration of how different texts produced by the same main participant – for example, Finance, JCPAA, or ANAO – and texts produced by different participants built upon or contrasted with each other.

Overall, the analysis process allowed the identification of different PB reform proposals put forward by the various participants and a comprehension of how these shaped relationships of managerial accountability in diverse ways, the latter by analysing texts to identify the identities of parties proposed as being in accountability relationships and the constituent elements of these relationships. The resulting empirical analysis is presented next, focusing first on the reform background followed by analysis of the alternative proposals.

5. Case study

5.1 *Background*

PB at the national government level in Australia operated historically as an informing and influencing device rather than a rigid-formula-based allocative system (see Schick 2007; OECD 2008). The framework at the time of this study required government departments to classify resource expenditure by programme and identify deliverables (products of programmes) and performance measures that would inform determinations of whether a programme was achieving its objectives. Coordinated by Finance, the budget statements of government entities under the responsibility of each

Table 1. Data sources.

Month,[a] Year	Authoring Entity	Title/Purpose	Pages
Mar 2012	Finance	Commonwealth Financial Accountability Review (CFAR): Discussion Paper	114
2012	Various	Submissions to the CFAR Discussion Paper	N/A
2012	Finance	CFAR Discussion Paper Feedback Summary	9
Nov 2012	Finance	CFAR Position Paper	76
Jun 2013	JCPAA	Report on the Public Governance, Performance and Accountability (PGPA) Bill 2013	75
May–Jun 2013	Various	Submissions to the JCPAA Inquiry on the PGPA Bill	N/A
May 2014	JCPAA	Inquiry into Public Governance, Performance and Accountability Act 2013 Rules Development	140
Feb–May 2014	Various	Submissions to the JCPAA Inquiry on the PGPA Rules Development	N/A
Mar 2014	Commonwealth of Australia	Transcript of JCPAA Inquiry Hearing on 27 March 2014	21
Apr 2014	Commonwealth of Australia	Transcript of JCPAA Inquiry Hearing on 7 April 2014	34
Aug 2014	Finance	Enhanced Commonwealth Performance Framework: Discussion Paper	73
2014	Various	Submissions to Enhanced Commonwealth Performance Framework: Discussion Paper	N/A
2014	Finance	Enhanced Commonwealth Performance Framework: Discussion Paper Feedback Summary	10
Nov 2014	Finance	Correspondence to JCPAA: Proposed Commonwealth Performance Framework, Rationale and Process of Consultation Undertaken including draft Guidance Documents	185
Feb 2015	Finance	Correspondence to JCPAA: Updated Proposed Commonwealth Performance Framework, Details of Extra Consultations and draft Guidance Documents	159
Mar 2015	JCPAA	Announcement of Inquiry into the Commonwealth Performance Framework and Terms of Reference	2
Mar 2015	Commonwealth of Australia	Transcript of JCPAA Inquiry Hearing on 19 March 2015	16
Mar 2015	Finance	Correspondence to JCPAA: Updated Proposed Commonwealth Performance Framework including performance information in budget statements and draft Guidance Documents	74
Mar–May 2015	Various	Submissions to the JCPAA Inquiry on the Commonwealth Performance Framework	N/A
May 2015	Finance	Updated Guidance on Commonwealth Performance Framework and Location of Performance Information in budget statements and corporate plans	2
Nov 2015	Finance	Submissions to the JCPAA Inquiry on the Commonwealth Performance Framework	23
Nov 2015	ANAO	Submissions to the JCPAA Inquiry on the Commonwealth Performance Framework	3
Nov 2015	Commonwealth of Australia	Transcript of JCPAA Inquiry Hearing on 26 November 2015	11
Dec 2015	Finance	Submissions to the JCPAA Inquiry on the Commonwealth Performance Framework	20
Dec 2015	Commonwealth of Australia	Transcript of JCPAA Inquiry Hearing on 3 December 2015	12

[a] Month details listed where available.

minister were tabled in Parliament in May of each year, and placed on the websites of central government and respective agencies soon after.

Budget statements provided the main source of information for politicians. Budget estimates committees comprising politicians from the upper house of Parliament were tasked with scrutinizing and questioning Departments about the budget allocations being proposed (see also Hawke 2007). Budget estimates committees held their main hearings two to three weeks after budget submission. As Mackay (2011, 24) notes, 'The parliament, particularly the Senate (upper house of Parliament), plays an important role in budget review and scrutiny, and in holding the government to account for its performance'. Thus possible judgements related to appropriateness of budget requests and the envisioned performance with likely consequences taking the form of reputational effects and media exposure. More broadly, Parliament could access other additional mechanisms in holding the executive branch to account, although these operated outside the budget approval process. Annual reports of individual departments contained actual results against individual performance measures for each year while the ANAO in its performance audit function provided independent assurance on the performance of government entities and programmes.

Continued observations indicated problems in relation to reporting of performance from public expenditure. The ANAO, in particular, was a vocal critic of performance measurement and the inability to link these to budgetary allocations and programmes, (ANAO 2011). A reasonable amount of responsibility for this (for example, by OECD, ANAO, and others) was attributed to the 'hands-off' approach taken by Finance to implementation (Mackay 2011). These perceptions related to how Finance had allowed individual Departments to self-determine performance measures and linkages between outcomes to resource use without sufficient guidance.

Partially in response to these observations but also concerns about growing societal demands on a finite amount of public resources, in December 2010 Finance commenced a broad consultation process to initiate reforms in public management. In relation to PB, the main concern appeared to be to strengthen the linkages between budget statements presented to Parliament and planning processes within government departments. In particular, Finance was concerned about variable planning practices and potentially short-term thinking in government departments when making resourcing decisions. Its key propositions in 2012 for enhancing transparency and accountability contained the following (Department of Finance 2012, 26):

> Align standards better for preparing appropriation bills, budget statements, annual reports and audited financial statements to enable comparisons and a clear read between budgeted and actual expenditure and performance.

5.2 *Proposing accountability relationships: narrowing accounts and alternative forums?*

In 2013 draft legislation was developed and refined through consultations held with key entities including the ANAO and the JCPAA, eventually being passed by Parliament into law mid-year as the *Public Governance, Performance and Accountability Act* (PGPA). While the changes introduced by the PGPA act were broad ranging, it had specific consequences for PB. Specifically, the PGPA act imposed legislative requirements requiring government entities to prepare a corporate plan for each year including planned performance and report on this planned performance at the end of the period. In particular, corporate plans were to focus government departments on describing their 'entity purpose', explaining how they would achieve this purpose and detail how they would measure and asses their performance in doing so. The annual performance statements would measure and assess entity performance in achieving this purpose in line with the methods disclosed in the corporate plan.

Corporate plans were to be given to the relevant Minister of the government entity and the Finance Minister and placed on departmental websites. They were to be developed at the end of August in the first year of introduction (2015) and the end of July for subsequent years. Annual performance statements were to be included in the annual reporting process and tabled in Parliament. While Finance saw the changes as enhancing external accountability, important questions were to arise as to whether the PB process would operate alongside these changes and what the effects would be for accountability relationships.

After engaging in further consultation with individual departments, Finance proposed an approach whereby planned performance information was to be removed from budget statements and only included in corporate plans. The timing of release of the two documents meant that budget statements and scrutiny over allocation of public resources were to occur in the absence of planned performance information because Budget statements were produced in May of each year while administrative procedures required the corporate plan to be produced later.

Budget statements were thus to no longer contain performance information, only resource expenditure information. This was to allow government departments to consider performance measures and targets as part of a corporate planning process once budgetary allocations were known rather than including them as part of a parliamentary budgeting process. These proposed changes to the design of the PB processes had a number of implications for relationships of managerial accountability. The proposal narrowed the account to be provided from government department (as actor) to Parliament (as accountability forum) down to resource expenditure information only. Concurrently, the proposed changes brought to the fore a managerial accountability relationship concerned with the public as forum. How the proposed PB process design shaped managerial accountability relationships is presented in Figure 1, with italics highlighting proposed changes to the status quo.

5.3 Contesting proposed accountability relations: specific accounts and privileging parliament

In response, the JCPAA decided in May 2015 to commence a new inquiry and invited submissions from government entities and the public. In the inquiry, Finance representatives spoke to their interest in enhancing the quality and longer-term orientation of planning processes in individual government entities as a means of improving resource management. This privileged corporate plans over budget statements as the home for planned performance information:

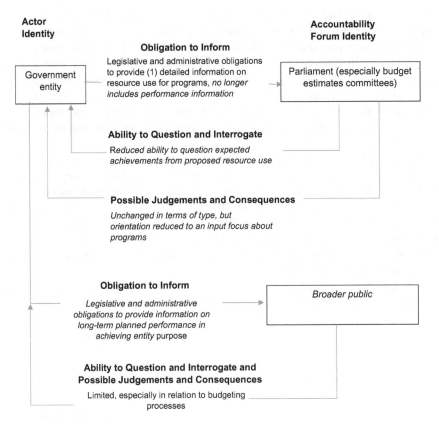

Figure 1. Performance budgeting and constitution of accountability relations [italics highlight proposed changes to existing situation].

Corporate plans are meant to provide a medium- to long-term narrative about what it is that an entity is seeking to do to achieve its purposes and to implement the policies of government. For that reason, we have come to a view that that is the better place in which to talk about planned performance information. … It is very difficult to see how information that has more than a 12-month horizon fits comfortably with the notion of an annual performance cycle and the annual resourcing that a parliament is giving to an entity. (Finance Representatives in Commonwealth of Australia 2015a, 5)

In addition, Finance also spoke for the government entities with which it had consulted, and which preferred to plan performance once parliamentary allocated resources were known rather than beforehand. Budget allocations were seen as relevant for improving how government departments planned performance rather than the reverse – planned performance information being seen as necessary for scrutiny over budget allocations:

The view of entities is strongly that they can construct more meaningful performance measures once the resourcing levels have been set by the government and the parliament than they can during the process of bidding for resourcing to do what they do. (Finance Representatives in Commonwealth of Australia 2015a, 5)

Simultaneously, Finance indicated that it was not opposed to external accountability. In its view, Departments would become more accountable for their longer-term planning through the legislative and administrative requirements that required corporate plans to be developed and placed on websites.

This proposal from Finance was opposed by the ANAO. In the inquiry, the Auditor-General argued that a different account was required by Parliament as part of accountability over the PB process. Key elements in the envisioned accountability relationship were account giving that included planned performance of publicly-funded programmes together with planned resource use and Parliament as a privileged accountability forum over other external users of PB information:

> The thing that we are seeking to raise with you – but it is a broader issue for the parliament and its committees – is: what do you need to be comfortable in passing the government's budget bills at any time? Just suggesting, 'This is the cash we need for particular programs and we will tell you about what we are going to deliver at some later stage' – after the budget is … not respectful of the parliament's role here. (Auditor-General in Commonwealth of Australia 2015a, 6)

The ANAO also drew attention to the nature of the accounts to be tabled in corporate plans. This was in response to Finance arguing that Parliament could always refer to a corporate plan if required. ANAO's concern related to how Finance proposed performance to be related to entity purpose rather than the effects of specific programmes consuming public resources.

In the inquiry JCPAA indicated similar perspectives to ANAO. During discussions, JCPAA voiced concerns about the proposed movement of performance information from budget statements, highlighting concerns about its ability to scrutinize budgetary allocations and hold government entities to account:

> I know that corporate plans do not necessarily reflect the type of information that a member of parliament requires to be accountable in an executive role. Why are we shifting from budget statements, which have the detail that all members of parliament can see very clearly, to corporate plans that are available three to 3½ months later, after we have allocated the budgets? (JCPAA representative in Commonwealth of Australia 2015a, 9)

In support of the perspective of the JCPAA, the Auditor-General also proposed an alternative PB process. This sought to maintain the status of Parliament as an important accountability forum and the nature of the account giving that was to occur:

> Minimum requirements for the inclusion of information on planned performance in entity budget statements … would include the expected achievements against program or activity objectives for which funding is being sought. (Auditor-General in Commonwealth of Australia 2015a, 4)

Thus by mid-2015 ANAO and JCPAA had contested the proposals of Finance and ANAO, in particular, had proposed an alternative. Important considerations for account giving for the ANAO comprised a focus on programmes rather than entity purpose, and planned performance combined with planned resource use. Expected programme achievements had to be known before adequate budgetary scrutiny could occur. Figure 2 presents the ANAO proposal for the PB process and how it shaped managerial accountability relationships, with italics indicating changes vis-à-vis the Finance proposal.

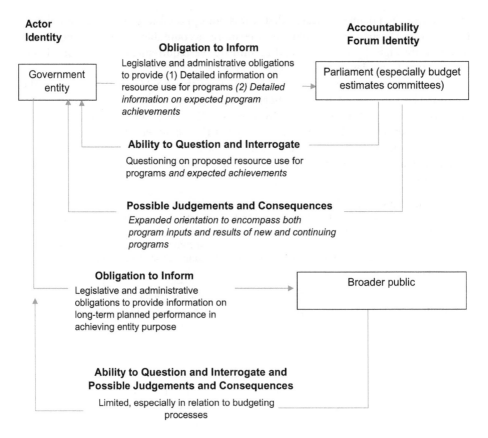

Figure 2. Alternative performance budgeting and constitution of accountability relations [italics highlight proposed changes to previous proposal].

5.4 *Compromise: connecting accounts and retaining forum status*

JCPAA subsequently wrote to Finance indicating that it wanted performance information to be retained in budget statements. Requiring parliamentary support for its proposed framework, Finance modified its approach, with planned performance information now to be retained in budget statements. According to Finance, Its compromise approach would create the required accountability relationships. It claimed:

> Under this proposal: (a) budget statements will continue to provide information to support Parliament's consideration of appropriation amounts being requested, including a strategic view of how the funding will be used to fulfil an entity's purposes, and how, at a high level, success will be measured. (Department of Finance 2015, 3)

High level success measures were to focus on the effectiveness of the entity in meeting its purpose (Department of Finance 2015). According to Finance, politicians could turn to the publicly available corporate plans if they required further information.

However, this approach was also to come under attack. The ANAO, in particular, saw the inclusion of only high-level performance information in budget statements as problematic given the importance of Parliament as an accountability forum. In its submission to the ongoing inquiry the ANAO argued:

> Budget statements have been stand-alone documents designed to contain sufficient performance information so that Parliamentarians do not need to unduly rely on other documents, such as the entity's corporate plan and annual report, when considering funding proposals. (ANAO 2015, 1)

Furthermore, it reiterated its earlier argument that a focus on measuring entity purpose was an insufficient account for the required accountability relationships surrounding PB. It noted that Finance's proposed PB approach created:

> a risk that the Parliament will have less measurable information available that links directly to the outcomes and programs for which funding is being sought at the time when it is considering the government's funding proposals. (ANAO 2015, 1)

The JCPAA appeared to accept the arguments of the ANAO. In a subsequent inquiry hearing, JCPAA representatives questioned why the reform process resulted in less accountability of the executive to Parliament when the original intent was that it was to enhance external accountability. They were also concerned about the nature of the account that was to be presented in terms of the 'higher' level performance measures under the compromise approach. They questioned the Finance representatives attending the inquiry:

> If we are changing the system to make it much more transparent and granular, why has that granular data not been included in the budget to privilege parliament's role of holding the executive accountable. (JCPAA representative in Commonwealth of Australia 2015b, 4)

And

> If the ANAO's letter is correct, why have you changed from a focus on the impact of programs and their effectiveness in achieving expected outcomes to differences made for each purpose? That seems quite woolly and vague. (JCPAA representative in Commonwealth of Australia 2015b, 4)

JCPAA also raised concerns with Finance that while corporate plans could be accessed on entity websites these may not be updated in May when budget statements were presented to Parliament in May or for budget estimates committees to conduct their budget scrutiny. Thus the argument that it could access corporate plans for more detailed performance information risked using out-of-date information.

In response, Finance indicated to JCPAA it would come back with a further refinement. One week later it submitted to JCPAA the refined compromise approach. One important change was that the high level performance measures would contain at least one measure of programme impact for continuing or established programmes. Lower level information on these established programmes was to be retained in corporate plans. Another material change involved new or materially changed programmes being presented for funding by Parliament. Here, budget statements would include detailed delivery information and performance measures of programmes. In this way they sought to address ANAO and JCPAA concerns about the primacy of Parliament as a privileged accountability forum and the nature of the account giving that was to occur through budget statements.

In a follow-up hearing on the latest proposal JCPAA indicated a greater level of comfort with the proposed PB process. However, it did express concerns with detailed performance information on existing programmes still being presented in corporate plans rather than budget statements and potentially being inaccurate or out of date at the time of budget presentation. Finance responded that it would suggest in guidance information to entities that corporate plans be updated as soon as practicable after budgets had been presented, which would both allow entities to know the amount of resource they had to allocate to the various programmes they delivered and Parliament to have updated corporate plans when they commenced the budget estimates process to scrutinize the proposed budgetary allocations.

This last (at time of writing) process had mitigated the concerns of JCPAA somewhat in how it would shape accountability relationships between the executive and legislative arms of the national government of Australia. Overall, Parliament and its estimates committees would receive accounts and be able to interrogate and pass judgements about new programmes in detail, receiving a 'higher-level' account about continuing programmes. Its ability to judge continuing programmes would largely depend on the voluntary obligation on government departments to update corporate plans at budget time. Figure 3 presents this third (iterated) version of managerial accountability relationships shaped by the proposed PB design, with italics highlighting how this compromise approach changed the previous alternative design proposed by ANAO.

Thus, there appeared to be consensus amongst the main protagonists in the PB redesign process. However, this consensus had been arrived at through contest and negotiation about how managerial accountability was to take place. The next section discusses the study's findings and contributions.

6. Discussion and conclusion

This study was motivated by concerns that prior research had devoted insufficient attention to how the design of PB processes affects managerial accountability relationships. The case study revealed alternative proposed designs for PB and how these shaped important elements of managerial accountability relationships in different ways including: the obligation of actors to inform; forum identity; a forum's ability to discuss and interrogate; and, albeit to a limited extent, potential forum judgements and consequences.

This is best illustrated through contrasting Figures 1 and 2. These figures indicate that how the PB process was designed would constitute important elements of the executive–legislature relationship as well as the legislature's status vis-à-vis the public as a forum that held the executive managerially accountable. PB design would influence whether Parliament and its budget estimates committees would interrogate and pass judgements about budget requests focused on expenditure or also programme achievements. PB design would also bring to the fore the accountability relationship with the public, with this forum receiving accounts of planned performance but a limited ability to interrogate and judge. While the various protagonists in the reform process moved towards consensus over time (refer to Figure 3), debates still occurred over the role of Parliament as an important managerial accountability forum focusing on new programmes or continuing programmes as well.

Thus one contribution the paper makes is to research on PB and accountability. Previous studies on PB and accountability have focused on the operation of PB and its role as an information device. This research concludes that context and the

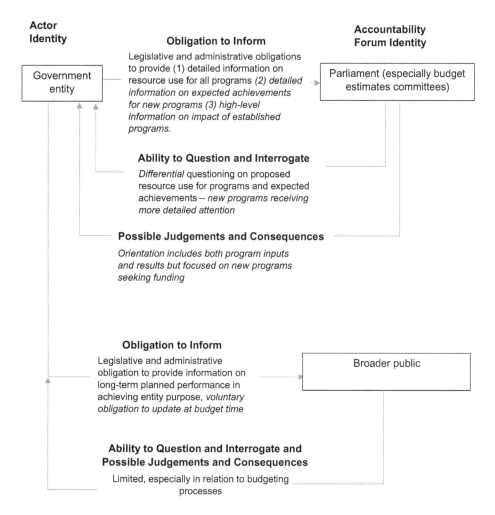

Figure 3. Compromise performance budgeting and constitution of accountability relations [italics highlight proposed changes to previous proposal].

dynamics between the executive and the legislature influence how PB information affects managerial accountability, with these factors existing independent of the PB process (Posner and Fantone 2007; Johnson and Talbot 2007; Bourdeaux 2008; Lu and Xue 2011; Ward 2015). The current study extends these understandings by showing how PB processes constitute the accountability context when one considers their design rather than operation. This occurs through PB design shaping important elements of managerial accountability relationships that include but also extend beyond information provision.

Importantly, it is not suggested that PB processes are deterministic. Numerous other factors are likely to shape how PB processes are ultimately enacted. Also, the constitutive effects between PB processes and accountability context are not one way. Indeed, the design of PB took place within a broader environment comprising expectations that government departments would be accountable externally to

Parliament and the public. However, as the case study shows, different managerial accountability relationships for performance resource use would have come into being contingent on the acceptance of the various proposals. PB processes and accountability context are mutually constitutive.

A second contribution of the paper is to public accountability literature interested in why accountability arrangements (such as PB) change over time and vary between geographies. This research emphasizes macro-level factors comprising country legacy and traditions (Reiss 2009; Overman, Van Genugten, and Van Thiel 2015) and entity-level characteristics such as policy field and size (Pollitt et al. 2004). Studying trajectories of accountability reforms, Overman, Van Genugten, and Van Thiel (2015, 1117) conclude that 'while country was a good predictor for the agency's accountability regime, future research should shed more light on the particular mechanisms'.

Here the study complements prior literature by indicating how accountability arrangements also come about through interactions at the 'micro-level', comprising contests between participants in redesign processes both interpreting accountability in different ways and seeking to persuade others to their points of view. Although the potential for conflict between executive and legislative branches of government (Wildavsky and Caiden 2001; Posner 2009) is widely acknowledged, this study shows that contest and conflict extend beyond the executive and the legislature to encompass significant agents who act on their behalf as well as in their own interests.

In the case study the particular managerial accountability arrangement that would ultimately come into being through PB (but also corporate plans and annual performance statements) was contingent on the interaction between Finance, JCPAA and ANAO. Finance sought to bring in enhancements in planning across the public administration component of the executive branch of government. Here Finance was interested in responding to criticisms for its previous 'light touch' approach to accountability reform and improving planning processes within the executive. Finance's proposed design, which disconnected inputs from results, arguably gave it greater control also over government departments in the preparation of budgets – if it wanted to focus on limiting spending levels it could prioritize and/or deny departmental budget requests without having to discuss formally the corresponding adjustments to performance.[2] In contrast, JCPAA focused on ensuring budgetary and accountability powers for parliament, while the ANAO, which saw its primary client as Parliament, was likewise interested in the accountability of the public administration to this branch of government as representatives of the public at large.

In these contests, NPM doctrine did not become a unifying theme that brought together different interests. Instead it comprised resources with a 'number of distinct personae, dependent upon the audience' (Osborne 2006, 379) that were appropriated by reform participants for their cause. The case study shows the highly contestable nature of account-giving that occurred in the name of managerial accountability, encompassing different aspects of performance and whether calculations of performance should orient to long-term entity purpose or short-term annual programme achievements. Future research on PB could thus pay attention to how micro-level contests between significant participants unfold in conversations about the design and reform of accountability arrangements, how doctrine or thinking about NPM or other beyond-NPM modes such as 'new public governance' (Osborne 2006) is appropriated in these contests, and how this contestation then shapes the accountability arrangements that emerge.

The practical implications of this study relate reforms of public budgeting processes and other arrangements that have accountability implications. While much of the focus of budgeting reforms is on limiting executive decision making and producing better information (Posner 2009; Caiden 2010), attention must also be devoted to other important elements of accountability relationships such as those examined in this study. Considering these multiple elements in budgeting reforms is especially important given increased calls for radical change of public budgeting processes (Caiden 2010). In relation to managerial accountability, consideration must also be given to the extent to which accountability for performance over multiple time horizons is important and how this is to be engendered. In the case study reported here a compromise solution of sorts was reached between accountability in the long-term oriented to entity purpose and accountability in the short-term focused on annual programme results.

In closing the limitations of this study should be acknowledged. As a single case study, observations and implications are no doubt influenced by the specific characteristics of the case setting. The use of discourse analysis also carries with it a number of limitations, such as the possibility of a partial selection of texts for closer analysis and the possibility of alternative interpretations about the relationships proposed within the analysed texts. While care was taken to ensure that texts important for the design of PB were selected it is conceivable that others were missed, especially those that were not in the public domain. Participant interviews and direct observations of design processes are important for future research to consider. Also, it is possible that the talk and text of actors did not reflect their underlying interests and motivations, although the significant effort and actions engaged in pursuit of espoused positions suggest otherwise. Finally, the reform of the budget process is still in flux (at time of writing) and it is likely that further changes and constitutive effects will occur. Despite these limitations, it is considered that the study contributes to prior research on PB and accountability by showing how the design of PB processes constitutes accountability context through shaping important elements of managerial accountability relationships.

Notes

1. PB takes two forms, a decision rule (direct performance budgeting) and a less defined analytical tool (performance-informed budgeting) (Schick 2007; OECD 2008). This study considers the second form of PB from the perspective of managerial accountability.
2. I thank the reviewer who pointed out this possibility.

Disclosure statement

No potential conflict of interest was reported by the author.

References

ANAO (Australian National Audit Office). 2011. "Development and Implementation of Key Performance Indicators to Support the Outcomes and Programs Framework." Performance Audit Report No. 5 2011-12. Canberra: Commonwealth of Australia.

ANAO (Australian National Audit Office). 2015. "ANAO Submission to JCPAA Inquiry into Commonwealth Performance Framework November." Accessed 14 March 2016. http://www.aph.gov.au/Parliamentary_Business/Committees/Joint/Public_Accounts_and_Audit/Performance_Framework/Submissions

Bourdeaux, C. 2008. "Integrating Performance Information into Legislative Budget Processes." *Public Performance & Management Review* 31 (4): 547–569. doi:10.2753/PMR1530-9576310403.

Bovens, M. 2007. "Analysing and Assessing Accountability: A Conceptual Framework." *European Law Journal* 13 (4): 447–468. doi:10.1111/eulj.2007.13.issue-4.

Bovens, M. 2010. "Two Concepts of Accountability: Accountability as a Virtue and as a Mechanism." *West European Politics* 33 (5): 946–967. doi:10.1080/01402382.2010.486119.

Bovens, M., T. Schillemans, and R. E. Goodin. 2014. "Public Accountability." In *The Oxford Handbook of Public Accountability*, edited by M. Bovens, R. E. Goodin, and T. Schillemans, 1–22. Oxford: Oxford University Press.

Brenton, S. 2014. "Ministerial Accountability for Departmental Actions across Westminster Parliamentary Democracies." *Australian Journal of Public Administration* 73 (4): 467–481. doi:10.1111/aupa.2014.73.issue-4.

Caiden, N. 2010. "Challenges Confronting Contemporary Public Budgeting: Retrospectives/Prospectives from Allen Schick." *Public Administration Review* 70: 203–210. doi:10.1111/puar.2010.70.issue-2.

Christensen, T., and P. Lægreid. 2015. "Performance and Accountability – A Theoretical Discussion and an Empirical Assessment." *Public Organization Review* 15: 207–225. doi:10.1007/s11115-013-0267-2.

Commonwealth of Australia. 2015a. *Transcript of JCPAA Inquiry Hearing on 19 March 2015.* Canberra: Commonwealth of Australia.

Commonwealth of Australia. 2015b. *Transcript of JCPAA Inquiry Hearing on 26 November 2015.* Canberra: Commonwealth of Australia.

Day, P., and R. Klein. 1987. *Accountabilities: Five Public Services.* London: Tavistock.

Department of Finance. 2012. *Is Less More? Towards Better Commonwealth Performance Discussion Paper.* Canberra: Commonwealth of Australia.

Department of Finance. 2015. "Submission to JCPAA Inquiry: November 2015." Accessed 14 March 2016. http://www.aph.gov.au/Parliamentary_Business/Committees/Joint/Public_Accounts_and_Audit/Performance_Framework/Submissions

Ezzamel, M., K. Robson, and P. Stapleton. 2012. "The Logics of Budgeting: Theorization and Practice Variation in the Educational Field." *Accounting, Organizations and Society* 37: 281–303. doi:10.1016/j.aos.2012.03.005.

Fairclough, N. 2003. *Analysing Discourse: Textual Analysis for Social Research.* London: Routledge.

Gray, A., and B. Jenkins. 1993. "Codes of Accountability in the New Public Sector." *Accounting, Auditing & Accountability Journal* 6 (3): 52–67. doi:10.1108/09513579310042560.

Hardy, C. 2004. "Scaling Up and Bearing Down in Discourse Analysis: Questions Regarding Textual Agencies and Their Context." *Organization* 11 (3): 415–425. doi:10.1177/1350508404042000.

Hawke, L. 2007. "Performance Budgeting in Australia." *OECD Journal on Budgeting* 7 (3). doi:10.1787/budget-v7-art17-en.

Hopwood, A. G. 1987. "The Archeology of Accounting Systems." *Accounting Organizations and Society* 12 (3): 207–234. doi:10.1016/0361-3682(87)90038-9.

Johnson, C., and C. Talbot. 2007. "The UK Parliament and Performance: Challenging or Challenged?" *International Review of Administrative Sciences* 73 (1): 113–131. doi:10.1177/0020852307075693.

Lu, E., Y. Z. Mohr, and A. Ho. 2015. "Taking Stock: Assessing and Improving Performance Budgeting Theory and Practice." *Public Performance & Management Review* 38 (3): 426–458. doi:10.1080/15309576.2015.1006470.

Lu, Y., and C. Xue. 2011. "The Power of The Purse And Budgetary Accountability: Experiences From Subnational Governments In China." *Public Administration and Development* 31: 351–362. doi:10.1002/pad.v31.5.

Mackay, K. 2011. "The Performance Framework of the Australian Government, 1987 to 2011." *OECD Journal on Budgeting* 11 (3): 1–48. doi:10.1787/budget-11-5kg3nhlcqdg5.

Miller, P. 1992. "Accounting and Objectivity: The Invention of Calculating Selves and Calculating Spaces." *Annals of Scholarship* edited by A. Megill. 9 (1–2): 61–86.

Mulgan, R. 2000. "Accountability: An Ever-Expanding Concept?" *Public Administration* 78 (3): 555–573. doi:10.1111/padm.2000.78.issue-3.

OECD (Organisation for Economic Co-operation and Development). 2008. *Performance Budgeting: A Users' Guide*. Paris: Policy Brief, Public Affairs Division, OECD.

Osborne, S. P. 2006. "The New Public Governance?" *Public Management Review* 8 (3): 377–387. doi:10.1080/14719030600853022.

Overman, S., M. Van Genugten, and S. Van Thiel. 2015. "Accountability after Structural Disaggregation: Comparing Agency Accountability Arrangements." *Public Administration* 93 (4): 1102–1120. doi:10.1111/padm.12185.

Parliament of Australia. 2015. "Duties and Powers of the JCPAA." Accessed 8 December 2015. http://www.aph.gov.au/Parliamentary_Business/Committees/Joint/Public_Accounts_and_Audit/Role_of_the_Committee#duties

Phillips, L., and M. W. Jorgensen. 2002. *Discourse Analysis as Theory and Method*. London: Sage.

Pollitt, C., C. Talbot, J. Caulfield, and A. Smullen. 2004. *Agencies: How Governments Do Things through Semi-Autonomous Organizations*. Basingstoke: Palgrave Macmillan.

Posner, P. L. 2009. "Budget Process Reform: Waiting for Godot." *Public Administration Review* 69 (2): 233–244. doi:10.1111/puar.2009.69.issue-2.

Posner, P. L., and D. M. Fantone. 2007. "Assessing Federal Program Performance: Observations on the U.S. Office of Management and Budget's Program Assessment Rating Tool and its Use in the Budget Process." *Public Performance & Management Review* 30 (3): 351–368. doi:10.2753/PMR1530-9576300303.

Reiss, D. R. 2009. "Agency Accountability Strategies after Liberalization: Universal Service in the United Kingdom, France, and Sweden." *Law & Policy* 31 (1): 111–141. doi:10.1111/lapo.2009.31.issue-1.

Schick, A. 2007. "Performance Budgeting and Accrual Budgeting: Decision Rules or Analytic Tools?" *OECD Journal on Budgeting* 7 (2): 109–138. doi:10.1787/budget-v7-2-en.

Sinclair, A. 1995. "The Chameleon of Accountability: Forms and Discourses." *Accounting, Organizations and Society* 20 (2–3): 219–237. doi:10.1016/0361-3682(93)E0003-Y.

Smyth, S. 2012. "Contesting Public Accountability: A Dialogical Exploration of Accountability and Social Housing." *Critical Perspectives on Accounting* 23 (3): 230–243. doi:10.1016/j.cpa.2011.12.007.

Smyth, S. 2016. "Public Accountability: Reforms and Resistance in Social Housing." *Public Management Review* 1–20. doi:10.1080/14719037.2016.1153703.

Ward, T. 2015. "The Irish Parliament and the Scrutiny of Departmental Performance Reports." *Public Money & Management* 35 (2): 153–160. doi:10.1080/09540962.2015.1007713.

Wildavsky, A., and N. Caiden. 2001. *The New Politics of the Budgetary Process*. 4th ed. New York: Addison-Wesley.

Willems, T., and W. Van Dooren. 2012. "Coming to Terms with Accountability." *Public Management Review* 14 (7): 1011–1036. doi:10.1080/14719037.2012.662446.

Balancing budget control and flexibility: the central finance agency as 'responsive regulator'

Michael Di Francesco and John Alford

ABSTRACT

This paper explores how the increasing need for budget flexibility might be reconciled with the necessity for control of public money by reframing the relationship between central finance agencies and spending agencies in 'regulatory' terms. The need arises because governments increasingly face complex, non-routine problems, which require them to develop greater capacity for collaboration and 'flexibility'. At the same time, the public expects government to be accountable for how resources are used, which is conventionally framed in terms of procedural regularity. After surveying the contours of flexibility and the different ways budgeting practices inhibit collaboration in the public sector, the paper uses responsive regulation perspectives to explore how reshaping the *type* of rules and the way they are applied, rather than fewer rules, is a preferred means of balancing central control and situational flexibility.

Introduction

In contemporary public management, 'flexibility' has assumed a place of importance alongside 'control'. In budgeting and financial management, the need for control historically was borne of the public's expectation that governments should be accountable to them for how compulsorily acquired resources are deployed. Budget systems are key means of operationalizing this accountability (Willoughby 2014, 25–56). They prescribe rules for the allocation, spending, transferring and accounting of public money. In every government, these rules are directed through some form of central finance agency, whose task is to promulgate, monitor and enforce the rules (e.g. Australia's Department of Finance or HM Treasury in the United Kingdom [UK]).[1] The ways in which a central finance agency (CFA or Finance) exercises control have enormous bearing on the scope of budget flexibility, and the nature of these interactions infuses both the design and implementation of budget systems, and by extension the theories explaining the impacts of alternative designs. These themes are central to this paper.

Increasingly, the traditional modus operandi of these agencies jostles with organizational and inter-organizational efforts to achieve results. There have, over time, been discernible shifts in the types of 'governance logics' that dominate organizational practices in the public sector, in structural forms, control foci and performance standards (Wiesel and Modell 2014). Quite often, the transposition from compliance-based public administration to market-directed new public management (NPM) and network-oriented new public governance (NPG) tended to gravitate towards a conception of performance facilitated by granting government entities and their managers 'autonomy' to define, negotiate and implement the best means to achieve mandated ends (Hood 1991). This movement sought to give managers more say about *how* results are to be achieved, while obliging them to respect the financial limits imposed by CFAs (Pollitt and Bouckaert 2004, 67–72). But as we shall explain below, this form of flexibility struggles to relate to non-routine problems.

We contend that the need for flexibility has nowadays burgeoned beyond the requirements of managerialist routines. The reason has been the emergence of more complex issues in more unsettled environments, which collectively we will call 'non-routine problems' (see below). In this new context, budgeting and financial management processes are increasingly caught between differing imperatives: the public's expectations that problems stemming from growing complexity and turbulence will be addressed with the help of some flexibility, and the same public's demands that the resources utilized by government to tackle those problems will be managed efficiently and fairly (Behn 2001; Kettl 2009). Sometimes, these imperatives are in conflict with each other, sometimes in harmony, and sometimes just different. It turns out that the variability of these interactions may point to ways of reconciling the imperatives, in particular through the instruments of 'responsive regulation'. Thus, the key research question for this paper is: *how can a central finance agency configure budget systems to enable greater situational flexibility for spending agencies while ensuring that public money is managed consistently with the purposes of the government as a whole?* In this question, we draw on the management sciences (e.g. Kickert 1985; De Leeuw and Volberda 1996) to initially define 'flexibility' as the capacity to reorient purposes, processes and resources quickly and substantially to meet changed circumstances, with the intent of explicating the concept in more detail below.

The research on budgeting is vast, spanning almost all the disciplines represented within the social sciences (Covaleski et al. 2003). A significant proportion is concerned with budget control and flexibility in the *private* sector where, as in many fields, the issue of flexibility is one where practice has tended to run ahead of theory. Many large companies, for example, have been exploring radical new methods, such as avoidance of the 'performance trap' and the use of continuous budgeting, espoused by the 'beyond budgeting' movement (e.g. Hope and Fraser 2003; Frow, Marginson, and Ogden 2010; Otley 2006). By comparison, research on *public* sector budgeting, whilst also substantial, tends to focus on long-standing practices and documents of budget decision and execution processes (Mitchell and Thurmaier 2012). In this context, research on budget *flexibility* in the public sector has been modest. An exhaustive literature search unearthed a small number of specialized studies in budget execution, generally focussed on 'rebudgeting' – i.e. revisions to the budget during the fiscal year to accommodate changing circumstances – in the United States (e.g. Hoskins 1983; Forrester andt Mullins 1992) and more recently in Italy (e.g. Anessi-Pessina, Sicilia, and Steccolini 2012, 2013).[2] The review also revealed that the principal subject of this paper – responsive regulation – had even fewer mentions (in fact, by our count, none) in the specific contexts of budget flexibility, public budgeting or budgeting more generally. Moreover, there appears to be limited research, including theorizing, on the impact of budget processes on *flexibility in the public sector*, at least outside the well-rehearsed criticisms of traditional public financial administration that inspired the NPM (e.g. Hughes 2003, 165–181). All of which, we contend, provide sufficient opening for exploring how the role of the central finance agency might be recalibrated to balance aspects of budget control and flexibility.

In this paper, therefore, we consider options available to central finance agencies for enabling flexibility while still maintaining control, and their implications for CFAs as 'regulatory' agencies. Our context is primarily the political institutions and norms of Westminster-type parliamentary systems, such as Australia and the UK, although the approach has broader application. We begin with an overview of how increasing complexity and turbulence require public sector agencies to become more collaborative but simultaneously comply with CFA control requirements. We outline the way in which budget processes are said to hinder those efforts and use the notion of 'rule variability' to explain the nature and scope of 'flexibility' within budgeting. We then examine ways of balancing flexibility with control, focussing on responsive regulation and the idea of 'earned autonomy'. This approach, which we discuss at length later in the paper, began in the UK National Health Service (NHS) and has more recently been investigated for its use in budgeting in Australia.

Non-routine problems and non-routine responses

The urge to standardize in public administration was propelled by the Weberian conception of impersonal administration of rules (Weber 1946). It took shape practically as consistency of processes, underpinning organizations' capacity to produce large-volume uniform services efficiently and normatively as a corollary of the need for equity in applying rules. In this way, public sector organizations have tended traditionally to orient themselves to what we might call the 'routine' services of government (Kettl 2009). Interestingly, this did not abate with the emergence of NPM from the early 1980s: its adoption of corporate planning, budgeting for outputs and performance measurement had the practical effect of further 'routinizing' programmes.

But at the same time, government organizations have been confronted by increasingly problematic issues in the world around them, to which their routine processes are not well suited. More and more, they have to make *non*-routine decisions and deliver *non*-routine services. There are three main types of non-routine problems. First, there are *complex* problems, where different issues, each the responsibility of a particular agency, are entangled with each other or straddle several agencies. The net effect is that agencies find that they have to interact with other agencies and seek their collaboration, or at least acquiescence. No single agency has the authority, resources, information or capabilities to deal with the problem on its own. The most extreme form of complex problem is the '*wicked* problem' – such as the use and effects of illicit drugs – which is intractable, involves multiple conflicting interests and is inherently resistant to clear definition and solution (Head and Alford 2015).

A second kind of non-routine problem is a *crisis*: an unexpected event or situation that generates uncertainty, is a threat to the organization or society and calls for urgent and complex change. A natural disaster, such as the Hurricane Katrina storm surge which in August 2005 devastated the metropolitan area of New Orleans in the United States, is an obvious example. Related to crisis is *turbulence*, a third variety of non-routine problem, where the organization is buffeted spasmodically but continuously by a series of difficult events. This can, for instance, take the form of political conflict that arises from problematic change, such as the disruptive social and economic effects of new technologies. These types of problems call for changes in policies, structures, resources and processes. We call these responses 'non-routine governance'.

Most noteworthy among them is 'collaboration' or 'networked governance' – where one or more government agencies work together with other government agencies, private firms or non-profits on particular tasks. Typically, it involves the participating parties sharing the decision-making, or the actual work or both (Donahue and Zeckhauser 2011; Sullivan and Skelcher 2002). The literature shows in abundance that successful collaboration between organizations relies on certain conditions, which the participating actors need to create or sustain (Huxham and Vangen 2005). One is agreement on purposes, which can be facilitated when the organizations involved have common interests. But, it is more likely that they will have different goals and almost certainly differing interests, in which cases different but complementary purposes, along with the interdependencies that underpin them, must form the basis for agreed goals (Lax and Sebenius 1986).

Another condition is mutual trust between the parties. Trust is recognized as an alternative to the carrots and sticks wielded in, for instance, classical contracting (Alford and O'Flynn 2012; deHoog 1990; Laughlin 1996). It involves each party developing confidence that the other parties will 'do the right thing' in situations where it is vulnerable to their actions. Following Gouldner's (1960) famous 'norm', building up trust stems from a pattern of mutual positive gestures, examples of which might be sharing information, bending rules or not taking advantage of unpredictable circumstances. At a minimum, it demands that organizations and those representing them in inter-organizational dealings deliver on what they promise.

This process of building trust takes considerable time, since each positive gesture is not sequenced but rather arises haphazardly in the course of organizational life (Covey 2006). This makes it susceptible to changes in personnel, policies, procedures and resources. For staff acting on behalf of their agency in a collaborative process with other organizations, it is also important that they have sufficient autonomy to make judgments about trust-enhancing offerings. However, these collaborative interactions can be constrained by the legitimate accountability requirements that surround public sector programmes and organizations. Rules relating to procurement, human resources and, of course, budgeting and financial management can affect the extent to which organizational representatives can make positive gestures and deliver on undertakings.

Rules and the control logic of institutional roles

These responses to non-routine problems necessitate a degree of flexibility in the structures and processes of government. But prima facie, they tend on the whole to have a different logic to the standard operating procedures of routine government, where 'inflexibility' is often associated with the bureaucratic pathology of 'red tape'. We tend to think of red tape as a surfeit of 'pointless' rules. In practice, its complexion is determined more by perception, framed by the function and institutional location of the beholder: one person's due process may be a vexatious constraint for another (Kaufman 1977). Public organizations are said to be 'inflexible' *precisely* because in conditions of non-routine problems, managers are prone to exercise control by applying existing rules (which may be inappropriate in the circumstances) or developing ever more detailed rules.

However, the way rule interactions impact on their intended purposes can also be used to explain how rules help or hinder 'organizational effectiveness'. On the plus side, rules define limits on arbitrary decision-making. They can facilitate efficiency, provide direction, encourage equity and help prevent corrupt behaviour. On the minus side, as Bozeman (2000) and Bozeman and Feeny (2011) propose, there are two key types of rule dysfunctionality. 'Rule-inception red tape' comprises rules that are 'born bad', such as when they generate unintended consequences due to faulty understanding of behavioural responses. 'Rule-evolved red tape' comprises rules that 'go bad' over time; for instance, the gradual accretion of rules that render the costs of compliance so high as to induce organizational paralysis. In short, the intent of rules and the way they interact, as well as the motives and priorities of institutional actors who either enforce or comply with them, are all important for understanding their role. Indeed, it is precisely in order to maximize the positive aspects of rules and minimize the negative ones, that we (and presumably many public officials) seek an optimal balance between flexibility and control. Specifically in public budgeting, two features contextualize rules: financial control as accountability and the symbiotic relationship between CFAs and spending agencies.

Earlier we noted that the routines of public budgeting sit within a broader institutional framework of government accountability. In the political systems we use to frame this paper – Westminster-type parliamentary systems – constitutional arrangements ensure that the principle of annual appropriation is not only the foundation for the accountability of executive government to the parliament but is also, through 'confidence and supply', the very basis for government formation. A cash-based system of government accounting that operated alongside consolidated 'fund' accounts was the primary mechanism of parliamentary control (Funnell, Cooper, and Lee 2012, 42–64). The set-piece importance of annual appropriations has meant that accountability has traditionally been effected through ministerial departments, with a *performance focus* on legal compliance and financial inputs.

The second defining feature is the place of routines in shaping the institutional roles and responsibilities of core actors in government budgeting. It has long been acknowledged that CFAs and spending agencies tend to assume distinct 'rationing' and 'claiming' roles: the 'guardians' (CFAs) protect the public purse, and the 'spenders' (spending agencies) advocate for or protect sectoral spending (Wildavsky 1964). Budget routines institutionalize these roles in two ways. Budgeting is a process of mutual adjustment characterized by distinct techniques of competition: guardians set and enforce decision processes and spenders deploy policy and operational expertise. At the same time, shared cultural understandings reinforce these formal rules of budgeting – the so-called closed budgetary village – that enabled guardians to exercise oversight through the continuous assessment of reputation (Heclo and Wildavsky 1974) and 'negotiated discretion' (Thain and Wright 1995). Over time, these techniques and cultural attitudes were entrenched as budget process routines designed to manage conflict by narrowing decisions to small changes (i.e. 'incremental budgeting').

During the 1980s and 1990s, these features of public budgeting came to be seen as root causes of public sector growth and inefficiency. An important part of the institutional response was for guardians to deploy budget reform as a type of procedural power. This comprised three strategies: centralizing the setting of expenditure ceilings (and excluding spenders from these processes); within the ceilings, decentralizing responsibility for allocative decisions to spenders and promoting the use of contracting to deliver public services (which diminished spenders' capacity to argue from expertise) (Kelly and Wanna 2001, 601–607). Intended primarily to force spenders to take on 'rationing' responsibilities, these changes disoriented CFAs who now found themselves under pressure to shift from a control-oriented 'command post' to a managerial-oriented 'strategic advisor' (Schick 2001).

In sum, the inflexibility attributed to rules in government – budgetary or otherwise – tends to reflect the perspective and location of organizational actors, and these in turn are framed by political system inherencies, such as strong institutional roles that impose accountabilities for detailed regularity. Against this background, there are valid reasons for spending agencies to seek flexibility, but there are equally valid reasons for CFAs to seek to exercise control. These contending imperatives must be reconciled, and as the custodian of the budget system, Finance has a core responsibility for setting the terms of reconciliation in the structures and rules it establishes. And, to a significant degree, they can be reconciled.

Budgeting as an inhibitor of flexibility

Budget rules are usually seen as 'hard' factors in the management of organizations; they derive their force from the simple fact that they govern the key resource for implementing government priorities: money. This happens in numerous ways, intended or unintended (Smith and Thompson 2010). We focus on three. First, budget rules *directly* inhibit flexibility by specifically prescribing or proscribing where, upon what, when, how and how much public money can be allocated, spent, accumulated or transferred, and who has authority to permit or prohibit these actions. This receives fuller treatment in the next section.

Second, the rules are more likely to constrict flexibility if they are cast in ex ante rather than ex post terms (Jones and Thompson 1986). Ex ante rules entail the regulator controlling the inputs and processes before or during the activity being regulated. By contrast, ex post rules are applied after the event so that the regulatee has some room to deviate. The shift from ex ante to ex post control is one of the defining trends in international public financial management reform (Ruffner and Sevilla 2004). For example, traditional financial control systems, in which payments were approved prior to commitment by a central controller (sometimes located in the CFA), have largely been replaced with devolved management systems that permit spending agencies to authorize transactions that are then audited externally after payment is made.

Third, budget rules can make it more difficult for government organizations to mount responses to non-routine situations, such as collaboration. Collaboration often requires devoting funds to a purpose transcending the organizational units involved. This often means that two or more organizations must agree to reallocate funds to the agreed purpose (see Raine and Watt 2013). However, budget rules usually mandate that one entity is the 'budget holder', which means that there needs to be either a high level of trust between the participating entities, or a mechanism to safeguard the over-riding purpose, especially when circumstances change. Either way, they complicate the ability of funding parties to contribute their fair share or to honour undertakings, which in turn undermines trust. Moreover, collaboration can be impeded where the parties at the 'coal-face' of the partnership lack sufficient decision rights and are constrained in the extent to which they can reallocate monies between organizations, programmes or time periods (O'Flynn et al. 2011; Campbell 2012).

Defining budgeting flexibility

As we noted earlier, flexibility in public budgeting concerns how readily allocations, expenditures and reporting processes can be varied to enable useful responses to both routine and non-routine problems. This in turn is largely a function of how much decision-making authority is *devolved* to those dealing with those problems. Those officials who are 'close to the action' are better equipped to deal with crises if they have some room to redeploy resources. Those involved in collaboration to tackle complex problems with other organizations will have more room to make trust-building positive gestures, and to limit trust-eroding breaches of undertakings, if they have greater authority to re-assign funds to purposes important to the cooperative relationships involved.

Our position is that flexibility in budget processes should be seen as largely a matter of *devolution* of decision-making authority. Whilst traditional approaches to public budgeting emphasize centralized and compliance-based 'ex ante' regulation of spending, throughout those processes, some actors have the authority to redirect funds to non-routine objects. Unfortunately, a key problem is that there is usually a disconnect between the actor with decision rights and those actually dealing with the circumstances requiring a response. Furthermore, the 'degree' of that authority may also fluctuate across the stages of budgeting. Flexibility should, therefore, be seen in multidimensional terms. In Table 1, we suggest that two dimensions – *levels of budget decision-making* and *budget rule variability* – operate across the generally recognized 'stages' of budgeting (Guess and Leloup 2010, 25–30). In a typical Westminster parliamentary system, these comprise a calendar of legal and administrative processes relating to budget preparation by the executive and its approval by the parliament, followed by the three elements of budget execution (operational management, spending approval and monitoring, and assessment of budget and programme performance). For analytical purposes, the processes described in Table 1 are highly stylized, conceived as separate and sequential, when in practice they can of course overlap or entail feedback loops.

The first dimension of flexibility is the *level* of budget decision-maker, whose authority is either endowed by the law or attached to the office they occupy. In Table 1, we distinguish a number of conventional levels, from high to low in terms of the power potentially wielded within the formal budget processes, and we provide an indication of where each level might be *routinely* expected to exercise influence. For instance, as the degree of influence will be delimited by the discretion attached to hierarchical positions, political and bureaucratic actors at higher levels would be

Table 1. Levels and dimensions of flexibility in budgeting.

Stages of budgeting	Budget formulation		Budget execution		
Dimensions of variability	Budget preparation	Budget approval	Budget management	Budget control	Performance assessment
	Fiscal rules (e.g. debt), Annual budget objectives, Budget process design	Budget program presentation, Legislative veto, Relationship between appropriations and budget presentation	Budget implementation, Relationship between appropriations and internal resource allocation	Budget compliance vs. program performance, Executive or legislative processes for adjustments	Budget compliance vs. program performance, Range of regular and ad hoc evaluation and review
Level of decision-maker (low to high)					
Parliament	■	■		■	
Prime Minister and/or Finance Minister	■	■		■	■
Portfolio Minister	■	■		■	■
Central Finance Agency	■	■	■	■	
Agency Head	■		■	■	■
Program Manager			■	■	■
Frontline public servant*					

*A 'front-line public servant' may play other informal decision roles, such as when exercising professional discretion in dealing with clients. The exemplar is the notion of the 'street level bureaucrat' (Lipsky 1980).

Table 2. General rules of budget control.

Rule	Description	Examples
1. Accountability	Who can spend	Parliamentary appropriations are to agencies or Ministers, and agency delegations specify staff positions authorized to spend
2. Amount	How much can be spent	Program structures specify budget allocation amounts, and agency delegations set upper limits on authority to spend
3. Purpose	What it can be spent on	Parliamentary appropriations specify purpose, and program structures categorize budgets on the basis of objectives or activities
4. Time	When it must be spent	Parliamentary appropriations authorize spending for a discrete time period, usually one financial year
5. Transfers	How spending can be changed	Most amounts cannot be reallocated between categories of appropriations, such as purposes or agencies
6. Information	How spending is accounted for	Regular financial reporting to monitor the expenditure of funds

expected *routinely* to possess greater scope to affect budget decisions than those actors operating in front-line service delivery roles.

When we say that discretion is delimited, we are in effect referring to the boundaries set for decision-makers by the 'rules' of budgeting. Therefore, the second dimension of flexibility – what we call budget rule *variability* – is the range of alternative possibilities for each type of budget rule. In Table 2, we distil six discrete rules that we suggest encapsulate basic control properties of budgeting: who can spend, how much can be spent, what it can be spent on, when it must be spent, how spending can be changed and how spending is accounted for. Each rule can be explained by the way it limits discretion, and how it does so in combination with other rules. We acknowledge that the exercise is artificial, but separating out properties allows us to scrutinize the way they are *designed* to interact, which we argue is equally important in explaining their endurance.

A useful illustration is the 'time' rule. This aligns with the principle of annuality, which requires budget allocations to be spent during a financial year. Annuality has well-known consequences for managerial behaviour – overspending can attract severe penalties while underspending can lead to the annual phenomenon of 'expenditure surge' – and the more strictly it is enforced, the more likely behaviour is oriented towards compliance with fixed budgets (Hyndman, Jones, and Pendlebury 2007; CFAR 2012a, 46, 70). Some of the defining features of public sector budget modernization during the 1980s and 1990s, many of which are in place today, include the carry forward of unspent balances from one fiscal year to the next and expanded latitude in determining the timing or assignment of funds (OECD 2007).

In summary, flexibility has both 'vertical' and 'horizontal' dimensions. The vertical dimension concerns how far down the hierarchy decision-making authority is devolved (or alternatively, how far out it is decentralized from central to spending agencies), whilst the horizontal dimension concerns the degree of latitude within the budget rules for varying decisions about purposes, allocations and performance assessment. In this way, flexibility can be seen as the *product* of the degree of vertical devolution and horizontal variability. A highly flexible system is one with significant devolution of budget decision authority to officials down a hierarchy, and broad latitude for them to vary their responses to rules.

Balancing flexibility and control: the 'regulator' role

At the core of any government financial management system is the relationship between the CFA on the one hand and spending agencies on the other. Historically, the CFA tended to act as a *command-and-control regulator* of spending agencies, with strict rule application to limit discretion at lower levels of management (Allen and Krause 2013, 100–102). Typically, this function was carried out in a controlling fashion: closely inspecting agencies' financial behaviours, detecting breaches and applying sanctions, all reinforced by the CFA's capacity to impose obligations *before* the fact (e.g. Weller and Cutt 1976). This stereotypical ex ante control implies that even were it inclined to break the rules, an agency would find it difficult to do so because the relevant transactions are controlled by Finance. The expected net result would be to inhibit flexibility in the ways we have discussed. But as discussed below, the application of sanctions can have perverse consequences, such as undermining working relationships between central and spending agencies based on trust (Hood et al. 1999).

One alternative to 'command-and-control' has already been widely adopted under the aegis of the NPM: *performance control.* Partly intended as a way of reconciling flexibility and control, its insistence on the achievement of mandated results simultaneously with its pragmatism as to how those results might be brought about allows flexibility in *how* things are done (OECD 2003; Van Dooren, Bouckaert, and Halligan 2015). But as this suggests, it entails not so much greater flexibility as it does flexibility in respect of different phenomena – that is means rather than ends. To the extent that outcomes are mandated, the spending agency has *less flexibility.* To put it another way, both command-and-control and performance control create silos, it is just that the silos in one are different from those in the other.

A second alternative, already introduced in many governments – although not quite as widely as performance control – is where Finance acts as an *encourager/facilitator.* This involves minimizing the controls wielded by the CFA, and encouraging agencies to comply voluntarily with budget rules, commonly through the transformative role CFAs can play in leading public sector modernization. As we saw earlier, CFAs have used budget reform to impose fiscal discipline *and* promote broader 'management improvement' focussed on devolved financial authority and capacity building (Ruffner and Sevilla 2004). However, this shift in budget control posture also required extensive *internal* cultural change in CFAs, which did not sit easily with 'old school' central budget officials (Schick 2001). The role changes have likely had some positive effect on the propensity of spending agencies to comply, but when combined with the dilution of enforcement measures, this approach has little chance *in itself* of ensuring the benefits expected from flexibility in financial processes. Ever-present is the temptation for some agencies to 'game' the laxity of the system. Equally, in the face of this behaviour, CFAs may have little alternative than to revert to their previous control mentality.

This brings us to our final alternative, which has been termed *responsive regulation.* This is one of the most widely cited frameworks in the broader field of regulation (Ayres and Braithwaite 1992) but has received little attention in the institutional design of regulation *within* government. Responsive regulation constitutes a way of mixing 'punishment and persuasion' in an optimal fashion (Braithwaite 1985). It starts from a recognition that people comply with their regulatory obligations for a variety of reasons, only one of which is the fear of punishment (others include material incentives, intrinsic motivations, social obligation and/or moral values) (Alford and O'Flynn 2012, 56–82). These impetuses affect regulatees' *willingness* to comply. In addition, people are more likely to obey rules if they feel more *able* to do so, which is a function of the simplicity of the compliance task and the capability of the regulatee. In sum, people tend to be complex bundles of motivations and capacities, which can be grouped into 'compliance postures' (Braithwaite 1995). For example, some people may adopt a posture of seeking to evade their obligations whenever it is both profitable and possible, whilst others may be disposed to obey rules in all circumstances because they attach moral weight to law-abidingness.[3]

The point about these varying postures is that it does not make sense to apply a uniform regulatory approach across all of them. If the regulator applies 'soft' methods such as education and persuasion, they will be insufficiently robust to influence opportunistic evaders, who will take advantage of the lax regime. If on the other hand 'hard' enforcement and compulsion is applied to everyone, this will alienate the law-abiding; moreover, it will have little effect on incompetent non-compliers (those who are willing to comply but find it difficult to do so). Thus, regulators need to apply different instruments to differing postures among regulatees. But, this in itself presents a problem: knowing which regulatees to target with which interventions. Responsive regulation offers an answer to this problem.

The framework can be illustrated by the regulatory pyramid (see Figure 1), which constitutes a hierarchy of regulatory instruments utilizing 'Tit-for-Tat' strategies, underpinned by the background possibility of heavy sanctions. For example, the regulator can start by offering regulatees help and information, and only become more directive – for instance by giving a warning, or applying a fine – where the

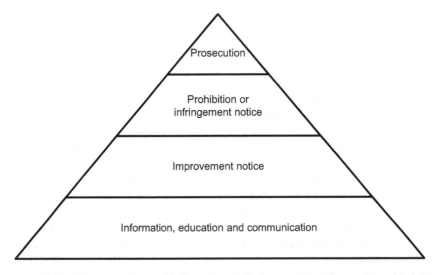

Figure 1. The regulatory pyramid: hierarchy of regulatory enforcement options. Source: Adapted from Ayres and Braithwaite (1992, 35).

regulatees engage in continuing non-compliant behaviour. These types of mutual responses can escalate up to higher levels of the pyramid for recalcitrants or remain lower down for compliant citizens. Thus, over the course of repeat encounters, responsive regulation 'varies' interventions in two ways. First, the regulatees in effect *select themselves* for either harsher or more lenient treatment, by the way they behave in the previous round; second, based on this information, regulators can assess the likelihood and consequences of non-compliance and *target interventions* to regulatees with higher risk compliance postures.[4]

The regulatory pyramid has been adopted across different systems of government and underpins a broad range of *external* regulatory functions, including corporations law, child protection and food and consumer product safety (Ivec et al. 2015). The approach has been most highly emulated in revenue administration, where traditionally regulation is heavily routinized and sanctions based. For example, the Australian Taxation Office (ATO) pioneered the 'cooperative compliance model' in the mid-to-late 1990s as a basis for interacting with individual and corporate taxpayers (Murphy 2004). This operationalizes the pyramid as a set of protocols for assessing the motivations for non-compliance and applying a scale of proportionate compliance strategies. Using compliance data to build profiles of compliance risk, the ATO subsequently developed a range of targeted interventions, such as its 'key client managers scheme' that locates its auditors at the corporate headquarters of large businesses assessed as high risk (Braithwaite 2005).

We submit that public budgetary processes are analogous to these regulatory arenas in the way CFAs seek to bring about compliance by spending agencies with budget rules. We have suggested that 'one-size-fits-all' approaches – such as 'command-and-control' and 'encourager/facilitator' – are by themselves ineffective for budgeting, just as they are in other types of regulation. In so far as it combines key aspects of these other regimes, 'responsive regulation' offers greater scope for flexibility without unduly compromising government's need to account for the effectiveness and integrity of budget systems.

How might this work in practice? Initially, Finance could establish a core set of budget regulations that modify the most salient control properties of the general rules described earlier in Table 2. These could, for example, further relax some of the existing controls over allocation of funds between programmes, underpinned by the type of training and cultural disposition discussed earlier. The rule set would be complemented by Finance monitoring for a discrete time period of how spending agencies behave under the freer regime, for instance the frequency, materiality and reasonableness of reallocation between programmes. This would inform Finance's application of 'rule variability', such as continuing flexibility for agencies that observe objectives encapsulated in the rules or, for the non-conformers, selective reimposition of control by Finance proportionate to the non-compliance. All of this would constitute the basis of a systematic cycle of monitoring, risk assessment and negotiation overseen by Finance.[5]

Some CFAs have implemented, or are exploring versions of, responsive regulation in the context of funding systems under the rubric of *earned autonomy*. This variant of responsive regulation uses tiered incentives to rate, compare and either reward or sanction regulated entities based on assessed performance. In the UK, for example, the 'principle' of earned autonomy underpinned the Blair Labour Government's targets-based approach to public service improvement (HM Treasury and Cabinet

Office 2004), although in practice, its application was concentrated in funding models for local government authorities and NHS trusts (Mannion, Goddard, and Bate 2007). Earned autonomy operated as a scaled incentive mechanism of rewards for high performing organizations and interventions for low performing ones. Performance was defined through publicly reported global ratings systems, and incentives were 'triggered' by predefined thresholds. The incentives available to funders ranged from lighter touch monitoring (such as less frequent reporting) to budgetary rewards (including retention of proceeds from asset sales) (Mannion, Goddard, and Bate 2007, 404). Conversely, the choice of interventions included a tighter monitoring role for the funder organization, the installation of greater contestability or, in worst case, management removal. In effect, this approach represents a nascent form of 'rule variability' in that the type of control properties identified in Table 2 (above) is modified in accordance with observed regulatory behaviours.

In Australia, the national Department of Finance has identified earned autonomy as a 'more nuanced and proportionate' alternative to the 'one-size-fits-all' approach to regulation (CFAR 2012b, 23; JCPAA 2013, 32). The motivation for this version is to construct a *financial regulatory framework* that applies across the whole of government and targets compliance more carefully. Whilst a set of *minimum* financial management requirements would initially apply across all government agencies, this would over time see varying levels of oversight and intervention calibrated by Finance's assessment of each agency's risk profile and performance (both financial and non-financial). The unfolding Australian regime is predicated on a clear link between performance and autonomy and anticipates the need to intervene in the case of poor performance. It too starts from a conviction that agencies 'set out to achieve results within the law and in accordance with government's policy priorities, including budgetary settings' (CFAR 2012b, 23).

In both versions of earned autonomy, the underlying rationale is to tie the winning of greater budgetary freedom to prior demonstrations of trustworthiness, at least as evidenced by predefined performance and risk data. In other words, the spending agency can demonstrate its trustworthiness and move beyond being subject to ongoing suspicion. Both stand in stark contrast to the command-and-control approach, where all agencies are continually subject to control founded in suspicion.

The application of responsive regulation *within* government has not gone completely unnoticed by scholars, nor is it without its critics. Some doubt that the necessary cultural conditions for 'enforced self-regulation' exist within the public sector (Hood 2004, 16–17; Hood et al. 1999, 65–67, 191–195). Can, for instance, 'hard' sanctions be credible when both regulators and regulatees can appeal to political superiors to discontinue the escalation process? We acknowledge such disquiet, but we also contend that responsive regulation is well equipped to deal with such problems *because* it has recourse to relational responses to areas of high risk, such as the demonstration effect of enforcement 'surges' in organizations assessed as higher risk (Braithwaite and Hong 2015). The introduction of earned autonomy as a variant of responsive regulation therefore entails a trade-off between the need to build trust between the CFA and spending agencies, and the need to avoid large-scale exploitation of a freer framework. In short, it calls for an appreciation of the relative risks involved, and indeed of those inherent in the other options. Table 3 summarizes a comparison of all four of the approaches discussed here.

Table 3. The central finance agency regulatory role: alternative approaches.

Approach	Impact on flexibility/control	Impact on trust building	Risk of opportunism by line agency
Command-and-control	Inflexible	Adverse	Low
Encourager/Facilitator	Very flexible, but insufficient control	Positive	High
Responsive regulation	High levels of flexibility and control applicable to each level	Highly positive	Low to moderate
Earned autonomy	Comparable to responsive regulation but emphasising control	Positive	Low

Conclusion

Many commentators have argued that budgeting practices within the public sector are constant brakes on flexibility, as illustrated by the behaviours required to manage non-routine problems. This contention is often asserted and rarely examined; it also disregards over 30 years of public sector budget modernization prosecuted in the name of managerial devolution. Here, we have assessed how the central finance agency can enable greater budget flexibility while safeguarding the integrity of the budget system. Our assessment proceeded in three steps. First, we noted that the incidence of non-routine problems requires government to develop greater capacity for collaboration, which is dependent on the ability of individuals and organizations to exercise flexibility, especially in the way resources are allocated and accounted for.

Second, we argued that budget flexibility can be defined as operating along two dimensions: how far down an organizational hierarchy decision-making authority is extended, and the latitude within rule sets that decision-makers at different levels have to vary decisions. Noting that the traditional approach to budgeting in the public sector operates through a small number of 'general rules' of budget control, we suggested that flexibility is a product of the capacity to vary budget rule application.

Third, we assessed a range of regulatory options for balancing these imperatives of control and flexibility. These options include the leadership/cultural role of central finance agencies in facilitating voluntary rule compliance, performance control and earned autonomy as a variant of responsive regulation. Whilst each of these options depends crucially on trust building, we submit that responsive regulation represents a potentially significant change in the practice of budgeting and financial management within government. Rule variability, as a novel form of internal-to-government regulation, could prove to be a powerful mechanism for governments to increase the flexibility of resource deployment and more effectively address contemporary problems, be they of a routine or non-routine nature.

Notes

1. Many terms are used to denote the executive government central agency responsible for budget and financial management functions, including 'central budget agency', 'finance ministry' and 'treasury' (see generally Allen and Krause 2013). We use the term 'central finance agency' as simply a shorthand.
2. As valuable as these studies are, they tend to target budget practices at the *sub-national* and *municipal* levels (although see Pitsvada 1983). Arguably, for reasons of political salience and fiscal materiality, implementing flexibility as 'rebudgeting' at the *central government* level can

be problematic, running the risk of appearing more like 'repetitive budgeting' which is an indicator of incapacity and high levels of uncertainty (Wildavsky 1986, 17–20).

3. In practice, of course, many regulatees are not individuals but rather organizations, especially corporations. As a result, and whilst acknowledging that individual motivations are mediated by more complex factors such as structure, culture and prior socialization processes, responsive regulation is commonly applied to organizations as well as individuals.

4. This capacity to 'vary' rule application, especially rewards and sanctions, in response to *regulatee* behaviour is the hallmark of responsive regulation approaches. It can be distinguished from other 'contingency-based' approaches to controllership in the public sector that emphasize the matching of management control systems to broad *cost and output categories* (e.g. Thompson and Jones 1986; Thompson 1993).

5. This has some equivalency with the idea of 'negotiated discretion' in which the CFA relationship with spending agencies is framed by relational characteristics such as reputation and competency, and issue salience such as the priority of policy and financial matters (Thain and Wright 1995, chapter 10).

Disclosure statement

No potential conflict of interest was reported by the authors.

Funding

This work was supported by an Australia and New Zealand School of Government (ANZSOG) Research Grant (2012–2013).

References

Alford, J., and J. O'Flynn. 2012. *Rethinking Public Service Delivery: Managing with External Providers*. Basingstoke: Palgrave Macmillan.

Allen, R., and P. Krause. 2013. "Role, Responsibilities, Structure and Evolution of Central Finance Agencies." In *The International Handbook of Public Financial Management*, edited by R. Allen, R. Hemming, and B. Potter, 98–115. New York: Palgrave Macmillan.

Anessi-Pessina, E., M. Sicilia, and I. Steccolini. 2012. "Budgeting and Rebudgeting in Local Governments: Siamese Twins?" *Public Administration Review* 72: 875–884.

Anessi-Pessina, E., M. Sicilia, and I. Steccolini. 2013. "Rebudgeting: Scope, Triggers and Players." *Budgetary Research Review* 5: 15–29.

Ayres, I., and J. Braithwaite. 1992. *Responsive Regulation: Transcending the Deregulation Debate*. New York: Oxford University Press.

Behn, R. 2001. *Rethinking Democratic Accountability*. Washington, DC: Brookings Institution.

Bozeman, B. 2000. *Bureaucracy and Red Tape*. Upper Saddle River, NJ: Prentice Hall.

Bozeman, B., and M. Feeny. 2011. *Rules and Red Tape: A Prism for Public Administration Research and Theory*. New York: M E Sharpe.

Braithwaite, J. 1985. *To Punish or Persuade: Enforcement of Coal Mine Safety*. Albany: State University of New York Press.

Braithwaite, J. 2005. *Markets in Vice, Markets in Virtue*. Sydney: The Federation Press.

Braithwaite, J., and S. H. Hong. 2015. "The Iteration Deficit in Responsive Regulation: Are Regulatory Ambassadors an Answer?" *Regulation & Governance* 9: 16–29. doi:10.1111/rego.12049.

Braithwaite, V. 1995. "Games of Engagement: Postures within the Regulatory Community." *Law & Policy* 17: 225–255. doi:10.1111/lapo.1995.17.issue-3.

Campbell, D. 2012. "Public Managers in Integrated Services Collaboratives: What Works Is Workarounds." *Public Administration Review* 72: 721–730. doi:10.1111/puar.2012.72.issue-5.

CFAR (Commonwealth Financial Accountability Review) 2012a. "*Is Less More? Towards Better Commonwealth Performance*." Discussion Paper. Canberra: Department of Finance and Deregulation.

CFAR (Commonwealth Financial Accountability Review) 2012b. "*Sharpening the Focus: A Framework for Improving Commonwealth Performance*." Position Paper. Canberra: Department of Finance and Deregulation.

Covaleski, M. A., J. H. Evans, J. L. Luft, and M. D. Shields. 2003. "Budgeting Research: Three Theoretical Perspectives and Criteria for Selective Integration." *Journal of Management Accounting Research* 15: 3–49. doi:10.2308/jmar.2003.15.1.3.

Covey, S. 2006. *The Speed of Trust: The One Thing That Changes Everything*. New York: The Free Press.

De Leeuw, A. C. J., and H. W. Volberda. 1996. "On the Concept of Flexibility: A Dual Control Perspective." *Omega: The International Journal of Management Science* 24: 121–139. doi:10.1016/0305-0483(95)00054-2.

deHoog, R. 1990. "Competition, Negotiation or Co-Operation: Three Models for Service Contracting." *Administration & Society* 22: 317–340. doi:10.1177/009539979002200303.

Donahue, J., and H. Zeckhauser. 2011. *Collaborative Governance: Private Roles for Public Goals in Turbulent Times*. Princeton: Princeton University Press.

Forrester, J. P., and D. R. Mullins. 1992. "Rebudgeting: The Serial Nature of Municipal Budgetary Processes." *Public Administration Review* 52: 467–473. doi:10.2307/976806.

Frow, N., D. Marginson, and S. Ogden. 2010. "'Continuous' Budgeting: Reconciling Budget Flexibility with Budgetary Control." *Accounting, Organizations and Society* 35: 444–461. doi:10.1016/j.aos.2009.10.003.

Funnell, W., K. Cooper, and J. Lee. 2012. *Public Sector Accounting and Accountability in Australia*. 2nd ed. Sydney: UNSW Press.

Gouldner, A. 1960. "The Norm of Reciprocity: A Preliminary Statement." *American Sociological Review* 25: 161–178. doi:10.2307/2092623.

Guess, G. M., and L. T. Leloup. 2010. *Comparative Public Budgeting: Global Perspectives on Taxing and Spending*. Albany: State University of New York Press.

Head, B. W., and J. Alford. 2015. "Wicked Problems: Implications for Public Policy and Management." *Administration & Society* 47: 711–739. doi:10.1177/0095399713481601.

Heclo, H., and A. Wildavsky. 1974. *The Private Government of Public Money: Community and Policy Inside British Politics*. London: Macmillan.

HM Treasury and Cabinet Office. 2004. *Devolving Decision Making. Volume 1 – Delivering Better Public Services: Refining Targets and Performance Management*. London: HMSO.

Hood, C. 1991. "A Public Management for All Seasons?" *Public Administration* 69: 3–19. doi:10.1111/padm.1991.69.issue-1.

Hood, C. 2004. "Controlling Public Services and Government: Towards a Cross-National Perspective." In *Controlling Modern Government: Variety, Commonality and Change*, edited by C. Hood, O. James, B. Guy Peters, and C. Scott, 3–21. Cheltenham: Edward Elgar.

Hood, C., O. James, G. Jones, C. Scott, and T. Travers. 1999. *Regulation Inside Government: Waste-Watchers, Quality Police and Sleazebusters*. Oxford: Oxford University Press.

Hope, J., and R. Fraser. 2003. *Beyond Budgeting: How Managers Can Break Free From the Annual Performance Trap*. Cambridge: Harvard Business School Publishing.

Hoskins, R. B. 1983. *Within-year Appropriations Changes in Georgia State Government: The Implications for Budget Theory.* Athens: University of Georgia Press.

Hughes, O. E. 2003. *Public Management and Administration: An Introduction.* 3rd ed. London: Palgrave Macmillan.

Huxham, C., and S. Vangen. 2005. *Managing to Collaborate: The Theory and Practice of Collaborative Advantage.* London: Routledge.

Hyndman, N., R. Jones, and M. Pendlebury. 2007. "An Exploratory Study of Annuality in the UK Public Sector: Plus Ca Change, Plus C'est La Meme Chose?" *Financial Accountability & Management* 23: 215–237. doi:10.1111/j.1468-0408.2007.00426.x.

Ivec, M., V. Braithwaite, C. Wood, and J. Job. 2015. *"Applications of Responsive Regulatory Theory in Australia and Overseas: Update."* Regulatory Institutions Network Occasional Paper 23. Canberra: Australian National University.

JCPAA (Joint Committee on Public Accounts and Audit) 2013. *"Advisory Report on the Public Governance, Performance and Accountability Bill 2013."* Report No. 438. Canberra: Parliament of Australia.

Jones, L., and F. Thompson. 1986. "Reform of Budget Execution Control." *Public Budgeting & Finance* 6: 33–49. doi:10.1111/1540-5850.00705.

Kaufman, H. 1977. *Red Tape: Its Origins, Uses and Abuses.* Washington, DC: The Brookings Institution.

Kelly, J., and J. Wanna. 2001. "Are Wildavsky's Guardians and Spenders Still Relevant? New Public Management and the Politics of Government Budgeting." In *Learning From International Experience with Public Management Reform,* edited by L. Jones, J. Guthrie, and P. Steane, 589–614. Amsterdam: Elsevier.

Kettl, D. 2009. *The Next Government of the United States.* New York: W.W. Norton.

Kickert, W. J. M. 1985. "The Magic Word Flexibility." *International Studies of Management and Organization* XIV: 6–31.

Laughlin, R. 1996. "Principals and Higher Principals: Accounting for Accountability in the Caring Professions." In *Accountability: Power, Ethos and the Technologies of Managing,* edited by R. Munro and J. Mouritsen, 225–244. London: International Thomson Business Press.

Lax, D., and J. Sebenius. 1986. *The Manager as Negotiator: Bargaining for Cooperation and Competitive Gain.* New York: Free Press.

Lipsky, M. 1980. *Street-level Bureaucracy: Dilemmas of the Individual in Public Services.* New York: Russell Sage.

Mannion, R., M. Goddard, and A. Bate. 2007. "Aligning Incentives and Motivations in Health Care: The Case of Earned Autonomy." *Financial Accountability & Management* 23: 401–420. doi:10.1111/fam.2007.23.issue-4.

Mitchell, D., and K. Thurmaier. 2012. "Currents and Undercurrents in Budgeting Theory: Exploring the Swirls, Heading Upstream." In *Foundations of Public Administration Series.* Washington, DC: ASPA.

Murphy, K. 2004. "Moving Towards a More Effective Model of Regulatory Enforcement in the Australian Taxation Office." *British Tax Review* 6: 603–619.

O'Flynn, J., F. Buick, D. Blackman, and J. Halligan. 2011. "You Win Some, You Lose Some: Experiments with Joined-Up Government." *International Journal of Public Administration* 34: 244–254. doi:10.1080/01900692.2010.540703.

OECD. 2007. *Performance Budgeting in OECD Countries.* Paris: OECD.

OECD (Organization for Economic Cooperation and Development) 2003. *"Public Sector Modernization: Governing for Performance."* GOV/PUMA 2003 (20). Paris: OECD.

Otley, D. 2006. "Trends in Budgetary Control and Responsibility Accounting." In *Contemporary Issues in Management Accounting,* edited by A. Bhimani, 291–307. Oxford: Oxford University Press.

Pitsvada, B. T. 1983. "Flexibility in Federal Budget Execution." *Public Budgeting & Finance* 3: 83–101. doi:10.1111/1540-5850.00603.

Pollitt, C., and G. Bouckaert. 2004. *Public Management Reform: A Comparative Analysis.* 2nd ed. Oxford: Oxford University Press.

Raine, J., and P. Watt. 2013. "Budgetary Models, Motivation and Engagement in Financial Collaborations." *Public Management Review* 15: 878–898. doi:10.1080/14719037.2012.725762.

Ruffner, M., and J. Sevilla. 2004. "Public Sector Modernization: Modernizing Accountability and Control." *OECD Journal on Budgeting* 4: 123–141. doi:10.1787/budget-v4-art11-en.

Schick, A. 2001. "The Changing Role of the Central Budget Office." *OECD Journal on Budgeting* 1: 9–26. doi:10.1787/budget-v1-1-en.

Smith, K., and F. Thompson. 2010. "Budgets? We Don't Need No Stinkin Budgets: Ten Things We Think We Think We Know about Budgets and Performance." *Yearbook of Swiss Administrative Sciences* 2012: 53–66.

Sullivan, H., and C. Skelcher. 2002. *Working Across Boundaries: Collaboration in Public Services.* Basingstoke: Palgrave Macmillan.

Thain, C., and M. Wright. 1995. *The Treasury and Whitehall: The Planning and Control of Public Expenditure, 1976-1983.* Oxford: Oxford University Press.

Thompson, F. 1993. "Matching Responsibilities with Tactics: Administrative Controls and Modern Government." *Public Administration Review* 53: 303–318. doi:10.2307/977143.

Thompson, F., and L. Jones. 1986. "Controllership in the Public Sector." *Journal of Policy Analysis and Management* 5: 547–571. doi:10.2307/3323261.

Van Dooren, W., G. Bouckaert, and J. Halligan. 2015. *Performance Management in the Public Sector.* 2nd ed. London: Routledge.

Weber, M. 1946. *From Max Weber: Essays in Sociology.* Translated and edited by H. H. Gerth and C. Wright Mills. New York: Oxford University Press

Weller, P., and J. Cutt. 1976. *Treasury Control in Australia.* Sydney: Novak Publishing.

Wiesel, F., and S. Modell. 2014. "From New Public Management to New Public Governance: Hybridization and Implications for Public Sector Consumerism." *Financial Accountability & Management* 30: 175–205. doi:10.1111/faam.12033.

Wildavsky, A. 1964. *The Politics of the Budgetary Process.* Boston: Little & Brown.

Wildavsky, A. 1986. *Budgeting: A Comparative Theory of Budgetary Processes.* Revised ed. New Brunswick, NJ: Transaction Publishers.

Willoughby, K. 2014. *Public Budgeting in Context: Structure, Law, Reform and Results.* San Francisco: Wiley.

Fiscal slack, budget shocks, and performance in public organizations: evidence from public schools

Abhisekh Ghosh Moulick and Lori L. Taylor

ABSTRACT
Some scholars equate fiscal slack with organizational inefficiency, while others argue that it is a useful environmental buffer. This study takes the first step in reconciling these opposing views, by classifying fiscal slack as *absorbed* and *unabsorbed* slack in public organizations. In a sample of 1,000 Texas public school districts over 17 years, fund balance (unabsorbed fiscal slack) does not seem to affect student performance, unless there is a major downward budget shock. In the absence of a negative budget shock, non-instructional spending per pupil (absorbed fiscal slack) has a negative impact on performance change in an average school district, but no meaningful impact on student performance during a major budget shock.

Introduction

Organizational resources that exceed the minimum amount needed to generate organizational outputs are classified as slack (Hendrick 2006), and there are at least two schools of thought regarding the usefulness of slack in the context of public organizations. The public choice literature argues that slack is synonymous with inefficiency and that budget-maximizing bureaucrats accumulate slack for personal gain. Management scholars take the opposite position and argue that slack is an essential cushion within an organization and serves a host of purposes, one of which is to buffer organizations from external turbulence.[1]

The empirical evidence suggests that slack is common in public and private institutions (e.g. Tan and Peng 2003; Johnes 2006; Vitaliano and Toren 1994; Casu and Girardone 2009; Grosskopf et al. 2001; Rose and Smith 2012) and that slack is buffer against fiscal stress at least some of the time and to some extent (Marlowe 2005; Hendrick 2006). Which raises an interesting question. Are some forms of slack more effective as a buffer against budgetary shocks than others?

Following the business management literature, we argue that slack can exist in public organizations in the form of either *unabsorbed* or *absorbed* resources (Tan and Peng 2003; Su, Xie, and Li 2009). Unabsorbed slack corresponds with 'currently uncommitted resources,' in an organization (Tan and Peng 2003). These monies typically accumulate in separate designated accounts. Examples of unabsorbed slack in local government would be unreserved fund balance, budget stabilization funds, or rainy day funds. Hendrick (2006) notes that unreserved fund balance and rainy day funds are the primary source of discretionary slack for public organizations. These are highly visible slack resources in local governments that are closely monitored by political stakeholders, taxpayers, external auditors, interest groups, and media. Thus, these slack reserves often trigger public scrutiny, and 'political pressure for tax cuts and spending increases' in local governments (Rose and Smith 2012, 187).

Given the scope for hostility towards visible savings in local governments, some managers pursue the alternative of absorbing slack into the current operations of local governments (Tan and Peng 2003). For example, when managers have two employees doing the job of one, arguably the source of such phrases as 'lazy bureaucrats,' managers have essentially built or absorbed slack into their operations by creating additional positions.[2] Since absorbed slack is 'tied up with current operations,' it 'amounts to excess costs in organizations' (Tan and Peng 2003, 1251). Because absorbed fiscal slack cannot be easily distinguished from other forms of spending, it is less open to oversight by the public and other external stakeholders. As such, absorbed slack is an easy breeding ground for inefficiencies that can make organization sluggish and hurt performance.

We investigate the buffering efficacy of absorbed and unabsorbed slack within the context of public school districts in Texas. School districts offer an excellent testing ground for such broader issues in public administration (Raffel 2007). They are one of the most widespread local governments in the United States, with richly detailed panel data and reasonably well-defined performance goals.

A focus on Texas takes advantage of the large number of diversely situated school districts in the state and makes a virtue out of the state's turbulent fiscal environment (Davis 2008; Trussel and Patrick 2012). For instance, the 82nd Texas Legislature that convened in early 2011 faced a $7.8 billion shortfall in the public education budget.[3] The expiration of federal funding from the American Recovery and Reinvestment Act of 2009 increased enrolment growth in Texas schools, settle-up cost in school districts, and declining values of local properties in Texas all contributed to this shortfall (Goff and Sanborn 2012). Lawmakers opted to balance the state's education budget by cutting projected state aid for school districts by $4 billion and delaying another $2.3 billion in payments to school districts. (The remaining gap in the education budget was closed with a $1.5 billion infusion from the state's General Revenue Fund.)[4] On average, nominal revenues per pupil declined by 2.8 per cent between 2010–2011 and 2011–2012, but some districts saw that revenues per pupil decline by more than 20 per cent. A similar version of this story played out in the public education sector across other US states as well.

Texas school district business managers made a concerted effort to prevent the 2011 funding shocks from affecting core instructional expenses and student learning (Goff and Sanborn 2012).[5] Several districts dipped into their fund balance reserves (unabsorbed slack) in the 2011–2012 fiscal year and were concerned about the unsustainability of these measures to cover repeated funding shortfalls (Goff and Sanborn 2012). Many districts cut non-instructional spending (absorbed slack). The three most common cost containment measures were deferred technological upgrades, deferred maintenance, and administrative salary freezes (Goff and Sanborn 2012). In other words, these local governments responded to a financial crisis by tapping into their absorbed and unabsorbed slack. Our question is to what extent can each type of slack successfully buffer the detrimental effects of negative funding shocks on their key deliverable, student performance?

Using a sample of 1,000 public school districts in Texas from 1994 to 2012, we show that the distinction between absorbed and unabsorbed fiscal slack is important when discussing slack as a buffer in public organizations. Our evidence suggests that unabsorbed slack can successfully buffer – but not fully negate – the impact of environmental turbulence on performance. In contrast, we find no evidence that absorbed slack systematically provides a meaningful buffer for negative budget shocks and some evidence that absorbed slack is negatively correlated with student performance. In public organizations, unabsorbed slack is visible and can be closely monitored. Hence, there is a greater chance that when these funds are made accessible to managers, especially in times of crisis, they use it for the betterment of the organization. Absorbed slack, on the other hand, is hidden in operations, difficult to redeploy, and does little to help firms in times of crisis. These findings help tie some of the loose ends in this line of research.

The literature on slack

There is a vast body of research on slack across various organizational settings. By definition, organizational slack should equal to zero in efficient organizations (Cyert and March 1963). To completely eliminate slack, an organization must leverage its internal and external environment such that it can fully optimize its resources (Bourgeois 1981). For most organizations, this is an ideal state. Slack is an inadvertent and inevitable outcome of group bargaining and decision-making process in an organization (Cyert and March 1963). But too much slack is undesirable. In excess, it is equated with inefficiency and causes organizational decline (Bourgeois 1981).

A rich literature specifically explores slack in public organizations (see Busch 2002; Busch and Gustafsson 2002). Rose and Smith (2012) note that fiscal slack – which we interpret as a form of unabsorbed slack – can be created in government organizations in three ways: first, expenditures can be set lower than anticipated revenues to create a general fund surplus; second, revenues can be underestimated or expenditures can be overestimated, while balancing the budget; and third, funds can be stipulated for budget stabilization (Rose and Smith 2012, 187).

Public managers, in charge of public resources, face constant pressure to minimize or give up slack altogether, or else they run the risk of being seen as wasteful (Boyne and Walker 2004; Stanbury and Thompson 1995; Salge 2011). The inherent suspicion of slack resources in public organizations has a long tradition of support in the public choice canon (see Niskanen 1971; Moe 1997; Migué et al. 1974; Milgrom and Roberts 1992). The general argument is that budget maximizing bureaucrats (Niskanen 1971) value slack in their organizations 'for political gain and can accumulate it when they possess more information about production costs relative to superiors, or when bureaucratic autonomy over budgetary matters is relatively high' (Hendrick 2006, 16). This suspicion is further buttressed by studies of local government finance that demonstrate that slack in municipal governments often far exceeds recommended amounts (Gianakis and Snow 2007; Stewart 2009; Marlowe 2005; Gore 2009). There is no evidence to make a case for large slack reserves supporting organizational performance in local governments (Marlowe 2011).

The general consensus among organization theorists is that the benefits of organizational slack far outweigh its costs. Slack offers inducement to members of an organization to remain in the organizational coalition, it works as a resource for conflict resolution, it facilitates strategic behaviour in an organization, it allows organizational risk taking and innovation, and it works as a buffer against environmental turbulence (Cyert and March 1963; Thompson 2003; Sharfman et al. 1988).

Tan and Peng contrast the organizational theory perspective on slack with a perspective arising from agency theory – namely that slack fosters inefficiency and inhibits performance. Using data on Chinese firms, they conclude that the distinction between absorbed and unabsorbed slack is important, and that while organizational theory appears to fit the data on unabsorbed slack, agency theory better fits the data on absorbed slack. The public finance literature has spent considerable effort in assessing various aspects of slack, such as the optimal amount (Marlowe 2011), its purpose in local governments (Hendrick 2006), and its counter-cyclical stabilization effects on key expenditure categories (Marlowe 2005; Hendrick 2006). Financial indicators and bond ratings have typically been the outcomes of interest in these studies. For example, Marlowe (2011) demonstrates that with 'some' unabsorbed slack,[6] as opposed none, US local governments have a 5–9 per cent improvement in credit ratings.

But bond or credit ratings offer, at best, an incomplete picture of the risks associated with declining organizational performance. Furthermore, questions are increasingly being raised regarding the reliability and consistency of credit ratings as indicators of fiscal health (Nanda and Singh 2004; Greenwald 2010; Trussel and Patrick 2012; Farmer 2015), and the relationship between slack and more direct measures of organizational performance remains largely unexplored.

Slack as a buffer

7Despite the theoretical argument that slack can work as a buffer against environmental turbulence, few studies have looked at the interactive effect of funding shocks and slack on aggregate performance in public organizations. O'Toole and Meier (2010) find that public schools with 10 per cent or greater budget shock can activate '(partial) slack in the managerial resources' in the short run and buffer performance from budget shocks (345). This partial slack (measured by the percentage of school district central office administrators and therefore, by our taxonomy, a form of absorbed slack) interacts with substantial budget shocks and dissipates the impact of these shocks on student performance. Marlowe (2005) argues that among a selection of fund balances, unreserved general fund balance (unabsorbed slack) has 'marginal counter-cyclical effect' during times of fiscal stress in US municipalities (49).

We believe that the distinction between unabsorbed and absorbed slack is important for understanding the potential role of slack as a buffer within public organizations. Despite accumulation and spending restrictions, unabsorbed slack is easy to redeploy. Since unabsorbed slack is not tied to a specific purpose or a spending category, managers have greater discretion over how they use these funds, although this discretion comes at a price. During times of crisis, public managers can easily redeploy unabsorbed slack where it may help the most. Public scrutiny, red tape, and regulatory bottlenecks restricting the use of these funds are relaxed during fiscal stress, and the core goal of salvaging performance takes centre stage (Goff and Sanborn 2012). Furthermore, using undesignated surplus funds during times of fiscal stress gives managers the best justification to accumulate these monies in the future. Various fund balance categories have been demonstrated to have important stabilization effects on current expenditures for municipalities, especially at the margins (Marlowe 2005). Therefore, unabsorbed fiscal slack should be an effective buffer for fiscal shocks.

Unlike unabsorbed slack, absorbed slack accumulates in public organizations with little transparency or monitoring. This slack category encompasses, but is broader than, the concept of 'administrative bloat' (Brewer 1996). For example, mission creep could be a mechanism for absorbing slack because, in times of fiscal stress, public organizations can retrench and refocus on core obligations. Thus, absorbed slack encompasses inefficiencies in various organizational processes.

Arguably, absorbed slack will be less effective than unabsorbed slack at buffering organizational performance against negative funding shocks. Managers in organizations with more absorbed slack will have a harder time coping with such shocks, because either they lead a sluggish organization or they put additional stress on their organizations as they try to reallocate these hidden resources. Such crisis management measures may cause organizational disruption in an already stressful environment. Organizations are forced to run leaner operations during times of fiscal stress, when they should have smoothly transitioned to more optimal usage of such resources before a crisis.

Model and estimation

The early organizational theory literature – which makes no distinction between absorbed and unabsorbed slack – suggests that on net, the organizational benefits of slack exceed the costs (for a discussion, see Tan and Peng 2003). However, when Tan and Peng (2003) distinguished between absorbed and unabsorbed slack, they found that agency theory better fits the data on absorbed slack. If true, then we would expect to see a positive relationship between unabsorbed slack and the primary objective of public education: student performance. On the other hand, we would expect to see a negative relationship between absorbed slack and student performance. This gives rise to our first two hypotheses:

H1: Unabsorbed fiscal slack will positively impact overall student performance in public school districts.

H2: Absorbed fiscal slack will negatively impact overall student performance in public school districts.

Furthermore, we argue that the distinction between absorbed and unabsorbed slack is crucial in the assessment of slack as an effective buffer. This leads to our second two hypotheses:

H3: Unabsorbed fiscal slack will successfully buffer the impact of a single major negative budget shock on performance in public school districts.

H4: Absorbed fiscal slack will be unsuccessful in buffering the impact of a single major negative budget shock on performance in public school districts.

To test our hypotheses, we model the performance of school district i in period t (P_{it}) as a function of unabsorbed slack (U_{it}), absorbed slack (A_{it}), a budget shock indicator (S_{it}), the interaction between budget shocks and slack, various controls (X_{it}), and an error term (ε_{it}):

$$P_{it} = \alpha + \beta_1 U_{it} + \beta_2 A_{it} + \beta_3 S_{it} + \beta_4 U_{it} S_{it} + \beta_5 A_{it} S_{it} + \gamma X_{it} + \varepsilon_{it}. \tag{1}$$

If the first two hypotheses are correct, then β_1 and β_2 should be significantly positive and significantly negative, respectively. If the buffering hypotheses are correct, then $\beta_1 + \beta_4$ should be positive and $\beta_2 + \beta_5$ should not be positive.

All reported models were estimated using ordinary least squares (OLS) regression, random effects regression, and fixed effects regression. Pooled diagnostic tests were performed to address common concerns regarding violations of key classical linear regression assumptions. Breusch–Pagan/Cook–Weisberg tests showed traces of heteroscedasticity in the OLS specifications. Thus, all models are report with robust standard errors clustered by the school districts. In addition, Wooldridge test for autocorrelation in panel data (Drukker 2003) shows presence of serial correlation in preliminary specifications. Thus, equations were adjusted with individual year dummies. Incorporation of year fixed effects gives us within year variation in all models.

Data

We test this in the data-rich context of K-12 education in Texas. There are more than 1,000 traditional public school districts in Texas.[7] These are highly professionalized organizations and independent local governments with their own taxing power. This study is conducted with 1,038 public school districts between 1994 and 2012 using administrative data from the Texas Education Agency.[8] As a result, our analysis captures a large array of public school systems in Texas over a significant time period, with significant variation in performance, organizational characteristics, and financial circumstances. While their status as a separate government somewhat insulates them from environmental turbulence, as we discuss earlier, they often face major funding shocks.

Slack

Unabsorbed slack is measured by the amount of surplus fund balance expressed as a per cent of the total budgeted expenditures (of the general fund) for the current year in a school district.[9] As Marlowe (2011) notes, Government Finance Officers Association and others define slack in public organizations with respect to fund balance. As the financial guidelines of school districts clearly state, fund balances are not rainy day funds. Instead, these are unreserved, undesignated funds from the end of the previous school year. Unreserved fund balance is 'that portion of the total fund balance that is not restricted for future payments to satisfy outstanding or future liabilities' (Hendrick 2006, 17). In most districts, this amount is equivalent to the fund balance at the beginning of the current school year.[10]

To manage cash flow during the fiscal year, state and local governments are expected to maintain 3–5 months of spending in unreserved fund balance accounts (Tyer 1993; Hendrick 2006). There has been an increasing tendency by districts to use surplus fund balance to meet shortages caused by budget cuts (Goff and Sanborn 2012). While not ideal, in practice, some local governments forgo separate contingency or rainy day funds and accumulate significantly higher unreserved fund balance for such contingencies (Tyer 1993; Hendrick 2006). Unreserved or surplus fund balance is also targeted by the public and media and used as justifications for funding cuts by legislators. Our analysis focuses on school districts with surplus fund balances less than or equal to 85 per cent of budgeted expenditures. We truncate this variable at 85 per cent to capture majority of the districts but exclude the outliers.[11] Our findings are sensitive to this truncation, as one would expect when adding or dropping outliers. However, in this way, we are able to capture the realities of average school districts in our sample which is the goal of this study.

Absorbed financial slack is hidden and tied up in current operations. Thus, by definition, it does not lend itself to a concise measure. However, we can look to school district behaviour to suggest the nature of absorbed slack. Survey responses indicate that in the wake of budget cuts during the 2011 legislative session, a majority of Texas school districts curtailed their spending on non-instructional categories, to protect instructional spending.[12] Districts deferred technological upgrades, deferred maintenance, and froze administrative salaries (Goff and Sanborn 2012). They also axed some administrative overhead (Goff and Sanborn 2012).[13]

This pattern of behaviour is what would be expected if non-instructional expenditures contained absorbed slack. The literature on administrative bloat also suggests that absorbed slack is more likely to be found in non-instructional spending (Brewer 1996). Thus, we use the share of the prior year's budget devoted to non-instructional functions (e.g. central administration, campus administration, facilities maintenance, etc.) as our (admittedly imperfect) proxy for absorbed slack. Following the literature on school district efficiency (e.g. Gronberg, Jansen, and Taylor 2011, 2012), we exclude spending on food and transportation services from both the numerator and the denominator of this budget share calculation because spending in those categories is clearly associated with non-academic outputs and not fungible with instructional spending, making it unlikely to represent absorbed slack.[14]

Intriguingly, we find no evidence that the two slack measures are correlated with one another. The Pearson correlation between them is only −0.0066, suggesting that districts with substantial unabsorbed slack are no more or less likely to accumulate absorbed slack.

Performance

The dependent variable is the change in the percentage of students in a district who passed all of the reading, writing, and math sections of the state's accountability test. Texas school districts administered the Texas Assessment of Academic Skills from 1993 to 2002, the Texas Assessment of Knowledge and Skills from 2003 to 2010, and the State of Texas Assessments of Academic Readiness from 2011 to at least 2016. All three are standardized, criterion-based tests that are required of all students in grades 3–8 and at least once at the high school level. Although the three exams are clearly different, the state's accountability system has consistently used passing rates as the primary measure of academic success. Thus, passing rates – regardless of the testing regime – are a key performance indicator for Texas school districts. The individual year indicators that are included in the analysis control for changes in the testing regime.

Budget shock

To measure budget shocks, we first regress total school district revenues per pupil (logged) in the present year on the previous year's school district revenue per pupil (logged) and current year values of the US Bureau of Labor Statistics' Consumer Price Index for urban consumers. This captures what the revenues of school districts, scaled by enrolment, would be if past trends continued, while also accounting for inflation.[15] Any year-to-year reductions in school district budgets that exceed 10 per cent of revenues are designated as a negative shock dummy (coded 1 for a shock).[16] A 10 per cent or more decrease in year-to-year school district revenue is a big loss for school districts and has been used as the cut point for fiscal shocks previously in the literature (Meier and O'Toole 2009; O'Toole and Meier 2010). Therefore, it is a solid benchmark for a major downward budget shock. Furthermore, the shock equation also takes into account enrolment trends. Revenue growth that is disproportionate with respect to enrolment helps us get at unanticipated dimension of these budgetary shocks. And since the model already controls for various expenditures, the coefficients of the shock variable estimate the impact of the shock, given the controls.

Controls

The vast literature on education production function offers some additional factors that may impact standardized test performance (for an overview, see Todd and Wolpin 2003). We control for the demographic characteristics of the students (the percentages of African-American, Hispanic, limited English proficient, special education, and economically disadvantaged students) and lagged indicators for the quantity and quality of the district's instructional staff (average teacher salaries, average teacher experience, and the number of students per teacher). Wealthier districts with higher property values per pupil may also fare better than poorer districts on standardized exams – either because such wealth is associated with higher quality school district capital stocks or because district wealth is a proxy for unobserved parental characteristics. Therefore, the district's property tax base per pupil (in logs) is also included as a control.

There is some debate on the impact of location on test performance (Butters, Asarta, and Thompson 2013) and evidence of significant variation in achievement based on location. Thus, all models include rural and metropolitan area dummies, using micropolitan areas as the base category. Logged enrolment is included as a measure of district size. Finally, while this study focuses on negative budget shocks, positive shocks can counterbalance the negative impact of a downward shock. Thus, key models (with the negative shock dummies) also include a 10 per cent or greater positive shock (extracted from the residuals) of the aforementioned shock equation. Summary statistics for all the variables are presented in Table 1.

Table 1. Summary statistics (N = 18,221).

Variable	Mean	Standard deviation	Minimum	Maximum
Change in passing rate	0.97	7.71	−51.20	51.90
Year-end fund balance (per cent)	23.92	15.43	−41.00	85.00
Non-instructional expenses (per cent)	42.51	10.38	10.28	93.81
Average teacher experience (years)	12.08	2.34	0.00	29.50
Student teacher ratio	12.69	2.46	3.30	57.40
Average teacher salary ('000s)	36.22	6.07	17.82	74.66
African-American student (per cent)	7.97	11.93	0.00	86.90
Hispanic student (per cent)	30.69	27.06	0.00	100.00
Low-income student (per cent)	50.80	19.28	0.00	100.00
Special education student (per cent)	12.87	4.22	0.00	49.10
Limited English proficient student (per cent)	7.20	9.71	0.00	87.10
District enrolment (in logs)	7.00	1.51	2.64	12.26
Property tax wealth, per pupil (in logs)	12.28	0.81	9.19	16.41
	0	1		
Negative 10% + budget shock	16,557	1,664		
Positive 10% + budget shock	16,364	1,857		
Metropolitan	9.706	8.515		
Micropolitan[a]	14,934	3,287		
Rural	11,802	6,419		

[a]Base, excluded from models.

Findings

Does unabsorbed fiscal slack resources have a positive impact on performance? Yes. Table 2 presents three alternative models of the relationship between slack, shocks, and changes in student performance. Each model represents an alternative strategy for estimating Equation (1), excluding the shock interaction terms. The first model was estimated using OLS regression; the second with random effects for school districts; and the third with school district fixed effects. All three models were estimated with robust standard errors that were clustered by district. The third model is our preferred specification because (unlike the OLS specification) it controls for unobservable differences among school districts, and it fits the data better than the random effects model (according to a Hausman test).

As we see in Table 2, there is a small, but statistically significant, positive relationship between the fund balance and the change in passing rates. Thus, unabsorbed fiscal slack has a minor, but positive, impact on overall student performance in school districts, which we interpret as support for H1. The coefficient on the absorbed slack measure is negative and statistically significant in the fixed effects specification, which we interpret as support for H2. A 10 per cent or greater negative budget shock in the current year and the past year causes a little less than a one-half point decline in performance. The impact of a negative shock in the prior year on performance is weaker than that in the current year and not statistically significant. Thus, we focus on shocks in the current year for the rest of the analyses.

When a 10 per cent or greater negative budget shock hits school districts in the current year, can unabsorbed fiscal slack resources in Texas school districts buffer changes in the passing rate? To examine this effect, we rearranged Equation (1) to yield

$$P_{it} = \alpha + \beta_1 U_{it}(1 - S_{it}) + \beta_2 A_{it}(1 - S_{it}) + \beta_3 S_{it} + (\beta_1 + \beta_4)U_{it}S_{it} + (\beta_2 + \beta_5)A_{it}S_{it} + \gamma X_{it} + \varepsilon_{it},$$

$$(2)$$

Table 2. Fiscal slack, budget shock, and performance.

	DV: Change in passing rate (all students, all tests)		
	Model 1	Model 2	Model 3
Prior year-end fund balance (per cent)	0.004	0.004	0.007
	(0.002)	(0.002)	(0.003)*
Prior year non-instructional expenses (per cent)	−0.006	−0.006	−0.011
	(0.004)	(0.004)	(0.004)*
Negative budget shock	−0.416	−0.416	−0.320
	(0.177)*	(0.177)*	(0.183)
Lagged negative budget shock	−0.189	−0.189	−0.163
	(0.176)	(0.176)	(0.181)
Positive budget shock	0.535	0.535	0.449
	(0.171)**	(0.171)**	(0.180)*
Average teacher experience (prior year)	−0.074	−0.074	−0.149
	(0.017)**	(0.017)**	(0.033)**
Student teacher ratio (prior year)	0.068	0.068	0.203
	(0.034)*	(0.034)*	(0.071)**
Average teacher salary (prior year)	−0.003	−0.003	0.014
	(0.016)	(0.016)	(0.032)
African-American student per cent	−0.000	−0.000	0.034
	(0.003)	(0.003)	(0.016)*
Hispanic student per cent	−0.002	−0.002	−0.001
	(0.002)	(0.002)	(0.015)
Low income student per cent	0.008	0.008	0.008
	(0.003)**	(0.003)**	(0.009)
Special education student per cent	−0.032	−0.032	−0.078
	(0.011)**	(0.011)**	(0.023)**
Limited English proficient student per cent	0.001	0.001	0.046
	(0.005)	(0.005)	(0.019)*
District enrolment (in logs)	−0.016	−0.016	−0.734
	(0.042)	(0.042)	(0.333)*
Rural	0.056	0.056	
	(0.064)	(0.064)	
Metropolitan	0.031	0.031	
	(0.059)	(0.059)	
Property tax wealth, per pupil (in logs)	0.049	0.049	0.825
	(0.055)	(0.055)	(0.203)**
Year fixed effects?	Yes	Yes	Yes
District random effects?	No	Yes	No
District fixed effects?	No	No	Yes
Number of observations	18,221	18,221	18,221

*$p < 0.05$; **$p < 0.01$.

and constructed two new variables. The first is the interaction between a negative budget shock in the current year and the measure of unabsorbed slack; the second is the interaction between one minus the budget shock variable and the measure of unabsorbed slack. Thus, the first new variable represents the measure of unabsorbed slack in a year with a negative budget shock, while the second represents the measure of unabsorbed slack in a year without a negative budget shock.[17]

As the first column of Table 3 illustrates, the marginal effect of unabsorbed slack is positive and statistically significant in years with a negative budget shock, and statistically insignificant in years without such a shock. We interpret this pattern as suggesting that unabsorbed slack has no effect on student performance in the absence of negative shocks (rejecting H1). But when hit by a negative budget shock (shock = 1), fund balance reserves buffer negative performance changes in an average school district (supporting H3).

Table 3. Can slack buffer a major budget shock?

	DV: Change in passing rate (all students, all tests)		
	Model 1	Model 2	Model 3
Prior year-end fund balance (per cent)		0.007	
		(0.003)*	
Prior year non-instructional expenses (per cent)	−0.011		
	(0.004)*		
Negative budget shock	−0.815	−1.620	−2.120
	(0.362)*	(0.736)*	(0.809)**
Prior year-end fund balance × negative budget shock	0.022		0.022
	(0.010)*		(0.010)*
Prior year fund balance × (1 − negative budget shock)	0.004		0.004
	(0.004)		(0.004)
Prior non-instruction expenses × negative budget shock		0.014	0.014
		(0.015)	(0.015)
Prior non-instruction expenses × (1 − negative budget shock)		−0.015	−0.015
		(0.005)**	(0.005)**
Positive budget shock	0.442	0.441	0.444
	(0.179)*	(0.179)*	(0.179)*
Controls?	Yes	Yes	Yes
Year fixed effects?	Yes	Yes	Yes
District fixed effects?	Yes	Yes	Yes
Number of observations	18,221	18,221	18,221

$*p < 0.05; **p < 0.01.$

The second column in Table 3 includes a similar set of interaction terms for our absorbed slack variable, and the third column includes the interaction terms for both absorbed and unabsorbed slack and represents the complete estimation of Equation (2). As the third column illustrates, the marginal effect of absorbed slack is not significantly different from zero in years with a negative budget shock, but the standard errors are large. We cannot reject (at the 5 per cent level) the hypothesis that the two non-instructional expenditures interaction terms are equal to one another, suggesting that there is no difference in the marginal effect of absorbed slack in years with or without a negative shock.[18] We find that absorbed slack has a negative impact on performance (supporting H2) and is ineffective in buffering a negative budget shock (supporting H4).

We performed a series of additional sensitivity analyses. There were no statistically significant findings to suggest that the two slack measures selected in this study, when squared, had a nonlinear impact on changes in the passing rate. Also, besides the 10 per cent shock thresholds, analyses were conducted with downward shocks of 5, 15, and 18 per cent (see Table 4). There were no statistically significant findings for 5 and 18 per cent categories. This is perhaps because 5 per cent shocks were too common and not powerful enough to perturb district performance outcomes and 18 per cent shocks were rare and impacted only a very small minority of the cases. At 15 per cent shock thresholds, the findings for the unabsorbed fiscal slack measure remain largely unchanged, suggesting that as fund balance reserves increased, districts were better able to cushion negative 15 per cent or greater budget shocks, although the coefficient estimates on the unabsorbed slack interactions are jointly significant only at the 10 per cent level. The findings regarding the absorbed slack measure were not sensitive to altering the budget shock threshold.[19]

Table 4. Robustness checks: Alternative definitions of shock.

	DV: Change in passing rate (all students, all tests)			
	5% Budget shock	10% Budget shock	15% Budget shock	18% Budget shock
Negative budget shock	−0.786	−2.120	−2.785	−0.308
	(0.548)	(0.809)**	(1.366)*	(1.886)
Prior year-end fund balance × negative budget shock	0.010	0.022	0.023	0.019
	(0.007)	(0.010)*	(0.015)	(0.019)
Prior year fund balance × (1 − negative budget shock)	0.005	0.004	0.005	0.005
	(0.004)	(0.004)	(0.004)	(0.003)
Prior non-instruction expenses × negative budget shock	−0.004	0.014	0.027	−0.016
	(0.010)	(0.015)	(0.023)	(0.032)
Prior non-instruction expenses × (1 − negative budget shock)	−0.014	−0.015	−0.015	−0.012
	(0.005)**	(0.005)**	(0.004)**	(0.004)**
Positive budget shock	0.236	0.444	0.468	0.905
	(0.126)	(0.179)*	(0.266)	(0.352)*
Controls?	Yes	Yes	Yes	Yes
Year fixed effects?	Yes	Yes	Yes	Yes
District fixed effects?	Yes	Yes	Yes	Yes
Number of observations	18,221	18,221	18,221	18,221

*$p < 0.05$; **$p < 0.01$.

Discussion and conclusion

This study makes several contributions. Marlowe (2011) demonstrates that slack resources can boost credit quality of US municipalities. The present study substantiates this claim with actual performance measures in school districts, another form of local government in the United States. Unabsorbed and absorbed resources have significant and divergent impacts on performance in for-profit organizations (Tan and Peng 2003; Su, Xie, and Li 2009). As we see here, in public organizations, two distinct forms of slack can exist as well. We show that the various diametrically opposed arguments about slack are in fact about two different kinds of slack. This is the key contribution of this study.

We ask, are some forms of slack more effective as a buffer against budgetary shocks than others? Our study suggests that is indeed the case. We find that unabsorbed slack can successfully buffer local governments during budget shocks, but absorbed slack cannot. Our evidence on unabsorbed slack is consistent with prior work using bond ratings as the measure of organizational performance for various US local governments and fund balances as measures of slack (see Marlowe 2005, 2011). Furthermore, our evidence on absorbed slack is consistent with the management literature (Tan and Peng 2003) and offers empirical support for the long held distrust of slack in the public choice literature (see Niskanen 1971; Moe 1997; Milgrom and Roberts 1992) and the 'administrative bloat' argument in the education economics literature (see Brewer 1996). But, we qualify this negative notion of slack and identify what types of slack may be specifically problematic in public organizations.

Marlowe (2005) argues that some US municipalities hoard large amount of slack, with no clear benefits. Our analysis indicates that unabsorbed slack does have benefits, but only when there is a major downward budget shock. This asymmetry may be propagating the false notion of uselessness of such reserves. Just as with any form of precautionary balances, rainy day funds and other sources of unabsorbed slack are only useful when it's raining. This is the first takeaway for practitioners from this study.

Absorbed slack in Texas school districts seems to be a manifestation of organizational inefficiencies. We see no evidence that absorbed slack can serve as a systematic buffer for fiscal shocks. Contrary to the implications of the organizational theory literature – but consistent with the agency-theory findings of Tan and Peng (2003) – our evidence suggests that absorbed slack has a negative association with schools district performance in the typical year.

Public school districts, like any public organization, can rarely work in an environment of fiscal austerity without registering a detrimental impact on performance. Our work and that of Meier and O'Toole (2009) finds that in the short run, public managers can activate slack to handle major budget shocks. Does this mean legislators should continue to slash funding for K-12 education or alternatively have no concern about excessive fund balances? The present study demonstrates that in the long run, public managers cannot cushion their organizations from performance drops when faced with funding shocks, even with access to unabsorbed slack – the most liquid slack resource. This is the second takeaway for practitioners from this study.

The marginal effects of some slack resources, as we uncover, can be crucial for distressed organizations. But if we keep removing visible unabsorbed fiscal slack reserves from public organizations, public managers will be incentivized to hide more slack in operations. This is the third takeaway for practitioners from this study and parallels the findings of Rose and Smith (2012), who demonstrate that political pressure can trigger building of less transparent surplus reserves in local governments. However, with less oversight, absorbing slack will breed inefficiencies and sluggishness in public organizations. This is not a desirable outcome for policy makers, managers who run these organizations, or the clientele who depend on them for access to crucial public services, such as health care, education, and transportation.

Notes

1. Public choice scholars focus on organizational efficiency (see Niskanen 1971). Management scholars, notably Cyert and March (1963), focus on organizational stability and effectiveness. These differences in focus lead to contradictory expectations about slack as a buffer.
2. See Walsh (2011, 2012) for a discussion on 'lazy bureaucrats'.
3. Legislative Budget Board Fiscal Size Up 2012–2013 Biennium.
4. http://www.texasalmanac.com/topics/government/82nd-legislature-cuts-school-funds-state-jobs.
5. The same concerns and strategies were revealed during personal conversations with several of these school district business managers.
6. Marlowe (2011) does not categorize slack as absorbed or unabsorbed but uses unreserved general fund balance, total general fund balance, and unrestricted net assets as three slack measures. We would categorize all three as unabsorbed slack measures.
7. Texas has a large and growing contingent of charter schools, which are not included in this analysis. We also exclude districts that were only operational during part of the analysis period and districts that lack reliable data for one or more key indicators.

8. The data come from TEA's snapshot (http://ritter.tea.state.tx.us/perfreport/snapshot/) and PEIMS (http://tea.texas.gov/financialstandardreports/).
9. Source: Texas Education Agency.
10. Source: Texas Education Agency.
11. Negative budget shocks hurt extremely poor district more than extremely rich districts. By excluding a few extremely rich school districts, that have over 85 per cent fund balance surplus, we lose fewer than 300 observations.
12. Despite their best efforts, Texas school districts could not entirely protect student performance from the detrimental effect of the 2011 funding shock. This was primarily because of a high volume of teacher attrition, which constituted 85 per cent of staffing losses from 2010–2011 to 2012–2013 school years that lead to larger classroom sizes leading to 'teacher fatigue,' and adversely impacted student performance (Goff and Sanborn 2012). Research suggests that besides remuneration, work environment plays a key role in influencing teacher attrition rates (Gritz and Theobald 1996; Falch and Strøm 2005). And, the cutbacks that were made directly and indirectly impacted the work environment in schools.
13. In school districts, a hierarchical administrative system controls the flow of resources and coordinates key activities (Brewer 1996). The administrative cadre in a typical district comprises of superintendents, at the district level, and their assistants and at the school level, this includes principals, assistant principals, departmental heads, professional/'para-professional' support staff, and 'nonprofessional' staff. Examples of paraprofessional staff would be psychologists, and teaching aides, and nonprofessional staff includes secretarial, transportation, and building maintenance workers (112).
14. Excluding food service expenditures also removes the potentially confounding correlation between student socio-economic status (which is measured by student participation in the National School Lunch Program) and non-instructional expenditures per pupil.
15. An analogous technique was used by Rattso (1999) to study shocks to the Norwegian national economy.
16. For sensitivity analysis shocks at 5, 15, and 18 per cent thresholds were also considered and their outcomes are reported at the end of the findings section.
17. We express the variables in this way to simplify interpretation.
18. The F-statistic for the hypothesis that the two coefficients are equal is 3.55 with one and 1,037 degrees of freedom. The probability of a greater F-statistic is 0.0597.
19. Bootstrapping the standard errors yields nearly identical results. The bootstrapped versions of Tables 2–4 are available upon request.

Disclosure statement

No potential conflict of interest was reported by the authors.

References

Bourgeois, L. J. 1981. "On the Measurement of Organizational Slack." *The Academy of Management Review* 6 (1): 29–39.

Boyne, G. A., and R. M. Walker. 2004. "Strategy Content and Public Service Organizations." *Journal of Public Administration Research and Theory* 14 (2): 231–252. doi:10.1093/jopart/muh015.

Brewer, D. J. 1996. "Does More School District Administration Lower Educational Productivity? Some Evidence on the "Administrative Blob" in New York Public Schools." *Economics of Education Review* 15 (2): 111–124. doi:10.1016/0272-7757(95)00032-1.

Busch, T. 2002. "Slack in Public Administration: Conceptual and Methodological Issues." *Managerial Auditing Journal* 17 (3): 153–159. doi:10.1108/02686900210419949.

Busch, T., and O. Gustafsson. 2002. "Slack in the Public Sector: A Comparative Analysis of a Private and a Public Enterprise for Refuse Collection." *Public Management Review* 4 (2): 167–186. doi:10.1080/14616670210130525.

Butters, R., C. Asarta, and E. C. Thompson. 2013. "The Production of Economic Knowledge in Urban and Rural Areas: The Role of Student, Teacher, and School Characteristics." *Journal of Agricultural and Applied Economics* 45 (01): 1–15. doi:10.1017/S1074070800004545.

Casu, B., and C. Girardone. 2009. "Testing the Relationship between Competition and Efficiency in Banking: A Panel Data Analysis." *Economics Letters* 105 (1): 134–137. doi:10.1016/j.econlet.2009.06.018.

Cyert, R. M., and J. G. March. 1963. *A Behavioral Theory of the Firm*. Englewood Cliffs, NJ: Prentice-Hall.

Davis, M. R. 2008. "Financial Crisis Now Striking Home for School Districts: Project Delays, Worries about Cash Flow Result of Tight Credit Markets." *Education Week* 28 (8): 1–20.

Drukker, D. M. 2003. "Testing for Serial Correlation in Linear Panel-Data Models." *Stata Journal* 3 (2): 168–177.

Falch, T., and B. Strøm. 2005. "Teacher Turnover and Non-Pecuniary Factors." *Economics of Education Review* 24 (6): 611–631. doi:10.1016/j.econedurev.2004.09.005.

Farmer, L. 2015. "Do Credit Ratings Matter Anymore?" Accessed March 15 2015. http://www.governing.com/topics/finance/gov-credit-ratings-still-matter.html

Gianakis, G. J., and D. Snow. 2007. "The Implementation and Utilization of Stabilization Funds by Local Governments in Massachusetts." *Public Budgeting & Finance* 27 (1): 86–103. doi:10.1111/j.1540-5850.2007.00870.x.

Goff, S., and R. Sanborn. 2012. *Doing More with Less? Public Education in a New Fiscal Reality. Texas Public Education Cuts: Impact Assessment*. Houston, TX: Children at Risk.

Gore, A. K. 2009. "Why Do Cities Hoard Cash? Determinants and Implications of Municipal Cash Holdings." *The Accounting Review* 84 (1): 183–207. doi:10.2308/accr.2009.84.1.183.

Greenwald, J. 2010. "Bond Insurer Exits Put Municipalities in a Bind." *Business Insurance* 44 (8): 14.

Gritz, R. M., and N. D. Theobald. 1996. "The Effects of School District Spending Priorities on Length of Stay in Teaching." *The Journal of Human Resources* 31: 477–512. doi:10.2307/146262.

Gronberg, T. J., D. W. Jansen, and L. L. Taylor. 2011. "The Adequacy of Educational Cost Functions: Lessons from Texas." *Peabody Journal of Education* 86 (1): 3–27. doi:10.1080/0161956X.2011.539953.

Gronberg, T. J., D. W. Jansen, and L. L. Taylor. 2012. "The Relative Efficiency of Charter Schools: A Cost Frontier Approach." *Economics of Education Review* 31 (2): 302–317. doi:10.1016/j.econedurev.2011.07.001.

Grosskopf, S., K. J. Hayes, L. L. Taylor, and W. L. Weber. 2001. "On the Determinants of School District Efficiency: Competition and Monitoring." *Journal of Urban Economics* 49 (3): 453–478. doi:10.1006/juec.2000.2201.

Hendrick, R. 2006. "The Role of Slack in Local Government Finances." *Public Budgeting & Finance* 26 (1): 14–46. doi:10.1111/j.1540-5850.2006.00837.x.

Johnes, J. 2006. "Data Envelopment Analysis and Its Application to the Measurement of Efficiency in Higher Education." *Economics of Education Review* 25 (3): 273–288. doi:10.1016/j.econedurev.2005.02.005.

Marlowe, J. 2005. "Fiscal Slack and Counter-Cyclical Expenditure Stabilization: A First Look at the Local Level." *Public Budgeting & Finance* 25 (3): 48–72. doi:10.1111/pbaf.2005.25.issue-3.

Marlowe, J. 2011. "Beyond 5 Percent: Optimal Municipal Slack Resources and Credit Ratings." *Public Budgeting & Finance* 31 (4): 93–108. doi:10.1111/pbaf.2011.31.issue-4.

Meier, K. J., and L. J. O'Toole. 2009. "The Dog that Didn't Bark: How Public Managers Handle Environmental Shocks." *Public Administration* 87 (3): 485–502. doi:10.1111/padm.2009.87.issue-3.

Migué, J.-L., G. Bélanger, and W. A. Niskanen. 1974. "Toward a General Theory of Managerial Discretion." *Public Choice* 17 (1): 27–47. doi:10.1007/BF01718995.

Milgrom, P. R., and J. Roberts. 1992. *Economics, Organization and Management.* Vol. 7. Englewood Cliffs, NJ: Prentice-Hall.

Moe, T. 1997. "The Positive Theory of Public Bureaucracy." In *Perspectives on Public Choice*, edited by D. C. Mueller, 455–480. New York: Cambridge University Press.

Nanda, V., and R. Singh. 2004. "Bond Insurance: What is Special about Munis?" *The Journal of Finance* 59 (5): 2253–2280. doi:10.1111/j.1540-6261.2004.00698.x.

Niskanen, W. A. 1971. *Bureaucracy and Representative Government.* Chicago, IL: Aldine-Atherton Press.

O'Toole Jr, L. J., and K. J. Meier. 2010. "In Defense of Bureaucracy: Public Managerial Capacity, Slack and the Dampening of Environmental Shocks." *Public Management Review* 12 (3): 341–361. doi:10.1080/14719030903286599.

Raffel, J. A. 2007. "Why Has Public Administration Ignored Public Education, and Does it Matter?" *Public Administration Review* 67 (1): 135–151. doi:10.1111/puar.2007.67.issue-1.

Rattso, J. 1999. "Aggregate Local Public Sector Investment and Shocks: Norway 1946-1990." *Applied Economics* 31 (5): 577–584. doi:10.1080/000368499324020.

Rose, S., and D. L. Smith. 2012. "Budget Slack, Institutions, and Transparency." *Public Administration Review* 72 (2): 187–195. doi:10.1111/puar.2012.72.issue-2.

Salge, T. O. 2011. "A Behavioral Model of Innovative Search: Evidence from Public Hospital Services." *Journal of Public Administration Research and Theory* 21 (1): 181–210. doi:10.1093/jopart/muq017.

Sharfman, M. P., G. Wolf, R. B. Chase, and D. A. Tansik. 1988. "Antecedents of Organizational Slack." *Academy of Management Review* 13 (4): 601–614.

Stanbury, W. T., and F. Thompson. 1995. "Toward a Political Economy of Government Waste: First Step, Definitions." *Public Administration Review* 55 (5): 418–427. doi:10.2307/976766.

Stewart, L. S. M. 2009. "Examining Factors that Impact Mississippi Counties' Unreserved Fund Balance during Relative Resource Abundance and Relative Resource Scarcity." *Public Budgeting & Finance* 29 (4): 45–73. doi:10.1111/pbaf.2009.29.issue-4.

Su, Z. F., E. Xie, and Y. Li. 2009. "Organizational Slack and Firm Performance during Institutional Transitions." *Asia Pacific Journal of Management* 26 (1): 75–91. doi:10.1007/s10490-008-9101-8.

Tan, J., and M. W. Peng. 2003. "Organizational Slack and Firm Performance during Economic Transitions: Two Studies from an Emerging Economy." *Strategic Management Journal* 24 (13): 1249–1263. doi:10.1002/(ISSN)1097-0266.

Thompson, J. D. 2003. *Organizations in Action: Social Science Bases of Administrative.* New Brunswick, NJ: Transaction Publishers.

Todd, P. E., and K. I. Wolpin. 2003. "On the Specification and Estimation of the Production Function for Cognitive Achievement*." *The Economic Journal* 113 (485): F3–F33. doi:10.1111/ecoj.2003.113.issue-485.

Trussel, J. M., and P. A. Patrick. 2012. "Predicting Significant Reductions in Instructional Expenditures by School Districts." *Journal of Education Finance* 37 (3): 205–233.

Tyer, C. B. 1993. "Local Government Reserve Funds: Policy Alternatives and Political Strategies." *Public Budgeting & Finance* 13 (2): 75–85. doi:10.1111/1540-5850.00976.

Vitaliano, D. F., and M. Toren. 1994. "Cost and Efficiency in Nursing Homes: A Stochastic Frontier Approach." *Journal of Health Economics* 13 (3): 281–300. doi:10.1016/0167-6296(94)90028-0.

Walsh, K. C. 2011. "Political Understanding of Economic Crises: The Shape of Resentment toward Public Employees." Paper presented at conference on Popular Reactions to the Economic Crisis, Oxford, June 24–26.

Walsh, K. C. 2012. "Putting Inequality in its Place: Rural Consciousness and the Power of Perspective." *American Political Science Review* 106 (3): 517–532. doi:10.1017/S0003055412000305.

Democracy, governmentality and transparency: participatory budgeting in action

Maria Isabel Brun-Martos and Irvine Lapsley

ABSTRACT
This paper examines initiatives in participatory budgeting (PB) in a city in the United Kingdom, a country which is a slow adopter of PB. While there are UK initiatives on PB, these are developmental. Nevertheless, this study underlines the potential of PB in an Anglo-Saxon context. The finance of local government and cities is notoriously opaque. PB has the potential to enhance both democratic accountability and effective city management through transparency. This study reveals a city which is profitably engaged with democratizing its budgetary activities and seeking to achieve greater transparency for its citizens and managers through the modernization of established practice.

1. Introduction

This paper examines an innovation in budgetary practice in the United Kingdom: the introduction of participatory budgeting (PB) in public services. While this budgetary practice was first introduced in Brazil some 30 years ago, it remains an **innovation** in the context of budgeting in UK cities and municipalities. To date, there has been limited adoption of PB in the United Kingdom. This has taken the form of pilot studies (Harkins and Escobar 2015). Given the UK position as a pre-eminent reformer in public management, the adoption of PB in the United Kingdom would represent a reverse diffusion process.

The declared intention of PB is to enhance transparency and democratic accountability in cities and municipalities. This paper mobilizes ideas of democracy, governmentality and transparency and uses the Biondi and Lapsley (2014) framework to investigate PB in the UK context. Specifically, this paper addresses the research questions of (1) Can PB enhance transparency in public finances and democratic accountability? (2) Can PB become a mediating instrument between managerialism and democratic accountability? The evidence presented in this paper underlines the significance of transparency in assessing the potential of PB.

This research is based on a case study of one city. This city is experiencing the difficulties of the era of austerity in public finances. This paper adds to our understanding of how austerity impacts on local government (Carmela, Guarini, and

Steccolini, 2016). This case reveals the receptivity of one UK city for the PB budgetary mechanism. In some ways, the evidence presented in this paper can be depicted as a story of a budgetary innovation which is operating at the margins. However, this interpretation understates the significance of PB, as this study shows how it could enhance both transparency and democratic accountability. While the evidence presented in this study may be seen as preliminary, it nevertheless identifies great potential for PB in the United Kingdom. To achieve its full potential, PB has to be regarded as an essential democratic process, not just another budgetary mechanism.

The adoption of PB in the United Kingdom would be a reverse diffusion process. There have been many public management initiatives from Anglo-Saxon countries which flowed across the world. This study is examining a practice which emanates from the developing world and which is actively under consideration in many advanced economies. Several studies attribute the emergence of PB to the experiences of the city of Porto Alegre, in Brazil (Aragonès and Sánchez-Pagés 2009). This initial conception of PB had the political aim of redistributing income to reduce poverty. It also had two distinct attributes by which it and by which subsequent manifestations of PB can be identified: (1) an insistence on *democratic participation* and (2) the need for *transparency* in the process and outcome of PBs (Goldfrank 2006).

While the diffusion of PB is impressive, there are complications: PB is being implemented in very different ways, largely as a result of legal, social, political and historical traditions that exist in different countries. In particular, it is noteworthy that there is limited PB in Anglo-Saxon countries. Within the United Kingdom, there have been tentative developments on PB, with some encouragement to develop PB approaches by having pilot studies (Harkins and Escobar 2015). Also, it is notable that PB takes a variety of forms. This paper contributes a more nuanced understanding of what PB is and what it might become in an Anglo-Saxon context by drawing on Sintomer, Herzberg and Röcke (2008) observations on the nature of PB.

This paper addresses the issue of the nature and effectiveness of PB in a number of stages. This study explores the theoretical lens of managerialism versus democratic accountability, governmentality and transparency. This addresses whether the mechanism of PB can enhance transparency and become a mediating mechanism which resolves the tensions between the aims of managerialism and democratic accountability. The lens of the Biondi and Lapsley (2014) framework is mobilized to evaluate PBs in a case study site. The research design elaborates how this was done. The Results section of this paper examines three variants of PB at the case study site. Finally, this paper offers conclusions and a management and research agenda.

2. Theory: democracy, governmentality and transparency

This study focuses on the experiences of one city in its development of PB. In this investigation of PB, three strands of contemporary thinking are mobilized:

(1) Managerialism versus democracy

The setting of cities has been at the centre of sustained managerial initiatives over the past three decades to reform their structures and processes as part of the worldwide phenomenon of NPM. Cities in the United Kingdom are political organizations with elected representatives having overarching responsibility for shaping the policies and direction of these entities, while working with city managers to deliver the pro-grammes for which elected members have overall responsibility (Lapsley, Miller, and Panozzo 2010).

Critics of the NPM trend see its spread as privileging management at the expense of citizens and their representatives (Box et al. 2001). This tension has often been depicted as a preoccupation with efficiency and result-oriented management which undermines democratic accountability (Ribot, Chhatre, and Lankina 2008) and where recasting the citizen as a consumer is highly problematic (Box et al. 2001). Nevertheless, there are proponents of the new managerialism in local government who suggest that the result-oriented reforms have the potential to enhance political accountability and representative democracy (Ospina, Grau, and Zaltsman 2004).

Within the literature, there is a point of convergence around the significance of transparency in both democratic accountability (Hollyer, Rosendorff, and Vreeland 2011) and in public management (Hood 2006). Indeed, it has been observed that transparency has a long history as a central principle for both public management and democratic accountability (Hood 2007). In a study of NPM reforms in a number of European countries, it was revealed that these reforms did not inhibit transparency (Opedal and Rommetvedt 2010), which indicates a means by which result-oriented managerial reforms may not undermine democratic accountability. The arch-proponents of NPM, New Zealand, placed transparency as a central feature of their reforms (Hood 2001).

Furthermore, a group of scholars advocate greater *participative* democracy rather than *representative* democracy (Young 1997; Häikiö 2010). This view supports giving more power to local citizens. The adoption of PB can be seen as resonating with this approach.

(2) Governmentality

In their discussion of governmentality, Miller and Rose (2008) distinguish between programmes of government and technologies of government. The programmes of government are the political rationalities of government actors. They are an assem-blage of visions, designs and policy articulations for governments. The programmes are the means by which government bodies seek to shape and influence life. In our case, city directives on education, social care, housing, transport and infrastructure provide the elements of the city programme. The technologies of government are a disparate set of techniques, mechanisms and practices which are mobilized to deliver on government programmes. There are interactions between these two concepts (Miller 2001). Indeed, it has been suggested that there is an essential reciprocity between the programmatic and technological aspects of government (Miller 1990). The technologies are often called upon by policymakers and political leaders within political argument and debate to enable, deliver and realize abstract aims and goals (Miller 1990).

Within the governmentality literature, prominence is given to accounting as a 'technology' or calculative practice. As Miller (2001) expressed it:

> (accounting) is always linked to a particular strategic or programmatic ambition to increase efficiency, to promote economic growth, to encourage responsibility, to improve decision making, to enhance competitiveness.

Indeed, accounting may serve as a mediating instrument between different worlds. Miller and O'Leary (2007) demonstrate the manner in which different spheres of life can be combined in a particular locale. This linkage may be achieved by a mediating instrument which functions in a fluid manner across diverse domains. This reveals a way in which accounting practices may be able to align the often different tensions inherent in the management and political leadership of cities.

This linkage may be confounded by the lack of appropriate, available tools to enhance democracy and social inclusion, which has been identified as a significant obstacle to more participative democratic institutions (Brugué and Gallego 2003). Indeed, it has been argued that the complexity of designing participative approaches to local government management is far from easy (Edelenbos 1999) and the shift from a centralist, policy content, top-down perspective to a more participatory approach and process orientation is challenging for all concerned. However, PB has the potential to become a mediating instrument between the interests of city management and democratically elected city politicians.

By focussing on a specific accounting practice (capital budgeting), Miller and O'Leary have shown how mediation can be detected. A study of PB could reveal similar results. However, given the experimental stage of UK PB practices, at best it is possible to *suggest* that PB has the potential to become a mediating instrument in the day-to-day activities of cities in which PB is undertaken routinely. Therefore, the aim of this study is to explore that potential, while recognizing that the extent of current practice may not yield a precise answer.

(3) Transparency

NPM influences can be seen as an antecedent of the present almost universal preoccupation with transparency in public finances. Furthermore, the mechanism of PB strikes a chord with a fundamental principle of both democratic accountability and the new managerialism: *transparency*. Hood (2006) has described contemporary usage of transparency in government as being 'quasi-religious'. However, the universal adoption of transparency as a desirable attribute is not straightforward. Nevertheless, the complex nature of this expression should not obscure its contemporary prominence. Despite the primacy of the aim of transparency in affairs of the state, there is some uncertainty about its actual meaning. Transparency is used widely in public finance without clear meaning and it is hard to assess its impact (Pollitt and Bouckaert 2000).

2.1. Framework for analysis

Given the centrality of transparency to both democracy and NPM, this offers a means of investigating the effectiveness of both in our study setting. A nuanced interpretation of transparency which captures its wider facets in management and democratic accountability is necessary to analyse its use and implications. To address this focus on local government PB as a mediating instrument between the worlds of democratic accountability and city management, this paper draws on the discussions by Biondi and Lapsley (2014) and Lapsley and Ríos (2015) which identified three levels of transparency:

(1) at one level, *access* to information is seen as achieving the aim of transparency (Kondo 2002);
(2) a second level of transparency which is best achieved when there is a genuine level of *understanding* of the phenomenon disclosed (Winkler 2000) and
(3) a third level of transparency, which is achieved where a sophisticated level of understanding, which extends to *shared meanings*, is held by potentially interested parties in the phenomenon disclosed (Christensen 2002).

The aim of this paper is to mobilize these three levels of budget transparency in the city of Edinburgh participative budgetary system to explore our research questions through the theoretical lens of managerialism versus democratic accountability, mediating instruments and transparency. If all three levels of transparency are achieved, the concerns of advocates of greater participative democracy are being met (Young 1997; Häikiö 2010). This finding also undermines the claim that NPM organizations, such as the city of Edinburgh (Lapsley, Miller, and Panozzo 2010), inevitability undermine democratic accountability (Box et al. 2001; Ribot, Chhatre, and Lankina 2008). The finding of all three levels of transparency also offers the **potential** that PB may be a mediating instrument between city management and the world of democratic accountability (Miller 2001; Miller and O'Leary 2007).

Therefore, the existence of a PB system which is transparent in its design, scope and practice may be regarded as providing a mediating instrument which enhances **both** city management and democratic accountability, and this is the key focus of this paper.

3. Research design

To investigate the adoption of PB in a landscape of financial austerity, we used a case study approach (Stake 1995). In particular, this city is a *critical case* because of its structural deficit. This financial circumstance has parallels with the adoption of innovations in public management which are associated with situations of financial distress (Hood 1995). This financial situation should mean that this city is a favourable setting for a budget innovation such as PB. This research focus recognizes the potential of cities as study settings for the exploration of social and economic phenomena using an accounting lens (Czarniawska 2002; Lapsley, Miller, and Panozzo 2010). The research design of this paper is set out in three stages:

(1) Study setting

Edinburgh exemplifies the contemporary city, where there is a conflict between high performing aspects of its services and the need to reduce public spending. The issues of both delivering essential services and ensuring a balanced budget have been a primary concern for the managers and elected leaders of this city, with the advent of the global financial crisis which has been identified as result-focussed NPM typesetting (Lapsley, Miller, and Panozzo 2010). Within this setting, we question whether this city offers a receptive context for the adoption and implementation of PB.

(2) Sources of data

Data have been collected over the period June 2014 to January 2016, from a wide variety of sources in this investigation of the impact of financial austerity on this city. This has included three categories:

(1) The first source of data is related to documentary evidence, collected
   - the annual reports and accounts of the city;
   - scrutiny of interim financial reports for the city, audit reports on the city, official policy documents, minutes of council meetings and debates on policy options.
(2) The second data source is represented by media commentaries. More specifically, they comprise
   - Commentaries on city websites. This included formal statements on city policy by its elected leader, comments by other elected members of the city council and statements by other stakeholders.
   - Media coverage of budgetary deliberations in the city. This perspective on both budgetary proposals and outcomes offers a more rounded perspective on the policies developed for the city.
(3) The third source of data was key informants. Interviews lasted approximately 45 min. These were open-ended interviews to explore views on PB.
   This included
   - Partnership development officers of Neighbourhood Partnerships (NPs).
   - Policy and Public Affairs Coordinator from the Edinburgh University Students' Association.
   - Finance Manager of the city of Edinburgh Council.
   - An informant from the PB partners organization.
   - COSLA (chief officer – communities)

     In addition, there was involvement in a budget meeting:
   - Observation of discussions at a NP meeting on budget priorities.

(3) Analysis of data

This adoption of multiple data sources allows triangulation (Eisenhardt 1989), providing stronger substantiation of constructs. These multiple sources of information have been deployed to make sense of PB initiatives in Edinburgh. The role of documents as the gathering of 'facts', which shapes both policymaking and judgement, has wider influences (Jacobsson 2016). It is recognized (Prior 2003, 21) that policy documents are not mere receptacles of information on the city, but important traces of policy debate and contest. The media can also be seen as framing, or attempting to frame, public perceptions on the merits of different policy options. This perspective – the media lens on city life – has been advocated as an illuminating way of visualizing the city (Czarniawska 2002), as a means of getting behind factual accounts of city life (Lapsley, Miller, and Panozzo 2010) and as a key way of understanding democratic processes in cities (Lapsley and Giordano 2010). Documentary and media analyses have been complemented with the perspectives of expert informants (Jones 1996). This informed our view on how committed these key actors were to PB initiatives. We also undertook some observation of budgetary discussions in pilot projects, such as the one in the area of Leith in May 2014, which enhanced our understanding of participant attitudes to these initiatives.

In the discussion of theory, we observed that Biondi and Lapsley (2014) identified three levels of transparency:

(1) *access* to information is seen as achieving the aim of transparency,
(2) a genuine level of *understanding* of the phenomenon disclosed and
(3) where a sophisticated level of understanding, which extends to *shared meanings*, is held by potentially interested parties in the phenomenon disclosed.

The aim of this paper is to mobilize these three levels of budget transparency in the city of Edinburgh participative budgetary system to explore our research questions through the theoretical lens of managerialism versus democratic accountability, mediating instruments and transparency. If all three levels of transparency are achieved, the concerns of advocates of greater participative democracy are being met and this finding also offers the potential that PB is a mediating instrument between city management and the world of democratic accountability (Miller 2001; Miller and O'Leary 2007).

In their 2014 paper, Biondi and Lapsley (op. cit.) only tested for level 1 transparency – access to information. However, a subsequent study (Lapsley and Ríos 2015) tested for all three levels of transparency. The latter approach is adopted in this paper.

4. Results (1) participative budgeting pilots

There are two strands to the city pilot initiatives on PB. The first was a pilot study for the care of the elderly. This first pilot study had considerable success. This pilot revealed significant participation and high levels of transparency at all three levels of the Biondi and Lapsley (2014) model, as used by Lapsley and Ríos (2015). This pilot reveals democratic accountability as elderly citizens exercised choice. This pilot shows how PB may be used as a mediating instrument between particular groups of citizens and the city management (Miller and O'Leary 2007). The targeted group had access to relevant financial information (level 1), the elderly people understood the options before them and had facilitators to elaborate upon different alternatives (level 2) and the targeted group of elderly citizens exhibited shared meanings in articulating spending proposals (level 3). However, while the nature of this pilot is positive, it only lasted for 1 year and was not repeated. The outcome for participative democracy of the kind sought by Young (1997) and Häikiö (2010) was therefore ephemeral.

The second pilot initiative was targeted at local communities through NPs. This setting raises a more significant possibility of the kind of participative democracy in which local people define problems and produce relevant and even creative solutions (Häikiö 2010). While the specific group of the elderly has more tightly focussed concerns, these NPs have a wider range of activities to focus on. However, the results of this pilot initiative are mixed. There are twelve NPs in this city. Only six of these had undertaken a participative budgeting exercise. Of the other six, four NPs had done nothing and two were at a planning or developmental stage. Within the six successful participative budgeting pilots in NPs, there is also unevenness of outcome. There are two projects (Leith Decides and South Central) which have all the hallmarks of the Biondi and Lapsley (2014) levels of transparency. However, the other four are more muted.

The results of these initiatives are examined in the following sections: (1) Canny wi' Cash: A PB initiative for older people, (2) PB Initiatives in NPs.

(1) Canny wi' Cash: A PB initiative for older people

The title of 'Canny wi' Cash' is Scots for careful with money, a circumstance which would be expected for many elderly people. Under the motto 'Our voice is being heard at last', the Edinburgh Voluntary Organisations' Council (EVOC) ran the PB project *Canny wi' Cash*[1] as part of the 10-year initiative of the Scottish Government 'Reshaping Care for Older People Change Fund' – see Table 1.

The aim of the project was to give older people the power to decide and consequently, under a scheme of small grants to local groups, they could make decisions about which events, activities and services they wanted to use, and how much money should be spent on them. Every group, which had to consist of people older than 65 years, could apply for up to £1500. This grants programme was developed from January 2013 to January 2014 and perhaps the most innovative aspect of this project was the decision of the EVOC Project Team to go where older people were facilitating the vote process and giving the same opportunities to everyone. Therefore, a group of seven facilitators, selected for the project, visited places such as drop-in centres, lunch clubs and day centres where they could explain and describe the proposals on which they could vote.

A total of 101 proposals were submitted and finally £56,112 was allocated into fifty-six different projects for the elderly. However, only 312 people voted in the thirty-seven different voting venues. Even so, Canny wi' Cash allowed older people in Edinburgh to feel included and according to the feedback obtained, they would like to participate again.

When they were asked about the chance they had to decide what they wanted or needed as an alternative to the politicians' decisions, expressions such as 'I was glad to have a chance to vote', 'People should be asked more often to vote for things' or 'It's democratic this way' arose. Additionally, the report of the project stated that one

Table 1. *Canny wi' Cash* in figures.

Projects	Submitted	101[a]		£106,540.05
	Awarded	56		£56,112
People involved	Voters		312	
	Steering Group		11	
	Facilitators		7	
Voting venues			37	
Budget allocation	Funding into selected proposals			£56,112
	Facilitators' costs			£815.5
	Co-ordination and management			£787.75
	Publicity and mailing			£300
	Materials			£450
	Final report (printing, copying etc.)			£294.75
	TOTAL			£58,760

[a]One project was considered as unsuitable by the Steering Group and it was removed from the list.
Source: compiled from *Canny wi' Cash* report by EVOC.

of the outcomes of the initiative was that these people have felt included in democracy and they understood the process and what was expected of them.

These findings are consistent with democratic participation and transparency in PB (Goldfrank 2006) and exhibit high levels of transparency (Biondi and Lapsley 2014) where we take the proxies of discussions over options and shared meanings over spending proposals (Lapsley and Ríos 2015) as proxies for level 2 and 3 transparency. It is important to note that this pilot was successfully managed by the city management working in partnership with a non-profit organization. The PB was an important focus as a mediating instrument between the interests of the citizens and the city. However, while this pilot is indicative of what can be achieved with PB, this result should be taken with some caution, because the pilot was only for 1 year and it has not been repeated.

(2) PB Initiatives in the NPs

Each NP is managed by a group of people including representatives from the local community, the police, health care, the voluntary sector, local organizations and local councillors. The NP Local Community Plan reflects key priorities to tackle local issues. Every NP offers grants to the local community groups through the programme Community Grants Fund, provided by the Council. Local groups can apply for a small grant to invest in projects for the community and to contribute to the achievement of the local priorities.

These bodies offer a setting of citizen involvement where it might be expected that PB initiatives would thrive and prosper. However, this perspective is based on the presumption that citizens wish to be involved in their local communities, actively defining local needs and devising appropriate courses of action (Häikiö 2010). In our discussions with Partnership Development Officers, it became clear that citizen apathy was undermining the pilot initiative in four of these NPs with two others striving to get the PB initiative started.

However, the remaining six NPs had established PB pilots. These addressed mainly issues around involving youths in their local community. Four NPs have performed PB initiatives between 2013 and 2014 in which local young people have been encouraged to submit proposals developing projects which benefit and give opportunities to the local youth. In this way, local young people have had the chance to decide about the allocation of local funds. In the Liberton & Gilmerton NP, the idea of a PB strategy arose after an event, *Youth Talk13*, at which a group of local young people showed their awareness of being more engaged in decision-making and being able to have a say in how local budgets are allocated (City of Edinburgh 2014a). Our informant from the NP, the Partnership Development Officer, highlighted after the voting event in which local youth selected seven out of nine projects to be awarded, how well they assumed their responsibility in the process as well as how they valued the possibility to express their views. This initiative allocated £11,000; however, the other three projects of PB for young people in the rest of NPs distributed between £2000 and £4000.

These initiatives are consistent with the key dimensions of PB, both an insistence on *democratic participation* and the need for *transparency* in the process and outcome of PBs (Goldfrank 2006). The manner and process of conducting these pilot studies are consistent with Biondi and Lapsley's (2014) model of access, understanding and shared meanings. Perhaps most importantly, engagement with the youth of these communities offers the potential of future development in PB initiatives.

The remaining active NPs, south-central NP and Leith NP, started PB projects in 2010. *Students in the Community*, an event hosted by the Edinburgh University Students' Association, has allocated £6000 of the south-central community grants budget every year since 2010. Students and people from the local community have worked together to improve their local area and this fostered closeness between students and non-students. Every year, applicants have presented their projects to improve their local community in an open forum where attendants, over sixty people each year, voted on their preferred ideas and the ones with the highest number of votes have been awarded. During this time, writing and art workshops, a film festival and cultural exchange activities have all been supported. The Partnership Development Officer affirmed that the provision of funding was attractive to student participants who understood the issues and worked together in developing proposals. These observations are consistent with the fundamental ideas of PB and are consistent with the Biondi and Lapsley (2014) model. However, this is a part of the city which has a large student population, which may skew the willingness and capacity of citizens to become involved in the PB pilot.

The most notable of the NP projects is *£eith Decides* which has been undertaken in Leith NP since 2010. COSLA, the organization with an overarching responsibility for local government in Scotland, provided a key informant who identified this pilot as an influential reference point for PB in the city. Indeed, in 2013, Leith NP received an award from COSLA for its work. This particular PB pilot resonates with Young's (1997) ideas of the renewal of democracy and Box et al.'s (2001) ideas of substantive democracy. This initiative has achieved the engagement and involvement of the people who work, live or study in the area of Leith, by letting them discuss local funding decisions and making them feel included in the community. This immersion in democratic processes and involvement in spending proposals and formulation of policies are consistent with Biondi and Lapsley's (2014) three levels of transparency. Exceptionally, this research team attended a 2015 meeting of the NP in which it proposed its spending plans. This confirmed the levels of engagement, of understanding and of commitment reported to us by the Leith Partnership Development Officer.

Table 2 reports the figures corresponding to each year of the *£eith Decides* PB, where it can be seen how the amounts of money and, especially, the people involved in the voting process increase over time. Furthermore, this includes people of all ages as well as from all of Leith (Leith NP Report 2011, 2012; City of Edinburgh 2013a, 2014b).

Table 2. Evolution in figures of *£eith Decides*.

		Projects		Voters		
	Funds allocated	To be considered for funds	Awarded	Public event	By post and in local libraries	Total
2010	£16,602	25	20	320	–	320
2012	£17,666	33	22	724	–	724
2013	£22,092	38	22	590	309	899
2014	£22,885	42	26	402	663	1,065
2015	£22,092	37	25	318	1,307	1,625

The reason for the success of this project might be due to the careful preparation and adaptation of PB to the participants' needs. When the pilot was presented for its approval in 2010 (Leith NP Report 2010), the report emphasized the need to promote the initiative widely within the local community and give applications sufficient time to prepare bids. £eith Decides has been coordinated by a steering group of local volunteers, NP members and Council staff, which has been responsible for planning the whole process, organizing the voting event, publicizing the initiative, supporting applicant local groups and encouraging participation. Organizers have widely publicized the PB project through local press, community newsletters, distribution of flyers and posters around the area, advertisements in the local radio, websites, email networks, local libraries provided information too and Facebook. In the 2010 and 2012 exercises, the only way to vote for the preferred projects was in a public event, while in 2013, 2014 and 2015, the chance to vote by post or in the local libraries was added to allowing those who could not attend the event to take part. The feedback received by the organization has always been positive and people are encouraged to carry on with PB in Leith. After the event in 2013, Councillor Blacklock for the Leith Walk Ward declared:

> For the first time, I heard people in the community meetings speaking about the NP as a tool for engagement, having real democracy where people can decide on how money is spent. (City of Edinburgh 2013a)

The PB in Leith is highly successful, complying with the fundamental ideas of PB. However, in any evaluation of the NPs involvement in pilot PB exercises in Edinburgh, we need to exercise caution and not overstate the case. In particular, in many NPs, there are low rates of participation, both in terms of applications for projects and in terms of participants in the voting process. Additionally, the pot of money allocated, usually corresponding with a percentage of the budget of the Community Grants Fund, is generally low.

Therefore, there is evidence of PB as a mediating instrument between the everyday world of citizens and city management, specifically not only in Leith NP and south-central NP but also in the youth initiatives. We conclude that the pilot PB initiatives in Edinburgh underline the potential for a more participative approach to budgeting, while recognizing that this is not a straightforward policy option.

5. Results (2) budget consultation exercise

In addition to their initiatives with pilot studies of PB for the elderly and for neighbourhood partners, the city has undertaken an extensive budget consultation exercise. This consultation exercise commenced in 2013/2014 and can be seen as part of a broad spectrum approach to enhancing democratic involvement in its financial affairs. This is consistent with Sintomer, Herzberg and Röcke (2008) classification of what may constitute PB. The Financial Manager at the City Council who was interviewed confirmed that the budgetary consultation exercise was regarded as an important part of its budget setting process.

This positioning by the city is consistent with the ideas of participative democracy (Young 1997; Häikiö 2010). We have said that this city is a *critical case* because of its structural deficit. This financial situation of financial distress makes this city a favourable setting for a budget innovation such as PB (Hood 1995). There is an issue over whether a budget consultation exercise can be regarded as PB. We have mentioned above that there is not a blueprint for PB, there is diversity in PB initiatives, which are shaped by social, political and legal contexts. According to Sintomer, Herzberg and Röcke (2008), this consultative process fits the 'Consultation on public finances' model in their typology of PB procedures. Specifically, to merit the descriptor of PB, a budget consultation exercise would have to demonstrate that the views of citizens had altered the budget (Sintomer, Herzberg, and Röcke 2008). Furthermore, the budget consultation exercise presents the possibility of the budget becoming a mediating mechanism between the citizens and city management where substantive exchanges occur. To achieve this, the budget consultation exercise has to exhibit both high levels of democratic engagement by, and with, citizens and high levels of transparency (Goldfrank 2006).

The City Council has addressed the issue of *transparency* in its public finances in many ways. It has opened up its municipal accounts to citizens before its budget is approved. The city draft budget is also presented to residents. It has devised a number of engagement exercises to ensure citizens have access to, and understand, its financial situation and its budget proposals. The city approach has been broadly based in interactive media. These include surveys, websites and social media inter-action. Online and paper surveys and phone interviews were undertaken. Interactive websites were placed at the disposal of citizens to make it easier to comment on the budget. People were also encouraged to post their comments and suggestions by using social networks such as Facebook and Twitter. The city also arranges public meetings at which local citizens have an opportunity to question elected representa-tives and city officials on budgetary issues. These points of contact were designed to be easily managed by ordinary citizens. In these various ways, city budget proposals and targeted savings were presented to citizens with the expectation that they would respond with comments, suggestions and recommendations on budget proposals.

These elaborate efforts by the city to make its financial situation transparent can be seen as meeting both level 1 (access) and level 2 (understanding) as proposed by Biondi and Lapsley (2014). The key issue of the level of engagement is crucial for achieving level 3 (shared meanings) (Biondi and Lapsley 2014); categorization as PB (Sintomer, Herzberg, and Röcke 2008); in forming a view on the budget as a mediating instrument (Miller and O'Leary 2007) and in achieving effective partici-pative democracy (Häikiö 2010).

The initial consultation exercises had limited success. In the 2013/2014 annual budget consultation, only 336 responses to the online survey were submitted (City of Edinburgh 2013b). In the 2014/2015 budget consultation, communications and involvement activities reached over 68,000 people and even so, there were only 341 responses to the survey and more than 200 social media comments and 250 email contacts were received related with the budget (City of Edinburgh 2014c).

However, the 2015/2016 budget consultation was much more successful. This coincides with deepening financial difficulties for the city and supports the observa-tions that financial distress can trigger substantive changes in public management (Hood 1995). During the last consultation (2015/2016), the highest record of responses was achieved, specifically 3,525 across the different formats (City of Edinburgh 2015).

Most importantly, after every period of public consultation, citizens' feedback has been reflected in changes to the final budget. This outcome resonates with ideas of local democracy and engagement (Häikiö 2010). This is indicative that this democratic process may have had impact on both the budget process and the budget outcome.

The amendments made to the draft budget after the analysis of the main proposals received from citizens in the consultation exercise on the city budget and saving proposals are set out in city budget documents. With reference to the 2015/2016 annual budget, citizens' proposals led to reductions in the expected savings in £3,094,000. For instance, in the draft budget, the Council expected to save £130,000 by reducing the provision of festive lighting and trees but after gathering respondents' suggestions and comments, the saving was withdrawn from the 2015/2016 revenue budget. On the budget consultation, Finance Convener Councillor Alasdair Rankin (Rankin 2015) said:

> I would like to thank the thousands of residents and businesses who took part in this open and democratic 11-week engagement and consultation process. A broad range of channels were used to ensure that everyone had their opportunity to have their say as an individual and/or as a group to influence how the council should invest and save money. We ensured it was promoted to all age groups and people from all walks of life to help us understand more fully where Edinburgh residents think council money should be invested and saved. The online planner has proven successful and will help us to make the right decisions for our residents now and in the future when setting our budget.

Councillor Rankin has subsequently reiterated this stance on the importance of giving voice to citizens' views in setting the city budget (Rankin 2016). These findings are indicative of a level of citizen engagement with city management which is congruent with the Biondi and Lapsley (2014) level 3 transparency as expressed by spending proposals (Lapsley and Ríos 2015). While this engagement exercise with citizens is publicly described as a consultation exercise, the substantive nature of the citizen engagement on budget proposals makes this exercise consistent with the Sintomer, Herzberg and Röcke (2008) categories of PB. The level of citizen engagement, particularly in the 2015/2016 budget consultation exercise, reveals key aspects of participative democracy (Häikiö 2010). This is suggestive of the budget as a mediating device between the democratic world of citizens and the managerial world of city officials (Miller and O'Leary 2007).

6. Conclusion

This research has addressed the important issue of budgetary reforms in cities by focusing on initiatives in PB. The topic of PB has its antecedents in South America as part of a political challenge to the establishment. This challenge to established practice, which had the intention of enhancing transparency and democratic accountability, is now spreading internationally, albeit with different interpretations and practices shaped by different institutional, social and political consequences. Given the flow of public management reforms from Anglo-Saxon countries, the adoption of PB represents a reverse diffusion process, which is significant in itself.

This study reaffirms the potential of the PB approach in the United Kingdom. The findings in this paper suggest that this form of budgeting is not an NPM type management tool which undermines democratic accountability (Box et al. 2001). Instead, the idea of PB enhances participative democracy (Young 1997; Häikiö 2010). The particular attraction of PB is the manner in which it may act as a mediating instrument (Miller and O'Leary 2007) between the two worlds of city management and citizens.

The official position in the United Kingdom on PB has been rather limited, being restricted to the recommendation of pilot studies. However, in this paper, the case study city reveals evidence of interesting developments with this innovative budgeting. In the initiative on the care of the elderly, and in the NPs, there was evidence of citizen engagement. There was also evidence of citizen apathy. But where citizens connected with the idea, these initiatives enhanced both democratic accountability and transparency in public finances. The expectation that citizens would act on the funds allocated to them was realized in certain of the above pilot studies. The other evidence in this study came from a budgetary consultation exercise by this city. This budgetary exercise is consistent with the Sintomer, Herzberg and Röcke (2008) classification of PB. While the levels of citizen participation were somewhat limited initially, in the year 2014/2015, as the fiscal crisis became more acute in the city, there was a more significant citizen engagement with the budget setting process. The examples of actual proposals made by citizens and the response of the city to such proposals were substantive. The evidence of these PB exercises indicates that they may lead to greater participation by citizens. There is evidence of citizens achieving high levels of transparency (Biondi and Lapsley 2014; Lapsley and Ríos 2015) by not only gaining access to budgetary information but also understanding it, and experiencing shared meanings with other participants in this budgetary process. Given the unevenness of this evidence, it is important to observe that this is a process, but, nevertheless, to recognize the potential of PB. In particular, PB has the potential to become a mediating instrument between city management and the electorate and their representatives, forging a bridge across the worlds of management and democratic accountability.

These findings suggest that policymakers should examine the case for a concerted action on PB. There is also a research and a management agenda to address how the PB processes may reach their potential. This study suggests that more significant funding could be allocated to NPs as the most likely means of achieving a more fundamental change in the case study city budgeting. Within these developments, there is a case for action research with study settings to identify successful practices to share and transfer expertise across other cities and indeed the whole of local government.

The wider adoption of PB offers a route to shifting from the traditional backward-looking silo approach to budgeting to a more participative approach which should achieve greater transparency and enhance democratic accountability, with the PB becoming a mediating instrument between the worlds of city management and democratic accountability. The findings in this paper, particularly in the budget consultation exercise, reveal the potential for this deep connection to be made between citizens, elected politicians and city managers.

Note

1. Full report available at http://www.evoc.org.uk/wordpress/wpcontent/media/2013/07/Jan21014_Canny_Wi_Cash_Report.pdf.

Disclosure statement

No potential conflict of interest was reported by the authors.

References

Aragonès, E., and S. Sánchez-Pagés. 2009. "A Theory of Participatory Democracy Based on the Real Case of Porto Alegre." *European Economic Review* 53 (1): 56–72. doi:10.1016/j.euroecorev.2008.09.006.

Biondi, L., and I. Lapsley. 2014. "Accounting, Transparency and Governance: The Heritage Assets Problem." *Qualitative Research in Accounting & Management* 11 (2): 146–164. doi:10.1108/QRAM-04-2014-0035.

Box, R., G. Marshall, B. Reed, and C. Reed. 2001. "New Public Management and Substantive Democracy." *Public Administration Review* 61 (5): 608–619. doi:10.1111/puar.2001.61.issue-5.

Brugué, Q., and R. Gallego. 2003. "A Democratic Public Administration?" *Public Management Review* 5 (3): 425–447. doi:10.1080/1471903032000146973.

Carmela, B., E. Guarini, and I. Steccolini. 2016. "Italian Municipalities and the Fiscal Crisis: Four Strategies for Muddling Through." *Financial Accountability & Management* 32 (3): 335–361.

Christensen, L. T. 2002. "Corporate Communication: The Challenge of Transparency." *Corporate Communications: An International Journal* 7 (3): 162–168. doi:10.1108/13563280210436772.

City of Edinburgh. 2013a. "£Eith Decides 2012-2013 Report." Leith Neighbourhood Partnership, May.

City of Edinburgh. 2013b. "Feedback on the Consultation on the Council's Draft Proposals Budget for 2013/14." Finance and Budget Committee, January 30.

City of Edinburgh. 2014a. "Liberton Gilmerton Neighbourhood Parternship Community Grants – Youth Participatory Budgeting Event." Liberton Gilmerton Neighbourhood Partnership, October 1.

City of Edinburgh. 2014b. "£Eith Decides 2013-14: Evaluation." Leith Neighbourhood Partnership, August 20.

City of Edinburgh. 2014c. "Budget Proposals 2014/15: Overview of Feedback and Engagement." Finance and Resource Committee, January 16.

City of Edinburgh. 2015. "Budget Proposals: Overview of Feedback and Engagement." February 3.

Czarniawska, B. 2002. *A Tale of Three Cities*. Oxford: Oxford University Press.

Edelenbos, J. 1999. "Design and Management of Participatory Public Policy Making." *Public Management Review* 1 (4): 569–576. doi:10.1080/14719039900000027.

Eisenhardt, K. M. 1989. "Building Theories from Case Study Research." *The Academy of Management Review* 14 (4): 532–550.

Goldfrank, B. 2006. "Lessons from Latin American Experience in Participatory Budgeting." Latin American Studies Association Meeting, San Juan, March.

Häikiö, L. 2010. "The Diversity of Citizenship and Democracy in Local Public Management Reform." *Public Management Review* 12 (3): 363–384. doi:10.1080/14719030903286649.

Harkins, C., and O. Escobar. 2015. *Participatory Budgeting in Scotland: An Overview of Strategic Design Choices and Principles for Effective Delivery*. Glasgow: GCPH, WWS. October.

Hollyer, J., B. P. Rosendorff, and J. R. Vreeland. 2011. "Democracy and Transparency." *The Journal of Politics* 73 (4): 1191–1205. doi:10.1017/S0022381611000880.

Hood, C. 1995. "The New Public Management in the 1980s: Variations on a Theme." *Accounting, Organizations and Society* 20 (2–3): 93–109. doi:10.1016/0361-3682(93)E0001-W.

Hood, C. 2001. "Transparency." In *Encyclopedia of Democratic Thought*, edited by P. B. Clarke and J. Foweraker, 700–704. London: Routledge.

Hood, C. 2006. "Transparency in Historical Perspective." In *Transparency: The Key to Better Governance?* edited by C. Hood and D. Heald. Oxford: Oxford University Press.

Hood, C. 2007. "What Happens When Transparency Meets Blame-Avoidance?" *Public Management Review* 9 (2): 191–210. doi:10.1080/14719030701340275.

Jacobsson, K. 2016. "Analyzing Documents Through Fieldwork." In *Qualitative Research*, edited by D. Silverman. 4th ed. Thousand Oaks, CA: Sage.

Jones, M. 1996. *Studying Organizational Symbolism.* Thousand Oaks, CA: Sage.

Kondo, S. 2002. "Fostering Dialogue to Strengthen Good Governance." In *Public Sector Transparency and Accountability: Making it Happen*, edited by Global Forum on Transparency, 7–12. Washington, DC: Organisation for Economic Cooperation and Development.

Lapsley, I., and F. Giordano. 2010. "Congestion Charging: A Tale of Two Cities. Accounting." *Auditing and Accountability Journal* 23 (5): 671–698. doi:10.1108/09513571011054936.

Lapsley, I., P. Miller, and F. Panozzo. 2010. "Accounting for the City." *Accounting, Auditing & Accountability Journal* 23 (3): 305–324. doi:10.1108/09513571011034316.

Lapsley, I., and A. Ríos. 2015. "Making Sense of Government Budgeting: An Internal Transparency Perspective." *Qualitative Research in Accounting & Management* 12 (4): 377–394. doi:10.1108/QRAM-01-2015-0014.

Leith NP Report. 2010. "Using a Participatory Budgeting Approach to Allocate the Community Grants Fund." Leith NP, February 24.

Leith NP Report. 2011. "£eith Decides Participatory Budgeting Pilot Project: Evaluation." Leith Neighbourhood Partnership, May 3.

Leith NP Report. 2012. "£Eith Decides 2011/12." Leith Neighbourhood Partnership, June 6.

Miller, P., and T. O'Leary. 2007. "Mediating Instruments and Making Markets: Capital Budgeting, Science and the Economy Accounting." *Organizations and Society* 20 (2/3): 219–237.

Miller, P. B. 1990. "On the Interrelations between Accounting and the State." *Accounting, Organizations and Society* 15 (4): 315–338. doi:10.1016/0361-3682(90)90022-M.

Miller, P. B. 2001. "Governing by Numbers – Why Calculative Practices Matter." *Social Research* 68 (2): 379–396.

Miller, P. B., and N. Rose. 2008. *Governing the Present.* Cambridge: Polity Press.

Opedal, S., and H. Rommetvedt. 2010. "From Politics to Management – or More Politics?" *Public Management Review* 12 (2): 191–212. doi:10.1080/14719031003616115.

Ospina, S., N. Grau, and A. Zaltsman. 2004. "Performance Evaluation, Public Management Improvement and Democratic Accountability." *Public Management Review* 6 (2): 229–251. doi:10.1080/1471903042000189119.

Pollitt, C., and G. Bouckaert. 2000. *Public Management Reform: A Comparative Analysis.* Oxford: Oxford University Press.

Prior, L. 2003. *Using Documents in Social Research.* London: Sage.

Rankin, A. 2015. "Have Your Say." *Edinburgh Evening News*, January 28.

Rankin, A. 2016. "The Budget Challenge." *Edinburgh Evening News*, January 15.

Ribot, J. C., A. Chhatre, and T. Lankina. 2008. "Institutional Choice and Recognition in the Formation and Consolidation of Local Democracy." *Conservation and Society* 6 (1): 1–11.

Sintomer, Y., C. Herzberg, and A. Röcke. 2008. "Participatory Budgeting in Europe: Potentials and Challenges." *International Journal of Urban and Regional Research* 32 (1): 164–178. doi:10.1111/ijur.2008.32.issue-1.

Stake, R. E. 1995. *The Art of Case Study Research.* Thousand Oaks, CA: Sage.

Winkler, B. 2000. *Which Kind of Transparency? On the Need for Clarity in Monetary Policy-making.* European Central Bank Working Paper Series, Working Paper No. 26. Frankfurt: ECB.

Young, S. C. 1997. "Local Agenda 21: The Renewal of Local Democracy?" *Political Quarterly* 68: 138–147. doi:10.1111/poqu.1997.68.issue-B.

Budgeting and the construction of entities: struggles to negotiate change in Swedish municipalities

Niklas Wällstedt and Roland Almqvist

ABSTRACT
Budgeting has endured changes in management ideals, because it supports an instrumental rationality in which organizations should use their own resources to produce their own results. Budgeting depends on and enforces traditional and transactional systems based on predefined entities, such as single-purpose organizations and measurable outputs. This study investigates this issue and asks what types of entities budgeting needs, and where and when these entities can be negotiated and reconstructed. This study shows that budgeting and its reinforcement of traditional and transactional systems makes it difficult to proceed towards new management ideals based on cooperation, sharing, and responsiveness.

Introduction

Public budgeting is persistent; it endures changes in management paradigms and withstands its own inherent contradictions. As Wildavsky (1978) argued, '[b]udgeting is supposed to contribute to continuity (for planning), to change (for policy evalua-tion), to flexibility (for the economy), and to provide rigidity (for limiting spending)' (501). Regardless of such contradictions, budgeting still stands strong – despite evident changes in administrative and managerial paradigms from the old public administration (OPA) over new public management (NPM) to what comes 'after NPM' (Almqvist and Wällstedt 2013; Hood 1991, 1995; Kurunmäki and Miller 2011) – for example, new public governance (NPG) (see Osborne 2006, 2009). We argue that this is because budgeting is an invaluable technology for defining and maintain-ing stable entities: with budgeting, resources are readily defined as monetary, perfor-mance can be defined as organizational outputs, and accountability can be allocated to those holding budgetary responsibilities in organizations. In Wildavsky's (1978) words, this means that the 'continuity' and 'rigidity' that budgeting contributes to have overpowered its usage for providing 'change' and 'flexibility.' This has conse-quences for the development of public sector management: in the era of NPG, based on cooperation, responsiveness towards clients and citizens, competence sharing, and societal outcomes (Almqvist and Wällstedt 2013; Needham 2010; Osborne 2006, 2009), such stable, uncontestable, entities may prove devastating.

In both the OPA and NPM eras, budgeting has been used to allocate (monetary) resources, define whether organizations are efficient and effective, and hold managers and politicians accountable (Agyemang 2010; Alford 2014; Gilmour and Lewis 2006; Heinrich 2002; Hood 1991, 1995; Jackson 2011; Kurunmäki and Miller 2011; Marti 2006; Robinson 2002; Wang 2000). The NPM reforms, aimed at a more transactional system, strengthened budgeting, because such practices as consolidated reporting and auditing (Grossi and Mussari 2008; Power 1997) put pressure on public sector organizations to prove that 'their own resources are used for their own output' (Almqvist and Wällstedt 2013, 225, italics in original). Budgeting worked well in a system that assumed that value creation could occur only through transactions within and between productive organizational entities (Broadbent and Laughlin 2009; Johansson 2008, 2015; Williamson 1996). In NPM, budgeting became the way to connect monetary resources with organizational output.

Consequently, public sector budgeting has been researched assuming that budgeting is an organizational project that has implications for the economy, which, purportedly, has to be understood predominantly from managerial or political perspectives (Anessi-Pessina et al. 2016; Wildavsky 1978). Critiques have focused on the implementation and use of budgeting in public sector organizations, for example its incrementality, top-down and bottom-up characteristics (Bozeman and Straussman 1982; Hendrick 1989; Kelly 2005; Long and Franklin 2004), or on how different stakeholders can influence the process (Ahrens and Ferry 2015; Ebdon and Franklin 2006; Wildavsky 1975). However, budgeting has not been challenged as a core control technology, as in the private sector (Wallander 1999). Instead, practitioners and researchers base their assessments and critique of budgeting on the same assumptions: from political, economic, and managerial standpoints. That is, budgeting has to live up to specific ideals of accountability, resource allocation, and manageability, and the focus has been on improving budgeting in line with those ideals.

In other words, budgeting has become a constant of public sector management: it is resilient to change, and if innovations are put in place, they have to adapt to the budget process, not the other way around. If, for example, cooperation is supposed to work, new accounting procedures, such as pooled budgets or open books, have to be put in place before new relations can be created (Kurunmäki and Miller 2011). Budgeting is a strong determinant when it comes to what can be done in the public sector: budgeting helps enable and constrain practices within and beyond public sector organizations. Consequently, budgeting needs to be analysed using a constructivist approach: because budgeting assumes – even demands – certain stable entities to function, these entities need to be investigated. This is because budgeting participates in constructing stable entities that hamper the types of flexible relations that may be needed in the new era of NPG. Otherwise, budgets become tools to prioritize the good of the organization – not the service users and citizens (Ahrens and Ferry 2015; Evetts 2009).

This study approaches budgeting in organizational practices with the assumption that entities are constructed and reinforced in such daily practices (Latour 1999, 2005; Law and Singleton 2005; Mol 2002; Thrane and Hald 2006). It is assumed that entities are constructed to 'fit' systems and rationalities; entities are made up to be useful in relation to dominant theories and practices in society and organizations (Mol 1999; Rose and Miller 1992; Wällstedt 2015). Therefore, we analyse budgeting in a broader context of management paradigms and organizational control systems in order to investigate how budgeting participates in the construction and maintenance of stable entities that makes it difficult to operationalize the ideas found in NPG. In particular, we focus on maintenance, because the contestation and reconstruction of entities – for example, single-purpose organizations and measurable outputs – is difficult, if not impossible, given the dominance of traditional and transactional systems stemming from the rationalities embedded in OPA and NPM.

We focus on budget negotiation in order to show how practically difficult it is to reconstruct entities to 'fit' an alternative system based on communication – a system that would enable the ideas of NPG, such as cooperation and responsiveness (Almqvist and Wällstedt 2013; Osborne 2006, 2009; Vigoda 2002). We ask the following questions. What types of entities does budgeting need? In which systems and in relation to which rationalities can these entities be negotiated and reconstructed? We examine how three Swedish municipalities undertake budgeting and organizational control, and how they make efforts to work more in line with the ideas of NPG – albeit with little success. Efforts to work according to a communicative rationality in which cooperative relationships are formed become hampered because budgeting works alongside an instrumental rationality that assumes that individual organizations have to be the source of production, and transactions are *the* way to organize public sector value creation (Broadbent and Laughlin 2009).

Management paradigms, organizational control systems, and budgeting

This study considers how budgeting in a broader context may be related to OPA, NPM, and 'after NPM' – using Osborne's (2006, 2009) notion of NPG as the dominant framework – and discusses the implications of such paradigms for budgeting and the setup of organizational control systems. We relate budgeting to the wider organizational context in which it is set to work – the rationalities behind control systems and the characteristics of such systems (Broadbent and Laughlin 2009). In addition, the organizational context is related to management paradigms, in that the organization and its means of control are different depending on the normative stipulations that follow from a management paradigm: organizations and organizational controls differed in the OPA versus NPM eras, and they continue to change as the rationalities underlying 'proper management' change. We use the value chain (Figure 1) used by, for example, Almqvist, Catasús, and Skoog (2011) and Jackson (2011) to illustrate the different rationalities.

Our research builds on a constructivist approach in which entities are understood to come into being in multiple practices: they are constructed and reconstructed in different contexts, following different rationalities (Mol 2002; Rose and Miller 1992). We engage in 'messy' practices in which little is clear or singular (Law and Singleton 2005), and analytical categories coexist. We subscribe to the argument that public

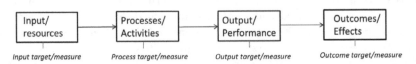

Figure 1. The traditional value chain. Source: Adapted from Jackson (2011).

sector practitioners live in a contradictory world in which several rationalities work simultaneously, and several paradigms coexist, although some may become dominant (Christensen 2014; Hyndman and Liguori 2016; Hyndman et al. 2014; Seo and Creed 2002; Wällstedt and Almqvist 2015). To provide analytical clarity, we have authored (Baxter and Chua 2008) the analytical framework as a rather 'clean' story of evolving paradigms.

OPA

Budgeting has been the dominant means of managerial control in public sector organizations (Wildavsky 1975, 1978). Together with legalistic and professional concerns, it formed the foundation for delivering public services to citizens (Almqvist and Wällstedt 2013; Osborne 2006, 2009). The budget worked as a means to allocate resources to professional groups responsible for serving public needs. Budget gaming ensued, by which professionals worked to secure resources for their activities while trying to maintain strong and lasting infrastructure for their endeavours (Covaleski and Dirsmith 1983; Dunleavy 1989; Wildavsky 1975).

Such gaming, together with administrators' planning efforts – in which resource allocation was coupled with sophisticated and statistics-based demographic forecasts (Porter 1996) – formed the basis for public budgeting during the OPA era. Hence, contemporary budget theory came to rest upon these basic characteristics: it was important to make budgeting work as a means for professional work and administrative planning as well as to provide transparency and allocate accountability. Thus, the debate came to circulate between the benefits of top-down versus bottom-up budgeting, as well as the problem that budgeting tended to focus on historical data, stability, and inputs when there was a need to consider future needs, promote change, and emphasize output and performance (Bozeman and Straussman 1982; Hendrick 1989; Hood 1991, 1995; Wildavsky 1978).

We refer to this as the *traditional system*, which builds on Wildavsky's (1975) budget games. In this system, budgeting is a means to allocate resources to professional groups so that they can perform their work in the way they see fit but should also secure equal resource allocation based on what society needs. Thus, there is a conflict of interest between taxpayer value and professional interest in performing duties. Budget negotiations are based on such conflicts, in which it is necessary to keep costs down in order to keep taxes down, and to maintain a high level of resources flowing to professional work of different organizations with different functions.

In the traditional system, *processual rationality* supports negotiation and incrementality. It is assumed that there is always conflict of interest among politicians, administrators, and service providers in budget negotiations, and that the conflicts are exacerbated by the difficulties of different organizational actors in understanding each other's interests, ways of communicating, motivations, and professional values (Lapsley 2008, 2009). Therefore, the system has to be rigid and change only slowly so that no one will get the upper hand: it has to reinforce certain entities, such as administrations, professional bodies, and political programmes, so that negotiations can focus on allocating resources to the relevant professionals and support prioritized political programmes (Moore 1980). Although the introduction of zero-based budgeting theoretically supported the idea that '[e]ach program would be on trial for its

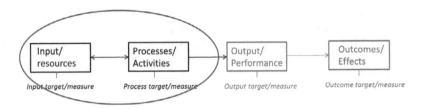

Figure 2. The OPA focus on inputs, professional processes, and negotiation.

life every year' (Lauth 1978, 420), this was seldom done in practice (Moore 1980). Stable entities of monetary funds that should be efficiently allocated to programmes, administrations, and professional bodies persisted. Figure 2 depicts the focus on professional processes and negotiation over resources, implying there is less focus on results, which arguably started to change with the introduction of programme budgeting in the public sector and efforts to couple organizational performance to programmes (Almqvist 2004; Lauth 1985). However, dramatic change towards results came with the advent of NPM.

NPM

Under NPM (Hood 1991, 1995; Osborne 2006, 2009), more effort was put into making organizations more efficient and cost-effective, and performance management and measurement, contracting out, and competition were introduced (Almqvist 2004). Western governments' approaches to public management divided them into purchasers and providers, followed by the need to allocate resources with transfer prices and evaluate performance through auditable standards (Lapsley 2008, 2009; Power 1997). Public management came to rest on agency theory and opportunistic behaviour was expected by all actors working in the public sector – professionals, administrators, and politicians (Almqvist and Wällstedt 2013). Budgeting had to keep up with changes and could do so because of the focus on single-purpose organizations and the emphasis on performance pay and evaluation techniques that relied on private sector auditing (Hood 1991, 1995; Power 1997).

Budgeting has always been focused on relating inputs to production or output (Wildavsky 1966, 1978). To ensure that organizations produced value for money, budgets were complemented with annual accounting reports (Grossi and Mussari 2008; Robinson 2002; Wang 2000). This was strengthened by concern about opportunistic behaviour, whereby legal standards promoted the idea that accountability should be allocated to individual purchasers and service providers (Laughlin and Broadbent 1993). Thus, there was a need to demarcate firmly where organizational and budgetary responsibilities began and ended. With NPM, organizational and budgetary entities became strengthened. Figure 3 depicts the ideal behind NPM: the focus on results.

The 'old' ideas of budgeting and negotiation were translated into a *transactional system* (Wällstedt, Grossi, and Almqvist 2014). It builds on *instrumental rationality* (Broadbent and Laughlin 2009) in which a specific output type is demanded from a specific input type – typically, costs are related to the amount of produced services or goods or a service quality level. The emphasis is on the transaction: a purchaser

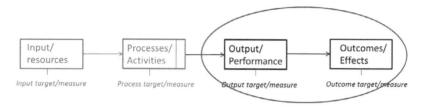

Figure 3. Instrumental rationality with the (ideal) NPM focus on results.

should be able to buy a certain output and hold the provider accountable for providing this output. The transactional system relates closely to an organizational structure of purchasers and providers, and an emphasis on competition and management by contracts (Almqvist 2004).

The instrumental rationality and focus on single-purpose organizations under the pressure of competition made organizational control deviate from the NPM ideal (Figure 3), in that it came to build on a rigid conception of a means–ends relationship (Hood 1991, 1995). This relationship is based on the idea that a quantity of input should be turned into quantities of output and outcomes by specialized organizations, complemented with recurring measurements to ensure this is accomplished efficiently and effectively and that the transactions produce as much value as possible (Jackson 2011). The rationality rests on stability: all quantities in the boxes in Figure 1 are defined clearly and the chain of cause and effect is well established. It should be possible to follow transactions from inputs to outcomes and to base accountability on these transactions. This implies stable productive entities and clear managerial roles.

If there is a problem with low output or outcomes in the system, this logic implies that the problem tends to be found 'to the left' in Figure 1: a problem with low output can be solved by improving processes in the productive unit. This makes the purchaser's role strong: it is always possible to criticize the work of providers. The argument that the provision of services can always be more efficient and effective is difficult to resist – processes can always be improved. However, there is an opportunity for providers to complain about resource allocation: the logic is that resources form the basis of service production (Knutsson et al. 2008). Although reasoning concerning efficiency and effectiveness may weaken arguments concerning low-resource allocation, this is a basis for conflict. Nevertheless, in a competitive environment coupled with standardized transfer prices, the purchaser may point to high achievers in the market and argue that high output can be achieved with the current level of resource allocation.

With instrumental rationality and within a transactional system, there is a tendency to stabilize budget items as much as possible: cost calculations and other calculation methods are used to establish transfer prices that cause 'fair' resource allocation between providers, markets are constructed with clearly demarcated productive entities bound by contracts to produce certain levels of outputs, and standardized output measures are constructed to benchmark the producers in the market and minimize transaction costs (Lapsley 2008, 2009; Triantafillou 2007). Purchasers are left with the possibility of working with their own budgets, and calculating prices based on what production level they expect and how many (monetary) resources they

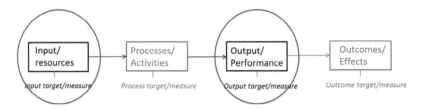

Figure 4. Instrumental rationality of NPM as carried out in practice.

can provide for a certain service area. The efficiency and effectiveness of purchasers and providers can then be assessed by 'objective' auditors (Power 1997).

Organizational entities are stabilized in the transactional system: the providers function in a competitive environment in which they can be measured against other entities that produce the same services for the same amount of resources, and they have to set their budgets based on these resource allocations and how performance is measured to show efficiency and effectiveness. The focus is on resource allocation in the form of transfer prices and cost-based formulas (Agyemang 2010) and the kind of results that could be directly tied to the individual organization: output (Almqvist 2004; Svärdsten Nymans 2012). In Figure 4, we depict how instrumental rationality came to be operationalized in practice, and within competing single-purpose organizations (Almqvist 2004).

NPG

NPM did not keep its promises for more cost-effective public service delivery. Excessive focus on narrow performance standards and high transaction costs related to competition and contract management made service delivery ineffective (Almqvist 2004; Lapsley 2008, 2009; Van Thiel and Leeuw 2002). Professional service delivery and personalized services were hampered by organizational control systems aimed at costs, efficiency, and auditable performance (Evetts 2009; Power 1997). The focus on single-purpose organizations and the heavy emphasis on efficient resource use by each organization made it difficult to share resources among competing organizations that should also be able to cooperate (Barretta 2008; LeGrand 1999).

NPG called for cooperation, sharing and outcome-based management (Osborne 2006, 2009). Budgeting had to follow, but recent evidence suggests it is falling short. The heavy emphasis on individual organizational performance, resource use and accountability makes sharing and cooperation especially difficult (Forrer et al. 2010). Strong adherence to budgets and their use for allocating resources to and within stable organizations causes resource sharing and work for the public good to be associated with considerable risk for public sector managers (Kurunmäki and Miller 2006, 2011). The penalties for managers and professionals who cannot provide evidence that their own resources are used to provide their own results are too high to use resources for the benefit of someone else.

We argue that NPG coheres with a *communicative rationality* that breaks with the processual rationality of OPA and the instrumental rationality of NPM. Communicative rationality builds on communication and negotiation among different stakeholders: it is realized in a *relational system* (Broadbent and Laughlin 2009).

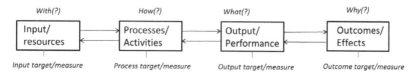

Figure 5. Communicative rationality. Source: Adapted from Almqvist, Catasús, and Skoog (2011).

Figure 5 depicts the means–ends relationships of communicative rationality. First, we highlight the communicative aspect by adding four questions that are generally used to discuss and problematize the relationships between the four boxes in the value creation chain (Almqvist, Catasús, and Skoog 2011). Open questions follow communicative rationality: with which resources should what be produced, how, and why? In this line of reasoning, resources do not necessarily equate to financial resources; the questions can be concerned with which competence a certain output should be produced. Measures used in the relational system are not more important than other bases for discussions and negotiations. The bidirectional arrows imply there are no predefined causal relationships between input and output.

The relational system builds on negotiation and the questions are open for budget items and organizational units. There is a possibility of negotiating competence characteristics and mixes as well as connections between processes, organizational relationships, and outcomes. In addition, the relational system assumes a possibility of opening up and deconstructing organizational entities and competences, sharing resources and aligning processes between different providers of services: because there is a possibility to start with a discussion about outcomes – the 'why' question – it becomes possible to discuss which resources are needed to accomplish something and how they should be aligned. This means that budget negotiations in the relational system may span organizational boundaries, question entities taken for granted and their functions, and problematize the simplistic value chain proposed by instrumental rationality.

Summary

We use three rationalities derived from Broadbent and Laughlin (2009) and Wildavsky (1975): processual rationality, which emphasizes internal coherence and builds on stability; instrumental rationality, which emphasizes that negotiations should concentrate on stable, theoretically coherent, and formal relationships of means and ends; and communicative rationality, in which virtually anything can be negotiated. For each rationality, we argue that budgeting becomes something different as it becomes situated within different management control systems. We refer to these different systems as traditional, transactional, and relational.

In any organizational practice, there is evidence of traditional, transactional, and relational systems, although, as we show, traditional and transactional systems tend to dominate. There is evidence of all three rationalities, although there are significant problems to operationalize the communicative rationality in practice: even if an organization attempts to reason in a communicative way, processual and instrumental rationalities tend to take over and emanate in traditional and transactional systems. We show how struggles to employ communicative rationality in practice are played out in three Swedish municipalities.

Method

'[I]n the study of human affairs, there appears to exist only context dependent knowledge' (Flyvbjerg 2006, 221). Therefore, we have studied multiple cases and the context(s) they are embedded in. In our study, we have simply exchanged Flyvbjerg's (2006) general question about 'context' for a slightly more specific one: we asked in which systems, and in relation to which rationalities, certain entities could be negotiated and reconstructed, and we studied this in three different settings. We developed empirical material from three Swedish municipalities: 'Suburb,' 'City,' and 'Town.' The municipalities have been researched within the confines of two different (but interrelated) research projects interested in general questions about management control within and beyond NPM. In these projects, we were interested in studying budgeting and other control technologies in practice. We came to understand budgeting as inescapable: in the Swedish municipal sector, budgeting is regulated by law, and thus one of the most important aspects of management control in the organizations studied. The municipalities are subordinate to the same legislation and work in a similar institutional environment: they are situated in a similar context despite their different sizes and approaches to administration and management.

In the first research project – a part of the Swedish national programme on local government research project (NatKom) – we researched all three municipalities to understand how they worked with their management control systems to deal with changing environment and new challenges. In the second project, we pursued a long-standing research engagement with 'City' municipality. We have followed City and its work with management control since the mid-1990s.

We were able to relate our data to evidence from the NatKom project as a whole, in which similar studies were undertaken on 47 municipalities (more than 200 interviews). Moreover, we developed our data collection and analysis based on our thorough and detailed knowledge of developments in City over the years. That is, we had ample opportunities to compare developments in our three municipalities with developments in Sweden as a whole, different municipalities in Sweden, and the developments in City over the years. Consequently, we could argue with confidence when similarities or differences among the studied municipalities seemed to be situated in a specific local context or were issues in a broader context.

We related the problem of budgeting to both the discussion on OPA, NPM, and NPG and to Broadbent and Laughlin's (2009) framework: these frameworks cohere with what we observed in the empirical material (Ahrens and Chapman 2006) and provide a way to analyse the practices in the organizations we researched. In an iterative process (Dubois and Gadde 2002) in which we went back and forth between the literature and the data collection in the two projects, it became clear that the struggles to 'break free' from the confines of single-purpose organizations and the traditional and transactional systems of OPA and NPM are highly contingent upon the budget process and how it helps reinforce specific entities and prescribes how resources should be allocated in relation to these entities. When comparing this with the extant literature, we found that these aspects of public budgeting are under-analysed.

In City, we collected 60 interviews at all organizational levels, and conducted 16 observations of budget and staff meetings. In Town, we conducted 33 interviews at all organizational levels, while in Suburb, we conducted 12 interviews focusing on management at different levels.[1] The interviews were recorded and transcribed. Although our understanding of management control in City is greater than our understanding of management control in Suburb, it is important to include Suburb in this study, because Suburb is an especially interesting case (Flyvbjerg 2006) of a municipality that relies heavily on the traditional budget process, which is not an unusual situation for Swedish municipalities.

Our interviews were formulated as analytical discussions with a range of different practitioners (Kreiner and Mouritsen 2005) about issues of management, control, and daily practice in the municipal organizations. From these discussions, it emerged (Charmaz 2006) that budgeting is an important part of everyday practice – from top management to the individual administrator, controller, teacher, or nurse – and in every organization – but in different ways, depending on how the management control system was rationalized and designed.

In addition to interviews and observations, we made use of administrative documents and followed public debates, allowing for the possibility of deducing dominant rationalities in society and the studied organizations. Our classifications in management paradigms, rationalities, and systems characteristics bring analytical clarity, but in practice, different rationalities are at work simultaneously. By using the empirical material, we attempt to show that certain rationalities dominate in practice. For example, differences between Town and City lie in their *efforts* – not success – to achieve certain things, and in how practitioners reason about this. Although their control models look similar, the intended uses of them in practice are radically different.

We exercise our role as authors (Baxter and Chua 2008) and take control of the narration of the data. We convey a narration of our studied cases predominantly with a vocabulary based on the theoretical framework, instead of letting our respondents talk. As a result, we sacrifice the kind of authenticity we obtain from using direct quotes for the benefit of making a critical exposé of the data, which focuses on the implications of our research for the budgeting literature (Golden-Biddle and Locke 1993). Although the struggles to 'break free' from traditional and transactional systems are full of nuances, we utilize the theoretical framework to extract the main problems emerging from our empirical work. This is a limitation of the study; further research would benefit from providing more nuance and detail regarding how budgeting constructs the entities that reinforce traditional and transactional systems.

Empirical data

In this section, we visit three Swedish municipalities. We argue that the organizational control systems are different in these municipalities because they rest on different dominant rationalities, although with contrasting inclusions of other rationalities. This determines how and where budget allocations, performance specifications, and organizational entities can be negotiated, and how the budget process participates in constructing and reinforcing such entities. Because budgeting is situated in a broader paradigmatic and organizational context, we discuss each municipality in the following subsections.

Suburb and the traditional system

Suburb is a municipality close to Sweden's capital, Stockholm. Suburb has about 65,000 inhabitants and is growing. It is considered to be in a beneficial position, since it has several growth possibilities for population and business. It is situated close to a large lake and owns several sites on which to build new residences. To use these advantages, Suburb's strategy rests on four pillars: 'open Suburb,' 'lake-side Suburb,' 'innovative Suburb,' and 'cooperative Suburb.' All aspects of organization and management control in the municipality should be connected to these pillars.

Based on the pillars, the municipality has constructed a 'portal objective,' which comprises two general directions: a high level of welfare and sustainable development. Suburb's budget document reads

> There are formulations about strategic and outcome-based objectives for the whole municipality. The objective that focuses on a high level of welfare is directed towards all programmes and operational areas, while the objectives that are located under the headline 'sustainable development' are prioritized areas of development that all municipal sub-committees[2] and administration units can contribute to.... The sub-committees have suggested target outcomes, which are derived from the municipality's strategic and outcomes-based objectives, and they have done so on the basis of their respective areas of responsibility. The suggested objectives regarding outcomes for the whole municipality are based on a citizen perspective, whereas the sub-committees' objectives regarding outcomes are based on a customer perspective.

Thus, the control system looks highly strategic, vision oriented, and outcomes based, obviously aiming for the ideals of NPG but with a strong focus on political programmes and clearly defined administrations. Nonetheless, this is a recent endeavour for the municipality. The formulations are far from operational in practice. Instead, the management control of Suburb is highly reliant on a strong budget process. The municipality has a history of financial crises from the 1970s to the early 1990s. The solution was to take control of the budget process to lower expenditure. Since the early 1990s, this has been the predominant form of management control and the municipality's internal motto has been 'a balanced budget.'

A significant part of taking control of the budget process was to move the budget decisions from the autumn to summer (the fiscal year ends 31 December), and to make budget decisions spanning over 2 years, instead of the usual span of 1 year. In addition, Suburb started to employ a 'salami strategy' of cutting costs by giving different administrations a little less each year. Normally, this is achieved by not compensating fully for inflation and salary increases. Together with the early budget decisions, this has had a clear effect on cost discipline. Because the budget for the following year is already made official in the summer of the current year, the administrations and operational units have the whole autumn to plan for the following year's income and cost levels.

These strategies were described in interviews as the product of a strong and small group of top managers, who had to lobby politicians intensely to make changes towards a strong, centralized budget process in which sub-committees were left with little say regarding resource allocation. This strong centralization, however, has some clear disadvantages. The financial director of Suburb told us the following:

> We work with a budget ceiling, which we can change depending on demographic forecasts. And then we work with transfer prices, which is educational because then people in the

administration know better how much money they can use. It is much more difficult with the politicians. When you have a forecast that points towards inflation and salary raises of 3% and we only give them 2%; then they [the politicians] ask 'but what are the effects of that?' and then we have to say that we don't know, and that it is up to the administration and operational units [to make do].

There are few negotiations other than within the top management team about resource allocation, which was problematic during the 2008 financial crisis. During 2008 and 2009, Suburb experienced increased unemployment, followed by rising social subsidies. Therefore, social services needed to raise allocated financial resources more than the ordinary, incremental, budget process would allow. To motivate this change, the social service administration commissioned a report from PWC, which they used to prove to top management and council politicians that more expenditure would be expected in the future as a result of higher unemployment. The report made the issue politically hot, and a strategic effort to reduce unemployment produced a new entity – an unemployment office – for inclusion in the budget process.

The centralization of resource decisions makes the system rigid but also results in strong decentralization of other decisions: because the top management is focused on financial management and the budget process, operational issues are left to professionals in operational units. This makes the control system quite heterogeneous. The elderly care administration implemented its own balanced scorecard, whereas the environment and planning administration constructed its own resource allocation model.

However, resource dependency persists: because the orientation towards objectives has been slow, and has only recently come into focus, there has been a tradition of lowering targets in the operational units in parallel with lowered resource allocations. There seems to be a valid argument that if fewer resources are obtained, then the service or output level cannot be maintained. The assumption is that everything hinges on resource allocation. Hence, there are difficulties in changing operations, and in incorporating all four dimensions of Figure 5 – something that, for example, the elderly care administration attempted to change by implementing the balanced scorecard but has not yet accomplished.

Overall, Suburb is a traditional municipality that favours a top-down, incremental resource allocation model. There are few negotiations – at least, not between top management and professionals at the operational level. The financial director even states that it is unclear what consequences the 'salami strategy' has on operations: as in Figure 2, the top management control focus lies in the resource dimension, while it is assumed that the operational level takes care of developing activities. Thus, operations remain unchanged: allocations are made to the same old entities – with the exception of the new effort towards unemployment. This focus on monetary resources and unchanging organizational entities is arguably a precondition for a stable, traditional budget process, and vice versa. If incrementality is to be achieved, there has to be stable organizational units to which resources can be allocated. We argue that this need for stability has made it difficult to implement the new focus on outcomes and strategic management, which is present only in the official documents of Suburb: the ambitions to move towards a more relational control system are hampered by the traditional focus on the budget process and the strong organizational entities that are a consequence thereof.

City and the transactional system

City has over 900,000 inhabitants, employs almost 40,000 people, and has a yearly budget of around 4.5 billion euro. City's administration consists of city council, 14 district committees with administrations (with responsibilities for e.g., elderly care, child care, and social services), 17 special committees (e.g., education, environment and planning, and culture), and 16 corporations (e.g., water supply and several companies providing rental apartments for citizens).

City is highly inspired by NPM, although it was a late adopter. Until the mid-1990s, it was a traditional, budget-oriented municipality. However, because of financial deficits and worries about productivity and output, it started to develop a new management control system which was implemented in the late 1990s. The system (Figure 6) rests on the notion that the city council decides on a few strategic objectives, which are broken down into a range of operational objectives, relating to the responsibilities of different committees. The committees are then obliged to formulate their own objectives for the council objectives. The committees buy services from providers, and the providers should work according to the 'wheel' at the bottom of Figure 6. Together with the management-by-objective system, City employed a purchaser/provider split and based most of its resource allocation on transfer prices based on cost calculations. This was done to encourage competition, so that in-house operations could compete on equal terms with private providers.

With technological development, City decided to found its control system on web-based computer software designed to follow the structure of Figure 6. This system can be accessed at all levels of the organization and is used to document budget stipulations at council level (within the square in Figure 6), committee level (below the square in Figure 6), and unit level (the 'wheel' in Figure 6). Hence, the council

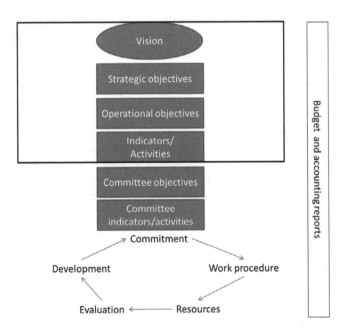

Figure 6. City's management by objectives system.

documents its objectives – strategic and operational – and defines the levels of quality or output it aims to achieve by the use of quantitative indicators. In addition, the council defines a range of activities it wants performed by the committees during the budget year (e.g., build youth centres in all districts). The committees respond to the formulations in the control system, formulate their own corresponding objectives and activities, and define levels of output or service qualities in accordance with council stipulations. Then, the provider units define their commitments in relation to the committee objectives and the quantitative levels on outputs and service qualities, define the procedures they will use to achieve their commitments, how they will use the allocated resources, how they will evaluate their work, and how they will develop it.

The data are registered in the highly standardized web-based system, making it possible to follow the chain of objectives from council down to the provider units (e.g., an individual school). Negotiations occur at all three levels regarding the objectives and levels of the indicators. First, the council politicians debate the objectives and discuss target levels with administration officials. Then, the same occurs at committee level, although the committee politicians and administrators are highly dependent on the council decisions. Eventually, the provider units have staff meetings and discuss commitments and indicator levels they consider achievable, and how they can achieve their commitments.

Thus, there is participative discussion at all levels, constrained from above: all discussions have to be adapted to the target levels determined at the higher level. This is particularly clear in the process when all organizational levels and units have decided on target levels for indicators: once done, these targets are evaluated at the council level and every committee considered to have decided on too low a target is called upon to raise it. The logic is one of aggregation: the targets and subsequent results of the whole municipality are the aggregated targets and results of the lower level organizational units. Table 1 shows an example of the aggregated targets and results at municipal level in City. Table 1 is based on City's budget documents and annual reports from 2010 to 2013 and shows the indicators used in elderly care (similar targets exist for all operations and administrations in City).

The limitations regarding negotiations also apply to resources: because almost all financial resources are allocated through cost-based transfer prices, they are non-negotiable. Only the question of 'how' can be negotiated at lower organizational levels. This follows the NPM logic that the definition of outputs and outcomes is centralized and discussions about work processes are decentralized. Resource allocations are rather a matter of cost calculation that builds the foundations of transfer prices. In this manner, costs are calculated for standard provider units, and then turned into 'pay per performance' prices: for example, by calculating the cost of running a school, and dividing it by the number of pupils in that school, it is possible to stipulate standard remuneration for each student. This can then be used to maintain a system based on choice, enabling pupils to choose which school to attend. This encourages competition and – so it is assumed – encourages providers to maintain quality standards to attract students and secure financial remuneration.

This system is complemented with other calculations based on other characteristics of customers (e.g., pupils or elderly people in need of care). It is assumed that some customers need more resources than others do. Therefore, additional allocation standards complement standard remuneration. If, for example, a pupil can provide a

Table 1. Elderly care budget targets and performance measures, city.

	2010		2011		2012		2013	
	Budgeted (%)	Outcome (%)	Budgeted (%)	Outcome (%)	Budgeted (%)	Outcome (%)	Budgeted (%)	Outcome (%)
Proportion of staff with basic training	87	88	89	89	No target	83	No target	Not measured
Generally satisfied customer	82	78	83	78	84	84	84	84
Satisfaction with meals	73	71	75	71	75	75	76	76
Customer's experienced security	88	84	89	85	89	86	90	89
The food tastes good	No target	Not measured	No target	Not measured	75	75	76	76

diagnosis of a neurodevelopmental psychiatric disorder (e.g., ADHD), he or she can bring higher remuneration to the provider to compensate for a higher need for teacher attention during classes, or even the need for personal assistance. Similarly, social workers at the purchaser side perform need-based calculations, which determine care levels and corresponding financial remunerations for elderly people moving into nursing homes. Providers thus have incentives to negotiate customer needs and provide professional evidence that their customers need more care than evaluated by the purchaser side. Although the financial well-being of the organization is in focus continuously because of the transactional system, it is possible to negotiate resource allocation 'outside' this system, with focus on the client and between purchaser and provider professionals.

Thus, resource allocation is negotiated centrally, when cost calculations are made, and turned into rigid transfer prices. However, there are often possibilities for negotiations 'outside the system,' involving other professional groups. Simultaneously, the determination of output and outcome objectives is highly centralized and follows a top-down logic. Although there are negotiations and discussions everywhere, the possibility of changing anything substantial is marginal. Hence, the system is a transactional one, and rests on stable organizational entities producing measurable outputs: it is very important to maintain organizational levels and the purchaser–provider division to maintain competition and allocate accountability for efficient resource use. This, in turn, makes it even more important for managers in, for example, provider units to work hard for *their* particular organization.

Town and the relational system

Town has about 41,000 inhabitants and is located in northern Sweden. Its major challenge is to retain and attract inhabitants, especially those with competences needed by industry and the municipality. In recent years, population growth has been stagnant, which is unsustainable in the long run. Town has two main areas of focus: tight financial control and being a strategic partner in developing local society. Top managers emphasize that the municipality has a long-standing tradition of competent financial management, and that they work hard to make the most of this for how to achieve societal outcomes.

Until recently, Town was a traditional municipality with a strong focus on the budget process. As an organization, it works hard not to adopt the principles of NPM: most service provision is in-house and there are few attempts to encourage competition between providers. Most resource allocation is negotiated in the traditional sense, that is, between the council politicians in charge of the municipal budget, and the committee politicians who want resources for their particular areas of responsibility – their administrations and programmes. These negotiations are strongly conditioned by a tight budget focus, and it is difficult for any proponent of expenditure to receive additional resources compared to the previous year. In this sense, Town's budget process is truly incremental.

The municipality was not satisfied with this focus, and for about the last 10 years, it has been working with an outcome-based control system. However, this system is far from the transactional and indicator-based system of City. Although it is accounting-based in that it relies on a strong budget process and monthly, 4-monthly, and annual reports used to follow up operations, these reports put measures in the

Figure 7. Town control system and quality chain.

background and instead focus on holistic analyses regarding the outcomes of municipal operations. The aim is to relate operations to outcomes in society. The control system builds on an organizational pyramid, and a quality chain made up of the analyses based on the recurring reports. It is depicted in Figure 7.

Therefore, the quality chain works on the logic that the annual report forms the basis for the budget, and that the achievements of the budget stipulations are evaluated on a monthly and/or 4-monthly basis. Although the model, on paper, is similar to City's transactional model, the reports focus on the holistic targets of the municipality, and the focus is *analysis* – not the achievement of, for example, quantitative target levels. Consequently, in the budget discussions and evaluation reports, there is a focus on the 'why' question in Figure 5.

This is, however, difficult to maintain. In part because it goes against the NPM logic that dominates in the surrounding society, and which relies heavily on an instrumental rationality and prescribes a more transactional system: other actors have problems understanding the model. For example, Town had trouble finding auditors able to audit the annual reports: most auditors simply claim that the report cannot be audited since it lacks standard quantitative indicators. A top manager stated the following:

> Some municipalities received awards for their cost-effective management, because they had achieved high levels on eight out of ten benchmark measures. Then I got disheartened. That is to diminish the distinctive character of municipal work! Our kind of work puts heavy emphasis on the analysis. And the auditors wanted to audit us based on these 'good examples' [municipalities that received awards]. They said that they could not make any conclusions regarding the cost-effectiveness of our operations. Then we got into a real discussion. You cannot put accounting-trained auditors to audit reports on municipal cost-effectiveness. It needs more. It is not a matter of measures. Finances are simple, whereas quality is much more complex.

As politicians have to draw conclusions from managers' analyses, there are serious demands on politicians to be up-to-date with municipal operations and understand the bigger picture at the same time. The idea is that resource allocation should follow this holistic model, underpinned by the analyses. It means that traditional budget games, in which every actor should try to obtain as much resources for his or her own operations as possible, should be abandoned. Instead, budget allocations should be made according to what the society needs and who is best equipped to meet these needs.

We found several attempts to go beyond the tradition of allocating resources to predefined budget entities and attributing certain outputs to predefined organizational entities. This, however, proved difficult for two reasons. First, laws demand that accountability should be specified to a distinct operating unit and organizational structures and governance systems should follow a particular pattern. Inspectors from oversight bodies use these demands to audit the efficacy of municipal organizations. Second, when resource allocation is based on traditional organizational entities, and one of the main objectives is to keep a balanced budget, it is difficult to refrain from traditional budget games. We heard several stories in which people at lower organizational levels acknowledged they always tried to negotiate resource allocation with cooperation and holistic outcomes in mind. Simultaneously, they could not risk financial deficits for their operations and therefore, attempted to secure additional financial resources.

Hence, Town is trying to apply communicative rationality and construct a relational system, but in practice is struggling with an overly strong traditional element, as well as some transactional characteristics imposed from the NPM-based environment – for example, auditors and instrumentalist oversight bodies. These powerful actors assume that certain, auditable, entities exist, and force Town into the transactional NPM system it is trying to avoid. Simultaneously, the budget process and financial pressure steer budget negotiations towards traditional incremental budgeting. The maintenance of traditional administrations and programmes exacerbates this, as do legal stipulations that demand that outputs should be attributed to specific organizational entities. Nevertheless, a few relational solutions are deployed in practice. First, the holistic focus makes it easier to share competence over organizational boundaries: although there is still competition over financial resources between the municipality's own operative units, there is no need to claim ownership over outputs, as long as the analyses show that resources and competences are used to obtain societal outcomes. Second, such sharing enables creation of new organizational entities in which, for example, social services and schools can cooperate closely. Such entities are not recognized by oversight bodies, and therefore, can operate 'below the radar' of external inspectors.

Discussion and conclusion

We show that the legacy of the budget process in OPA remains strong, in terms of how entities, such as programmes and administrations, are maintained. Although negotiation is located in somewhat different places within traditional and transactional systems, they are remarkably similar in many ways. Both traditional and transactional systems have a strong distinction between a governing entity with an interest in constraining expenditure and a producing entity interested in securing resources, although the focus on cost-based formulas and transfer prices makes it difficult to negotiate resource allocations in the transactional system (Agyemang 2010). However, the case of Suburb illustrates that such a difficulty can be maintained in the traditional system: just because resource allocation can be negotiated, does not mean that it is.

It is clear that the transactional system strengthens organizational entities, exacerbated further by NPM notions, such as competition and auditing. This makes it difficult to employ a relational system: not only is it difficult to refrain from budget games, it is also difficult to manage for societal outcomes and cooperation as long as the focus is on organizational performance and performance auditing. Thus, although it is possible to negotiate which entities should do what, and who should be prioritized in the resource allocation in a relational system, it is difficult to operationalize these negotiations: the practice is in itself conditional upon the entities specified by budgeting, resource allocation technologies, and accountability relationships (Miller and O'Leary 2007; Miller and Power 2013). In effect, the negotiations become all talk and no action – and seemingly, so becomes the transition towards NPG (Hyndman et al. 2014).

This answers our research questions: the entities that are constructed to fit the traditional and transactional systems can seldom be negotiated, challenged, and reconstructed. Following communicative rationality, they can be negotiated, although it is quite difficult to operationalize the negotiations in practice: the relational system cannot be developed as long as rationalities other than the communicative one are allowed to dominate.

The main problem here – to paraphrase Wildavsky (1978) – is that the rigid traditional–transactional system that dominates public sector management today is highly theoretical, based on economic and managerial concerns, and devoid of practical nuance (Broadbent and Laughlin 2009). This system and its characteristics constrain practice to what works, and to the entities that 'fit' in economic theory: theories about transactions and the role of managers (Almqvist 2004; Hood 1991, 1995) define what can be done. Studies on, for example, negotiation, incrementalism, budgeting for results, or sharing of resources and competence will miss important practical aspects if they do not consider that the rationalities that underpin budgeting and other characteristics of organizational control constitute part of what can be negotiated, incrementally changed, seen as results, or shared in the first place (Kurunmäki and Miller 2011). Table 2 summarizes our arguments regarding which entities 'fit' which rationalities and management paradigms.

This study shows that practitioners who want to challenge the status quo encounter trouble because the alternatives they suggest (i.e., competence sharing and holistic views on results that problematize the existence of stable, productive organizational entities, or challenge organizational output as the primary matter of concern) do not fit the views in the dominant traditional–transactional system. Strong organizations, powerful managers, quantified measures of organizational efficiency, and effectiveness, and influential auditors and inspectors are still seen as integral for successful control of the value-creating process: they form the conditions for what can be negotiated and what can be done.

Earlier research on budgeting needs constructivist approaches to complement the economic and managerialist research that dominates contemporary research on public budgeting (Anessi-Pessina et al. 2016). Economic approaches themselves rely on instrumental rationality and assume transactional systems (Broadbent and Laughlin 2009; Johansson 2008, 2015; Williamson 1996). Therefore, research using

Table 2. Management paradigms, control systems, budgeting and entities.

Management paradigm	OPA	NPM	NPG
Dominant rationality	Processual	Instrumental	Communicative
Control system characteristics	Traditional	Transactional	Relational
Budget focus	Negotiation, resource allocation, incrementalism, programmes	Accrual budgeting, budgeting for results	Participation, resource pooling, sharing
Entities constructed to fit the budget focus, rationality, and system characteristics	Monetary funds, administrations, professions, programmes	Purchasers and providers, single purpose organizations, measurable outputs, transaction costs	Outcomes, competences
Context in which the entities are set to function	Budget games, negotiation	Competition, marketization, auditing	Cooperation, sharing, responsiveness
Analytical framework	Political, economic	Economic, managerial	Political, constructivist

the economic approach is likely to reinforce, rather than problematize, entities that make it difficult to operationalize NPG ideas in practice.

In addition, we argue that the managerial approach might not be helpful in analysing how budgeting can work in a relational, post-NPM world. Managerial assumptions rest on the notion that there has to be well defined, stable entities that can be managed – for example, in the form of single-purpose organizations, inputs, outputs, and established relationships between low input and high output – and managerialist research is built on the same assumptions (cf., Coe 2008; Jääskeläinen and Lönnqvist 2011; Kaplan 2001; Moe 1994). This means that neither economic, nor managerialist approaches might be helpful in critically discussing and analysing what might lead to more communicative, relational, and cooperative practices. However, constructivist and political approaches, which deconstruct and criticize entities taken for granted in economic and managerial research, might help to innovate practices in line with the demands that the new landscape of public administration places on them.

Further research needs to dig deeper into practices than ours does. Because we aimed to show several examples of how budgeting reinforces the construction of certain entities, we did not show the practices in detail. It would be possible to dig deeper into single cases and follow how certain entities – such as outputs – are constructed, reinforced, and reconstructed in different organizational systems and following changes in rationalities (e.g., Svärdsten Nymans 2012). In addition, it is necessary for practitioners to start debating if all entities supported by NPM and NPM-inspired budgeting practices are necessary when developing services. Textbook budgeting and the maintenance of traditional and transactional systems and the entities that 'fit' them may give a sense of control, but it may very well be a false sense. If elements of control are constructed primarily in relation to what 'functions' in economic and managerialist theories, effective control will remain a dream; and as Mol (2008, 95) argues: 'dreams of control do not make you happy, they make you neurotic. And one way or the other they end in disappointment.'

Notes

1. In City, we studied elderly care, education, environment and planning, and traffic. In Town, we studied social services, elderly care, environment and planning, library services, and childcare. In Suburb, we studied social services, elderly care, and environment and planning.
2. A Swedish municipality is governed by a municipal council, which is subject to re-election every fourth year in open elections. The subcommittees are political bodies subordinate to the council, and with responsibility for special operational or geographical areas. Each subcommittee has an administration responsible for executing the political decisions of the council and subcommittee. A municipality could have, for example, a social committee responsible for social services, and a corresponding social service administration.

Disclosure statement

No potential conflict of interest was reported by the authors.

References

Agyemang, G. 2010. "Accounting for Needs? Formula Funding in the UK Schools Sector." *Accounting, Auditing & Accountability Journal* 23: 82–110. doi:10.1108/09513571011010619.

Ahrens, T., and C. S. Chapman. 2006. "Doing Qualitative Field Research in Management Accounting: Positioning Data to Contribute to Theory." *Accounting, Organizations & Society* 31: 819–841. doi:10.1016/j.aos.2006.03.007.

Ahrens, T., and L. Ferry. 2015. "Newcastle City Council and the Grassroots: Accountability and Budgeting under Austerity." *Accounting, Auditing & Accountability Journal* 28 (6): 909–933. doi:10.1108/AAAJ-03-2014-1658.

Alford, J. 2014. "The Multiple Facets of Co-Production: Building on the Work of Elinor Ostrom." *Public Management Review* 16 (3): 299–316. doi:10.1080/14719037.2013.806578.

Almqvist, R. 2004. *Icons of New Public Management*. Stockholm: School of Business, Stockholm University.

Almqvist, R., B. Catasús, and M. Skoog. 2011. "Towards the Next Generation of Public Management: A Study of Management Control and Communication in the Swedish Armed Forces." *International Journal of Public Sector Management* 24: 122–145. doi:10.1108/09513551111109035.

Almqvist, R., and N. Wällstedt. 2013. "Managing Public Sector Organizations: Strategic Choices within Changing Paradigms." In *Management – An Advanced Introduction*, edited by L. Strannegård and A. Styhre, 203–229. Lund: Studentlitteratur.

Anessi-Pessina, E., C. Barbera, M. Sicilia, and I. Steccolini. 2016. "Public Sector Budgeting: A European Review of Accounting and Public Management Journals." *Accounting, Auditing & Accountability Journal* 29: 491–519. doi:10.1108/AAAJ-11-2013-1532.

Barretta, A. 2008. "The Functioning of Co-opetition in the Health-care Sector: An Explorative Analysis." *Scandinavian Journal of Management* 24: 209–220. doi:10.1016/j.scaman.2008.03.005.

Baxter, J., and W. F. Chua. 2008. "The Field Researcher as Author Writer." *Qualitative Research in Accounting & Management* 5: 101–121. doi:10.1108/11766090810888917.

Bozeman, B., and J. D. Straussman. 1982. "Shrinking Budgets and the Shrinkage of Budget Theory." *Public Administration Review* 42 (6): 509–515. doi:10.2307/976120.

Broadbent, J., and R. Laughlin. 2009. "Performance Management Systems: A Conceptual Model." *Management Accounting Research* 20: 283–295. doi:10.1016/j.mar.2009.07.004.

Charmaz, K. 2006. *Constructing Grounded Theory: A Practical Guide through Qualitative Analysis.* London: Sage Publications.

Christensen, T. 2014. "New Public Management and Beyond: The Hybridization of Public Sector Reforms." In *Global Themes and Local Variations in Organizations and Management: Perspectives on Globalization,* edited by G. S. Drori, M. A. Höllerer, and P. Walgenbach. New York: Routledge.

Coe, C. K. 2008. "Preventing Local Government Fiscal Crises: Emerging Best Practices." *Public Administration Review* 68: 759–767. doi:10.1111/j.1540-6210.2008.00913.x.

Covaleski, M. A., and M. W. Dirsmith. 1983. "Budgeting as a Means for Control and Loose Coupling." *Accounting Organizations and Society* 8 (4): 323–340. doi:10.1016/0361-3682(83)90047-8.

Dubois, A., and L.-E. Gadde. 2002. "Systematic Combining: An Abductive Approach to Case Research." *Journal of Business Research* 55 (7): 553–560. doi:10.1016/S0148-2963(00)00195-8.

Dunleavy, P. 1989. "The Architecture of the British Central State, Part I: Framework for Analysis." *Public Administration* 67 (3): 249–275. doi:10.1111/padm.1989.67.issue-3.

Ebdon, C., and A. L. Franklin. 2006. "Citizen Participation in Budgeting Theory." *Public Administration Review* 66 (3): 437–447. doi:10.1111/puar.2006.66.issue-3.

Evetts, J. 2009. "New Professionalism and New Public Management: Changes, Continuities and Consequences." *Comparative Sociology* 8: 247–266. doi:10.1163/156913309X421655.

Flyvbjerg, B. 2006. "Five Misunderstandings about Case-Study Research." *Qualitative Inquiry* 12: 219–245. doi:10.1177/1077800405284363.

Forrer, J., J. E. Kee, K. E. Newcomer, and E. Boyer. 2010. "Public–Private Partnerships and the Public Accountability Question." *Public Administration Review* 70 (3): 475–484. doi:10.1111/(ISSN)1540-6210.

Gilmour, J. B., and D. E. Lewis. 2006. "Does Performance Budgeting Work? An Examination of the Office of Management and Budget's PART Scores." *Public Administration Review* 66 (5): 742–752. doi:10.1111/puar.2006.66.issue-5.

Golden-Biddle, K., and K. Locke. 1993. "Appealing Work: An Investigation of How Ethnographic Texts Convince." *Organization Science* 4: 595–616. doi:10.1287/orsc.4.4.595.

Grossi, G., and R. Mussari. 2008. "Effects of Outsourcing on Performance Measurement and Reporting: The Experience of Italian Local Governments." *Public Budgeting & Finance* 28 (1): 22–38. doi:10.1111/pbaf.2008.28.issue-1.

Heinrich, C. J. 2002. "Outcomes-Based Performance Management in the Public Sector: Implications for Government Accountability and Effectiveness." *Public Administration Review* 62 (6): 712–725. doi:10.1111/puar.2002.62.issue-6.

Hendrick, R. 1989. "Top-Down Budgeting, Fiscal Stress and Budgeting Theory." *The American Review of Public Administration* 19 (1): 29–48. doi:10.1177/027507408901900103.

Hood, C. 1991. "A Public Management for All Seasons?" *Public Administration* 69: 3–19. doi:10.1111/padm.1991.69.issue-1.

Hood, C. 1995. "The 'New Public Management' in the 1980s: Variations on a Theme." *Accounting, Organizations and Society* 20 (2–3): 93–109. doi:10.1016/0361-3682(93)E0001-W.

Hyndman, N., and M. Liguori. 2016. "Public Sector Reforms: Changing Contours on an NPM Landscape." *Financial Accountability & Management* 32: 5–32. doi:10.1111/faam.12078.

Hyndman, N., M. Liguori, R. E. Meyer, T. Polzer, S. Rota, and J. Seiwald. 2014. "The Translation and Sedimentation of Accounting Reforms. A Comparison of the UK, Austrian and Italian Experiences." *Critical Perspectives on Accounting* 25: 388–408. doi:10.1016/j.cpa.2013.05.008.

Jääskeläinen, A., and A. Lönnqvist. 2011. "Public Service Productivity: How to Capture Outputs." *International Journal of Public Sector Management* 24: 289–302. doi:10.1108/09513551111133461.

Jackson, P. M. 2011. "Governance by Numbers: What Have We Learned over the Past 30 Years?" *Public Money & Management* 31: 13–26. doi:10.1080/09540962.2011.545542.

Johansson, T. 2008. "Municipal Contracting Out: Governance Choices, Misalignment, and Performance in Swedish Local Government." *Financial Accountability & Management* 24: 243–264. doi:10.1111/fam.2008.24.issue-3.

Johansson, T. 2015. "A Critical Appraisal of the Current Use of Transaction Cost Explanations for Government Make-or-Buy Choices: Towards a Contingent Theory and Forms of Tests." *Public Management Review* 17: 661–678. doi:10.1080/14719037.2013.848922.

Kaplan, R. S. 2001. "Strategic Performance Measurement and Management in Nonprofit Organizations." *Nonprofit Management & Leadership* 11: 353–370. doi:10.1002/(ISSN)1542-7854.

Kelly, J. M. 2005. "A Century of Public Budgeting Reform: The "Key" Question." *Administration & Society* 37 (1): 89–109. doi:10.1177/0095399704268626.

Knutsson, H., O. Mattisson, U. Ramberg, and T. Tagesson. 2008. "Do Strategy and Management Matter in Municipal Organisations?" *Financial Accountability & Management* 24 (3): 295–319. doi:10.1111/fam.2008.24.issue-3.

Kreiner, K., and J. Mouritsen. 2005. "The Analytical Interview: Relevance beyond Reflexivity." In *The Art of Science*, edited by S. Tengblad, R. Solli, and B. Czarniawska. Solna: Liber.

Kurunmäki, L., and P. Miller. 2006. "Modernising Government: The Calculating Self, Hybridisation and Performance Measurement." *Financial Accountability & Management* 22: 87–106. doi:10.1111/fam.2006.22.issue-1.

Kurunmäki, L., and P. Miller. 2011. "Regulatory Hybrids: Partnerships, Budgeting, and Modernising Government." *Management Accounting Research* 22: 220–241. doi:10.1016/j.mar.2010.08.004.

Lapsley, I. 2008. "The NPM Agenda: Back to the Future." *Financial Accountability & Management* 24 (1): 77–96. doi:10.1111/j.1468-0408.2008.00444.x.

Lapsley, I. 2009. "New Public Management: The Cruellest Invention of the Human Spirit?" *Abacus* 45 (1): 1–21. doi:10.1111/abac.2009.45.issue-1.

Latour, B. 1999. *Pandora's Hope – Essays on the Reality of Science Studies*. Cambridge, MA: Harvard University Press.

Latour, B. 2005. *Reassembling the Social*. New York: Oxford University Press.

Laughlin, R., and J. Broadbent. 1993. "Accounting and Law: Partners in the Juridification of the Public Sector in the UK?" *Critical Perspectives on Accounting* 4: 337–368. doi:10.1006/cpac.1993.1019.

Lauth, T. P. 1985. "Performance Evaluation in the Georgia Budgetary Process." *Public Budgeting & Finance* 5: 67–82. doi:10.1111/1540-5850.00673.

Lauth, T. P. 1978. "Zero-Base Budgeting in Georgia State Government: Myth and Reality." *Public Administration Review* 38: 420–430. doi:10.2307/975500.

Law, J., and V. Singleton. 2005. "Object Lessons." *Organization* 12: 331–355. doi:10.1177/1350508405051270.

LeGrand, J. 1999. "Competition, Cooperation, or Control? Tales from the British National Health Service." *Health Affairs* 18 (3): 27–39. doi:10.1377/hlthaff.18.3.27.

Long, E., and A. L. Franklin. 2004. "The Paradox of Implementing the Government Performance and Results Act: Top-Down Direction for Bottom–Up Implementation." *Public Administration Review* 64 (3): 309–319. doi:10.1111/puar.2004.64.issue-3.

Marti, C. 2006. "Accrual Budgeting: Accounting Treatment of Key Public Sector Items and Implications for Fiscal Policy." *Public Budgeting & Finance* 26: 45–65. doi:10.1111/j.1540-5850.2006.00846.x.

Miller, P., and T. O'Leary. 2007. "Mediating Instruments and Making Markets: Capital Budgeting, Science and the Economy." *Accounting, Organizations and Society* 32: 701–734. doi:10.1016/j.aos.2007.02.003.

Miller, P., and M. Power. 2013. "Accounting, Organizing, and Economizing: Connecting Accounting Research and Organization Theory." *The Academy of Management Annals* 7: 557–605. doi:10.1080/19416520.2013.783668.

Moe, R. C. 1994. "The 'Reinventing Government' Exercise: Misinterpreting the Problem, Misjudging the Consequences." *Public Administration Review* 54: 111–122. doi:10.2307/976519.

Mol, A. 1999. "Ontological Politics. A Word and Some Questions." *The Sociological Review* 47: 74–89. doi:10.1111/sore.1999.47.issue-S1.

Mol, A. 2002. *The Body Multiple: Ontology in Medical Practice*. Durham: Duke University Press.

Mol, A. 2008. *The Logic of Care: Health and the Problem of Patient Choice*. New York: Routledge.

Moore, P. 1980. "Zero-Base Budgeting in American Cities." *Public Administration Review* 40: 253–258. doi:10.2307/975379.

Needham, C. 2010. "Debate: Personalized Public Services—A New State/Citizen Contract?" *Public Money & Management* 30: 136–138. doi:10.1080/09540961003794246.

Osborne, S. P. 2006. "The New Public Governance?" *Public Management Review* 8 (3): 377–387. doi:10.1080/14719030600853022.

Osborne, S. P. 2009. "Debate: Delivering Public Services: Are We Asking the Right Questions?" *Public Money & Management* 29 (1): 5–7. doi:10.1080/09540960802617269.

Porter, T. M. 1996. *Trust in Numbers: The Pursuit of Objectivity in Science and Public Life*. Princeton: Princeton University Press.

Power, M. 1997. *The Audit Society: Rituals of Verification*. Oxford: Oxford University Press.

Robinson, M. 2002. "Output-Purchase Funding and Budgeting Systems in the Public Sector." *Public Budgeting & Finance* 22 (4): 17–33. doi:10.1111/1540-5850.00087.

Rose, N., and P. Miller. 1992. "Political Power beyond the State: Problematics of Government." *The British Journal of Sociology* 43: 173–205. doi:10.2307/591464.

Seo, M.-G., and W. E. D. Creed. 2002. "Institutional Contradictions, Praxis, and Institutional Change: A Dialectical Perspective." *The Academy of Management Review* 27: 222–247.

Svärdsten Nymans, F. 2012. *Constituting Performance: Case Studies of Performance Auditing and Performance Reporting*. Stockholm: Stockholm Business School, Stockholm University.

Thrane, S., and K. S. Hald. 2006. "The Emergence of Boundaries and Accounting in Supply Fields: The Dynamics of Integration and Fragmentation." *Management Accounting Research* 17: 288–314. doi:10.1016/j.mar.2006.06.001.

Triantafillou, P. 2007. "Benchmarking in the Public Sector: A Critical Conceptual Framework." *Public Administration* 85: 829–846. doi:10.1111/padm.2007.85.issue-3.

Van Thiel, S., and F. L. Leeuw. 2002. "The Performance Paradox in the Public Sector." *Public Performance & Management Review* 25: 267–281. doi:10.1080/15309576.2002.11643661.

Vigoda, E. 2002. "From Responsiveness to Collaboration: Governance, Citizens and the Next Generation of Public Administration." *Public Administration Review* 62: 527–540. doi:10.1111/puar.2002.62.issue-5.

Wallander, J. 1999. "Budgeting – An Unnecessary Evil." *Scandinavian Journal of Management* 15 (4): 405–421. doi:10.1016/S0956-5221(98)00032-3.

Wällstedt, N. 2015. *Managing Multiplicity: On Control, Care and the Individual*. Stockholm: Stockholm Business School, Stockholm University.

Wällstedt, N., and R. Almqvist. 2015. "From 'Either Or' to 'Both And': Organisational Management in the Aftermath of NPM." *Scandinavian Journal of Public Administration* 19: 7–25.

Wällstedt, N., G. Grossi, and R. Almqvist. 2014. "Organizational Solutions for Financial Sustainability: A Comparative Case Study from the Swedish Municipalities." *Journal of Public Budgeting, Accounting & Financial Management* 26 (1): 181–218.

Wang, X. 2000. "Performance Measurement in Budgeting: A Study of County Governments." *Public Budgeting & Finance* 20 (3): 102–118. doi:10.1111/0275-1100.00022.

Wildavsky, A. 1966. "The Political Economy of Efficiency: Cost–Benefit Analysis, Systems Analysis, and Program Budgeting." *Public Administration Review* 26: 292–310. doi:10.2307/973301.

Wildavsky, A. 1975. *Budgeting: A Comparative Theory of Budgetary Processes*. Boston: Little, Brown.

Wildavsky, A. 1978. "A Budget for All Seasons? Why the Traditional Budget Lasts." *Public Administration Review* 38 (6): 501–509. doi:10.2307/976027.

Williamson, O. E. 1996. *The Mechanisms of Governance*. New York: Oxford University Press.

Index

Page numbers in **bold** refer to tables and those in *italic* refer to figures.